Nine Women Revealed

♀♀♀♀♀♀♀♀♀

Intimate Revelations of Nine Real Women in Images and Words

Brittney

Jessica

Jess

Marilyn

Roxy

Rashell

Joelle

Jasmine

Stephanie

By Gary D. Melton

Goofy Rooster Publishing
Wylie, Texas
www.goofyrooster-publishing.com

Nine Women Revealed

Intimate Revelations of Nine Real Women in Images and Words

By Gary D. Melton

Goofy Rooster Publishing   PO Box 2904 Wylie, Texas 75098
www.goofyrooster-publishing.com

ISBN-10: 0-9843940-4-4

ISBN-13: 978-0-9843940-4-3

Contents:

Introduction

For some time, I have been wanting to create a book to showcase my artistic work - my female figure study photographs. The problem is that there are hundreds, if not thousands, of coffee table collections of nudes out there. While I felt that my photos were not necessarily like those of everyone else, I wanted to create something that was a bit different. I wanted to publish a book that stood apart from other similar ones on the bookshelf. My photos are mostly what I like to call "artistic snapshots" - photographs that look candid and unposed, but are actually carefully produced. I wanted to find the right "showcase" for my creations.

A few months ago, I had the beginnings of a "light bulb over the head" idea. I decided I wanted to create a book that 1) featured several women, 2) that showed them in typical "natural" settings around the home, and 3) that included some details about each of the subjects. That original idea grew over time to include the following concept goals:

- The photos will be tasteful, artistic, but "real and gritty" (i.e.: minimally retouched).
- They will be of a type that tells us something about what the subjects are like "under their skin".
- Attire for the photos will range from casual outfits to lingerie, topless, implied nude and nude.
- The book will not be too graphic - it will be something like "PG-16" rated.
- Accompanying each group of photos will be text providing glimpses into the essence of the subject - telling a bit of each woman's "story".
- A key concept for the book will be "intimacy" - not necessarily just sexual intimacy (though there will be some of that) but a kind of "sharing secrets/welcome to my inner sanctum" kind of intimacy. I want readers of the book to feel like they're visiting a part of each subject's world that is normally only seen by someone really close to them - like a lover or best friend.
- Many of the photos will be of women doing everyday, routine activities. Also included will be photos of activities that they might indulge in when they're home alone - like amusing themselves by acting silly - dancing in front of a mirror in their underwear, for example.
- The "feminine perspective" will be visited as much as possible in both the photos and the text in an attempt to create a book about women that will appeal to women themselves almost as much as it does to men. The book will be designed to attract a wide audience - something that will be compelling to a range of different people with a variety of interests.

My original idea included finding ordinary women who had never posed nude before (or at least, had never posed nude for anyone other than a significant other in private). It also included photographing each subject in their own home - their own environment. Unfortunately, these two concepts proved to be more difficult to achieve than I had originally thought.

I conducted my search for nude models on a popular networking web site for models and photographers that I have been a very active part of for more than three years. I was truly amazed at the large response

I received for my casting call, and by the women who responded to it. Even with the time it took me to perform the necessary "due diligence" to find the sort of models that I was looking for (using a three-tiered screening/interviewing process) - I was able to find my nine amazing subjects in about three weeks. Oh, and in case you're curious why I picked "nine" as the number of women - nine has always been my lucky number. It also seemed like a nice round number - not too many and not too few.

I'm one of those men who feel that most women have at least some beauty in them - that it just needs the right eyes and a little coaxing to bring it out - so I was not necessarily looking for nine beautiful women. As you can see by looking through this book, though, that's exactly what I wound up with. The women range in age from 20 to 40. Seven of them live in north Texas, while the other two live in central Texas. One of them is a student, three are married, four are mothers, one is an ex-cop and one is a Playboy model (in fact, she is one of the Playboy Special Edition Top Ten Models for 2010 - the number one of these top ten to be announced in July 2010).

Having selected the women for the book, I began and completed the wonderful task of photographing and interviewing them all - which I did over a period of six weeks (if you do the math - that's one every four and two thirds days).

This project has really been one of the most incredible experiences of my life. All ten of us - the nine models and I - had a wonderful time creating this book! We had a lot of fun in the process as well, and I hope that our spirit of fun comes across in the final product here.

All of the women were great to work with, and all contributed ideas and concepts to the project. For that, I want to thank them all, sincerely, from my heart. Thank you Brittney, Jessica, Jess, Marilyn, Roxy, Rashell, Joelle, Jasmine and Stephanie!

I especially want to acknowledge the contributions that Jessica made (especially for her help with "shaping" the book once I started putting it all together). She went well beyond the call of duty! Thank you Jessica!

Gary Melton

Hopefully, my introduction has given you some insight into how this book project came to be. To learn more about how it all went - both from my perspective, and from the perspective of each of the "Nine Women" - see the chapter "The Making of 'Nine Women Revealed'".

♀♀♀♀♀♀♀♀♀

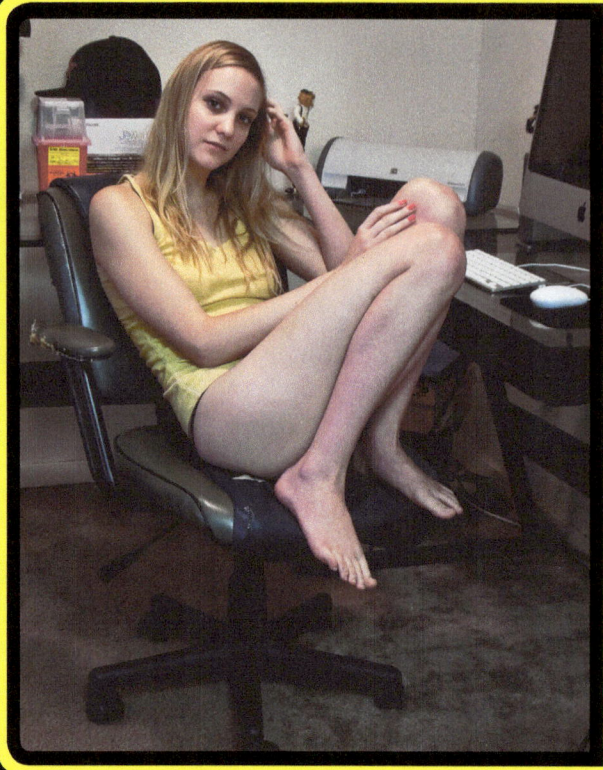

Brittney

♀♀♀♀♀♀♀♀♀

"Whether you think you can or you can't - you're right."

At 20, Brittney is the youngest of the "Nine Women." She's a working model in the DFW area who seems wise beyond her years. I found her to be an utterly charming and adorable breath of fresh air.

I've wanted to act and model since I was a kid - though there was a long period where I wanted to be a veterinarian - I love animals!

Right now, I am at such a happy point in my life. I have an amazing relationship (with my boyfriend of three years) and some amazing friendships. I'm making good money, doing things I truly enjoy (modeling), and I'm going to film school. I'm really doing everything artistically that I desire, and going after everything that I want - which is what everyone should do.

Things weren't always so rosy - my childhood wasn't the best, to be honest. I was born in Colorado, a beautiful state which I still consider my home. My mother and father divorced when I was about two. Then I lived with my mother and the oldest of my three younger brothers in Colorado for about three years (he was born about the time of the divorce). When I was five, we moved to Texas to be with my mother's new husband.

It was hard for us all. My mother had some emotional problems. A couple of years after we moved down here, the youngest of my brothers was born with Asperger's Syndrome (an autistic spectrum disorder). We all had to grow up fast - especially me, being the oldest. We all helped take care of our autistic brother, and ourselves as necessary. My three brothers are 13, 15 and 18 now, and we all love each other more than words can say. We've all stuck together through everything.

I matured really fast as a kid because I had to (people have often said I had an "old soul"). I saw a lot of bad in my world and I lost some innocence - but I became wiser in the process. So there were some benefits as well.

♀♀♀♀♀♀♀♀♀

I don't have any regrets in my life. To be truly honest, I wouldn't do anything differently - just because I've learned so much from my mistakes.

♀♀♀♀♀♀♀♀♀

I have so many passions - but if I could do anything at all, I'd love to be a film director making music videos. I'd really love to change the whole direction that they're going in today. So many of the music videos you see on MTV today are crap: no artistic value. Heck, a lot of the time, they aren't even about the songs that they feature. Too often, the music isn't even very good. I'd love to work with some great bands - creating videos that elevate and illustrate their music!

♀♀♀♀♀♀♀♀♀

I haven't been many places, but I'd love to travel when I get the chance one day. I'd love to see the countries of western Europe - experience their way of life and culture first hand. I'm a very open minded person - I don't have many reservations about life. It seems that most of the cultures over there aren't so super conservative compared to the US. I'd like to see a lot of the gorgeous architecture over there as well!

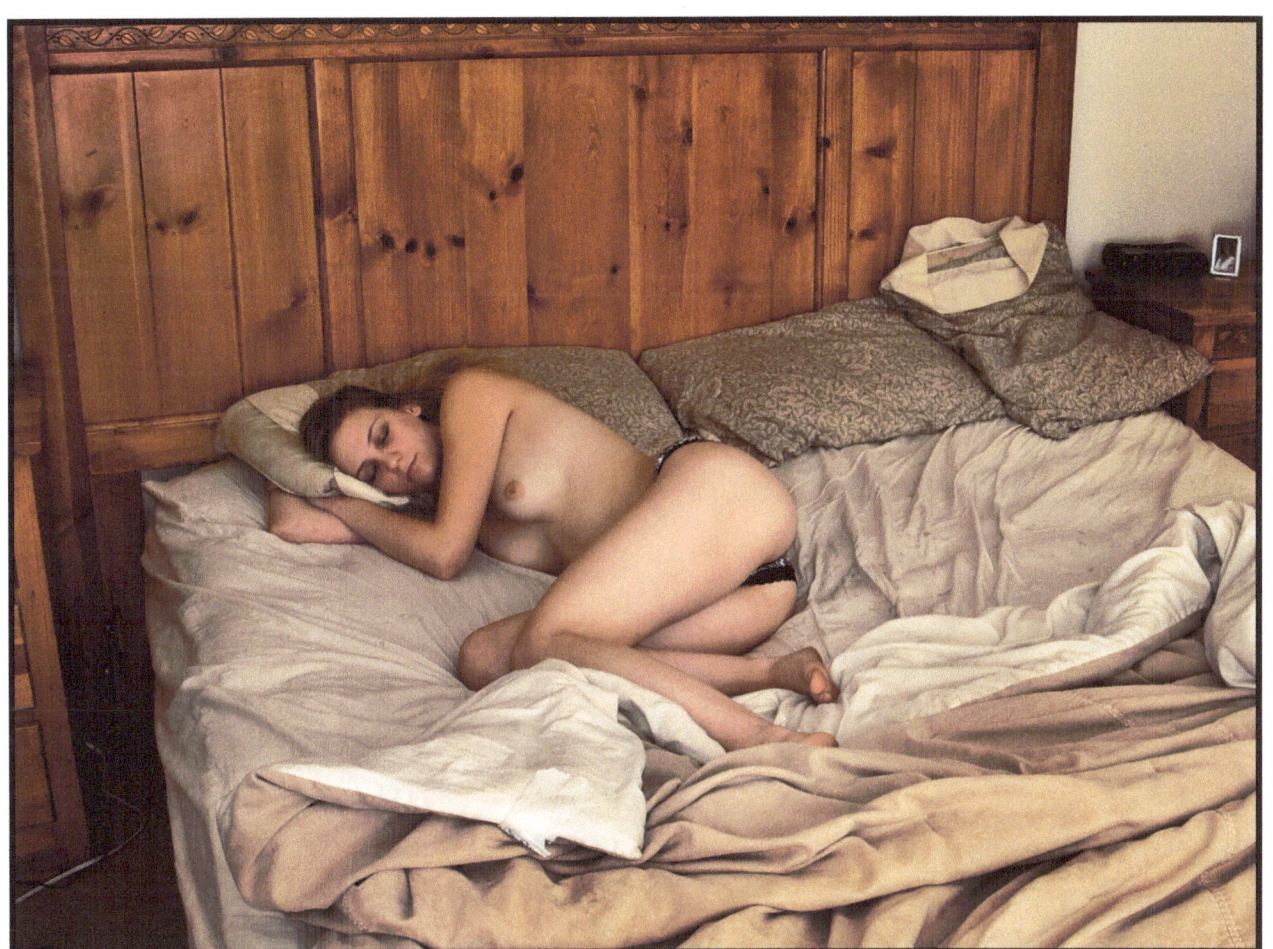

♀♀♀♀♀♀♀♀♀

I love being a woman, especially in today's world. I mean, I am SO meant to be a woman! I'm not a typical woman though - more of a "guy's girl" because I'm always hanging out with the guys.

I hate the stereotypes and misconceptions about women. Myself - I'm not into materialistic things, and I don't really like to go shopping. I don't even nag my boyfriend!

I'm attractive, so I get hassled by guys all the time - and that can suck (uh-oh, I'm sounding a bit vain, aren't I)! At the same time, the best part of being a woman to me is that feeling you get when you know you really look good! A woman's body is just SO beautiful! It's so wonderful on those days when you come to the realization of confidence where you're like, "I look like a work of art today!" It's an amazing feeling!

♀♀♀♀♀♀♀♀♀

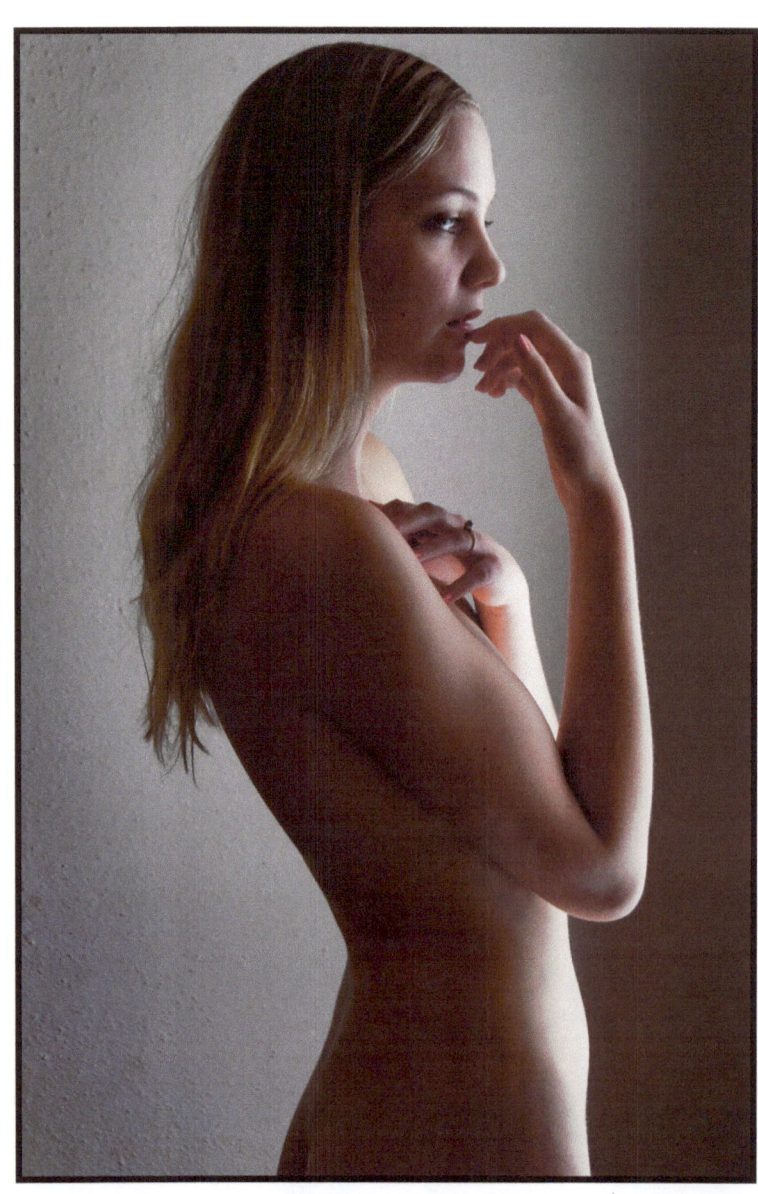

I love guys, I really do - but they can get away with so much more than women when it comes to appearance. For example, male actors don't HAVE to be in peak physical condition to get roles in films (just look at some of the popular comedic actors today like Seth Rogan). They can be overweight and unattractive but still get roles based on their talent.

How many talented but unattractive females do you see getting a lot of jobs in films these days? Not many!

And the double standard is STILL with us! If a guy sleeps around - he's just a "player" or he's "just bein' a guy"! But a girl who does the same thing - she's a "slut"! She's not "exploring her sexuality" or "just bein' young"!

Men do get some bum raps though. They have stereotypes to deal with, too: "all they want is sex!", "they never listen", "they're not emotional", etc. I can tell you, from all the time I've spent hanging out with the guys - they are JUST as emotional as us women, and have many of the same feelings that we do. It's just that society has deemed it "uncool" for men to express their emotions, their feelings - so they have to suppress them.

♀♀♀♀♀♀♀♀♀

I'm a pretty open person. My fiancé (we've been engaged for a year) and I tell each other everything. I think my best quality, though, is that I really care about people! Some of my friends think that I let some people get away with too much, but I just feel that everyone makes mistakes. I like to give, I like to be generous. I like to do things for other people and buy things for other people (but not for myself so much).

Oh - and I like to think I'm pretty funny most of the time!

On the other hand - I can be downright stubborn at times, especially when it comes to discussing opinions. I do like to argue - though I try real hard to avoid saying things like "no, your opinion is wrong."

♀♀♀♀♀♀♀♀♀

Not much scares me these days. I used to be afraid of death and of the unknowns of my future. After a lot of thinking on it, though, I came to the realization that there just isn't any point in being afraid of things that you can't help, or things that are simply inevitable.

♀♀♀♀♀♀♀♀♀

If I could change anything about myself, though - it would be my immune system. I get sick a lot, and I have a whole list of medical and physical conditions that sometimes keep me from doing a lot of the things that I want to do.

♀♀♀♀♀♀♀♀♀

Don't tell anyone, but I have SUCH a star-crush on Johnny Depp! What can I say - he's a great actor, too!

Oh - and I'm such a music freak, and a total sucker for guys in bands! I guess my biggest band guy crush would be on Brandon Boyd - the lead singer for the group Incubus!

♀♀♀♀♀♀♀♀♀

If I could be any animal - it would be a horse! They're so free, and they get to run around, and they're just so gorgeous! I love horses a lot!

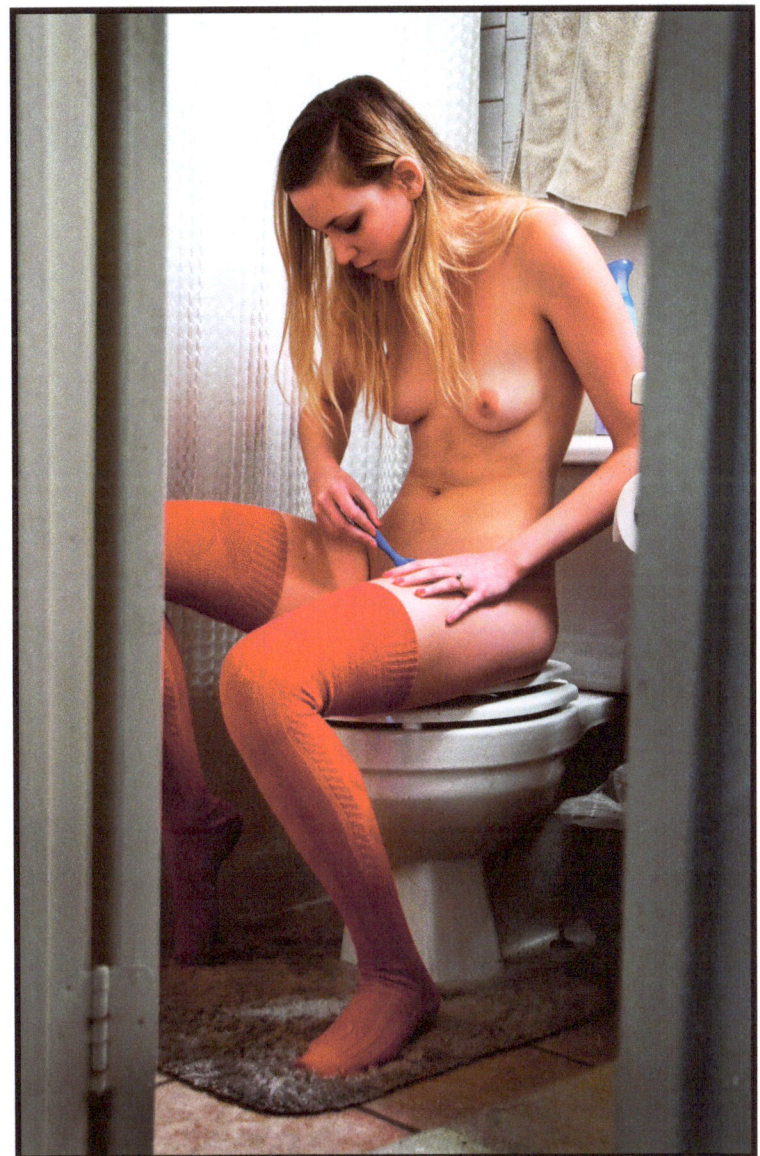

♀♀♀♀♀♀♀♀♀

My favorite fairy tale is Rumpelstiltskin - I'm not sure exactly why. Maybe because it's kind of a dark story.

♀♀♀♀♀♀♀♀♀

I was never in to sports as a kid, but I was in to dance. I still love to dance a lot! I have studied all types, including ballet - my favorite. I'd love to get back to it - if I could only find the time.

I don't care much for watching conventional sports like football - they just don't interest me. I like watching extreme sports - like x-games, snowboarding and motocross.

♀♀♀♀♀♀♀♀♀

Favorite sexual position? Uh - well it depends. I like to change it up. Sometimes I like to be in control and sometimes I don't. I like just about all positions equally - it depends on my mood that day!

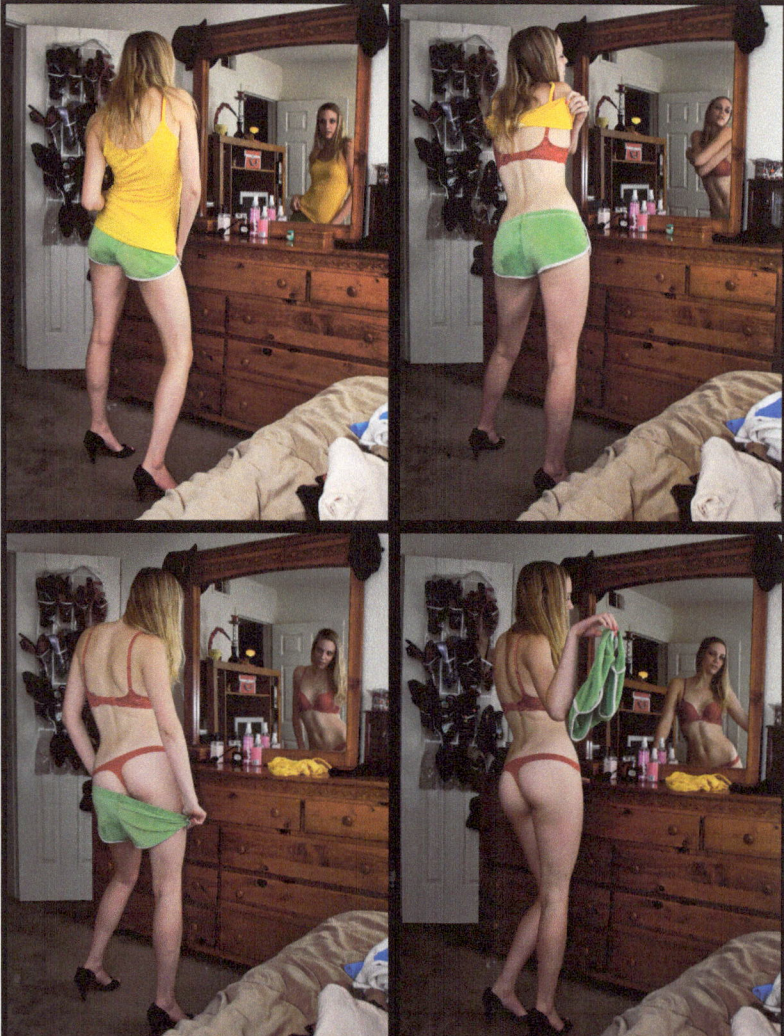

♀♀♀♀♀♀♀♀♀

I love food, but my favorite comfort food is fried chicken! And my favorite place to get fried chicken? Chicken Express - it's delicious!

♀♀♀♀♀♀♀♀♀

Yellow and red are tied for my favorite colors. I love red to wear - it's a color that looks great on me. Yellow is just a color that I love in general.

♀♀♀♀♀♀♀♀♀

I think I've already mentioned that I really love music. I love it when it's real obvious that a band has true musical talent, like when they actually compose things - things that sound unique and quirky, or crazy and fun. I guess I mostly like music that is rock-ish, all forms of rock really!

♀♀♀♀♀♀♀♀♀

Favorite TV show: I'm currently OBSESSED with "Dexter"! I love that show!

I have kind of a crude sense of humor.

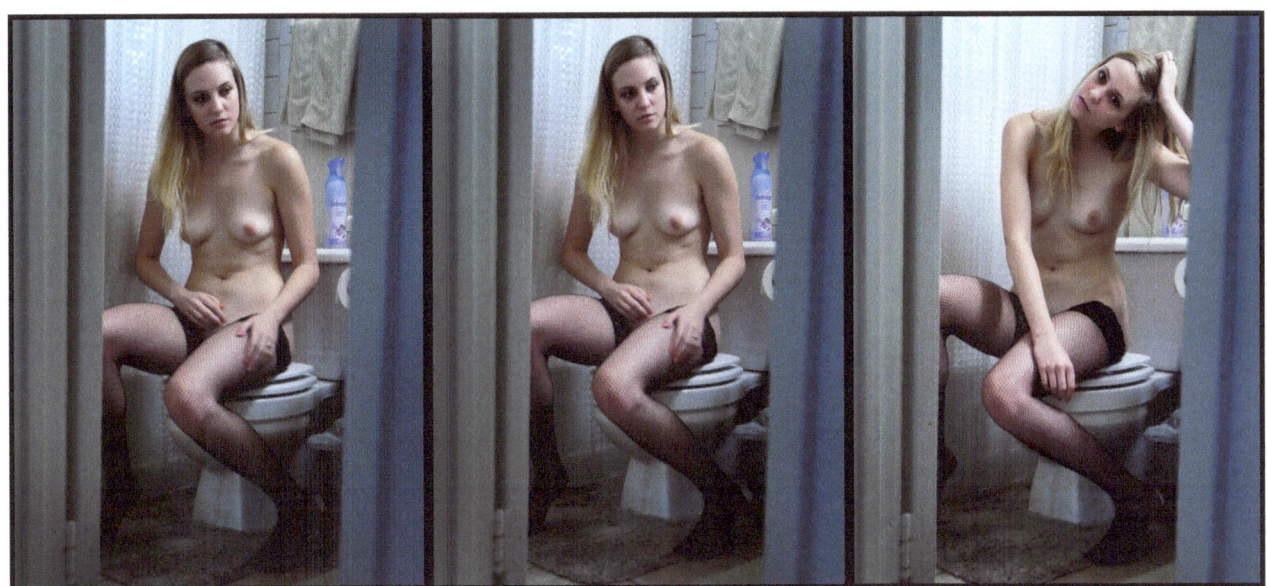

I love me some movies! Quentin Tarentino is one of my favorite directors. I love the two "Kill Bill" films and "Pulp Fiction" and "Reservoir Dogs"! I love how he can take comedy and action and drama and roll it up into this quirky, little fun mix.

Some other favorite films of mine: "There Will Be Blood" and "No Country For Old Men".

♀♀♀♀♀♀♀♀♀

The best way for a man to win my heart is to take me as I am - to really and truly like everything about me. Now that's pretty simple, isn't it?

♀♀♀♀♀♀♀♀♀

I love art - I'm really passionate about it in general. I paint, I write scripts, short stories and poems, I dance, I'm into photography and modeling, and everything connected with that - like makeup and styling.

♀♀♀♀♀♀♀♀♀

My biggest pet peeve is when people try to push their beliefs on you and say things like "you're wrong"

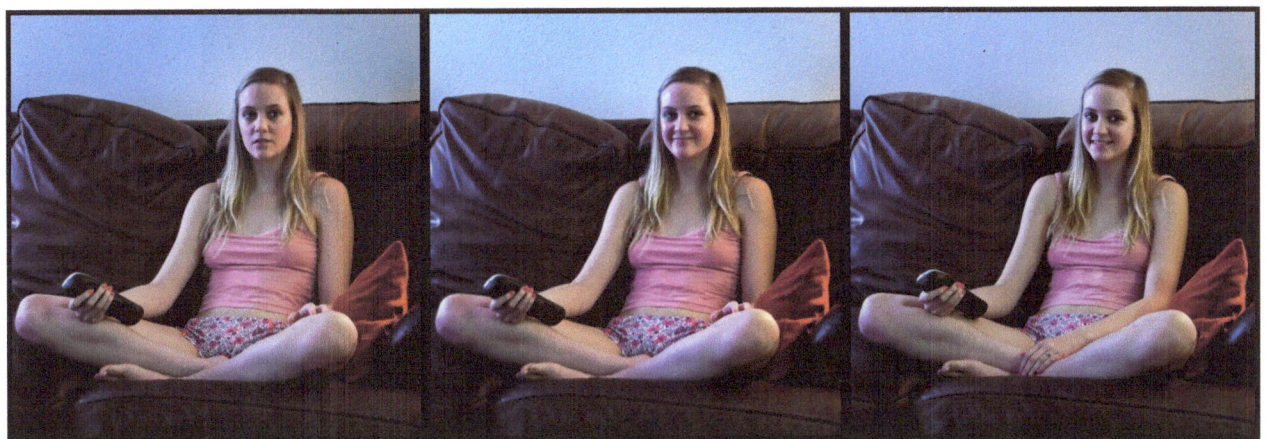

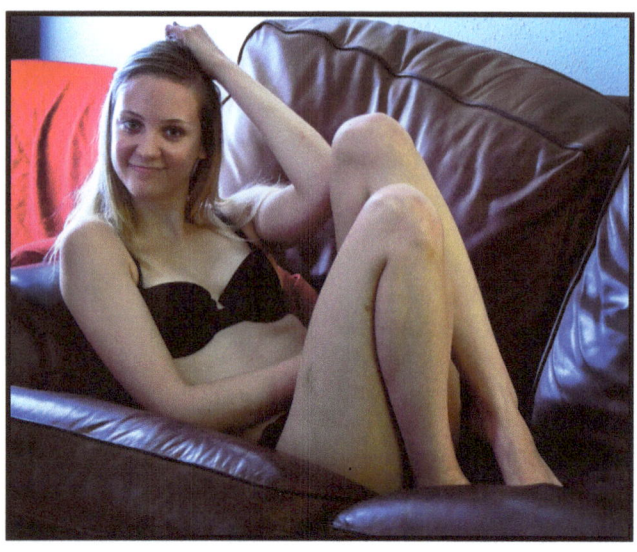

for what you do, or for what you believe. I really, REALLY hate that!

♀♀♀♀♀♀♀♀♀

My favorite time of the year is winter - I love the snow and cold.

♀♀♀♀♀♀♀♀♀

Do you want to know what the craziest, wildest thing I've ever done is? Well, recently - my fiancé and I threw a party, just for our closest friends (so it was a fairly small group). After we all drank quite a bit - we decided that we'd go swimming in our apartment complex's closed swimming pool. So - we all just jumped over the gate, stripped off all our clothes and dove into the pool. It was all pretty insane. I don't remember a lot of it, which is probably a good thing!

♀♀♀♀♀♀♀♀♀

I had one of the best days of my life not too long ago. My fiancé and I celebrated our three year anniversary together by taking a little trip to a nearby lake. It was late in the season and hardly anyone else was there. At times it felt like we had the place completely to ourselves. It was such a serene and peaceful time together - hiking and swimming and just enjoying each other's company!

The worst day of my life? I don't think I want to tell you about that one.

♀♀♀♀♀♀♀♀♀

I can be shy sometimes, but I'm also one of those people who would like to both direct and star in a

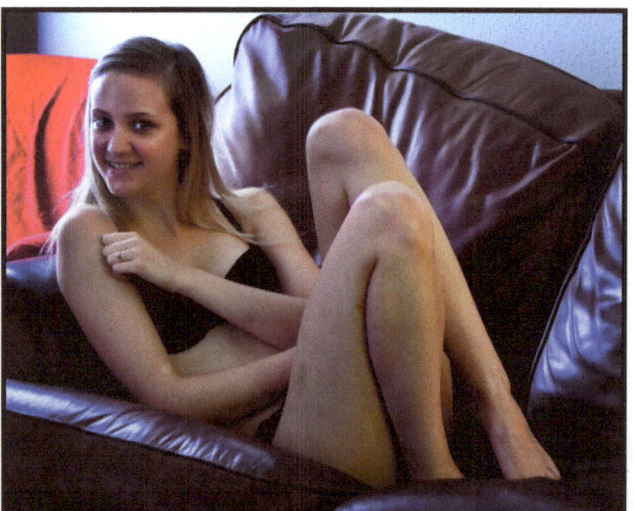

movie. I like to be in front of the camera - I like to be noticed. I like to wear fun, crazy and sexy outfits wherever I go.

♀♀♀♀♀♀♀♀♀

I think that everyone has something beautiful about them!

♀♀♀♀♀♀♀♀♀

The color of my eyes seem to change, or so people tell me. They can look slightly different, depending on what I'm wearing at any given time. Mostly, they're kind of "honey colored" - yellowy brown with a little bit of green.

♀♀♀♀♀♀♀♀♀

So what do I think it's like to be a woman in today's world? It's obviously a lot more empowering, but at the same time - self-image is a big issue today. Self esteem is difficult to deal with - given all the images on TV, in the movies and in magazines of perfect looking women. It's hard for a lot of women to accept that they don't have to look like that.

♀♀♀♀♀♀♀♀♀

My parting words: I haven't had a real easy life at all, but just experiencing and learning all that I have - I

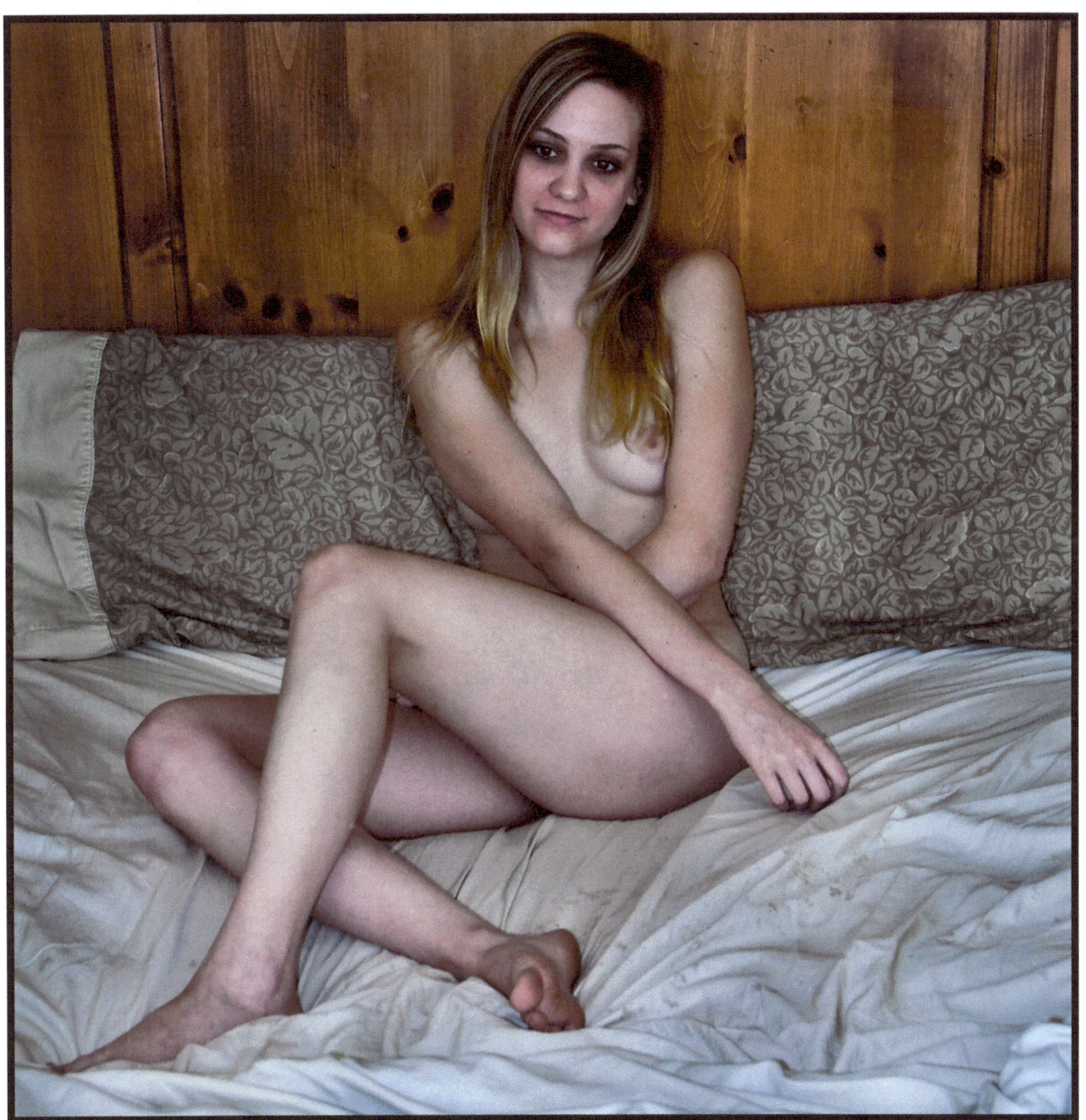

feel like I'm very mature for my age. I've really learned to just absorb everything I can, and to love life with a passion! I'm so thankful for everything I have. What I really want to do is just contribute to doing something that is different and unique.

Brittney

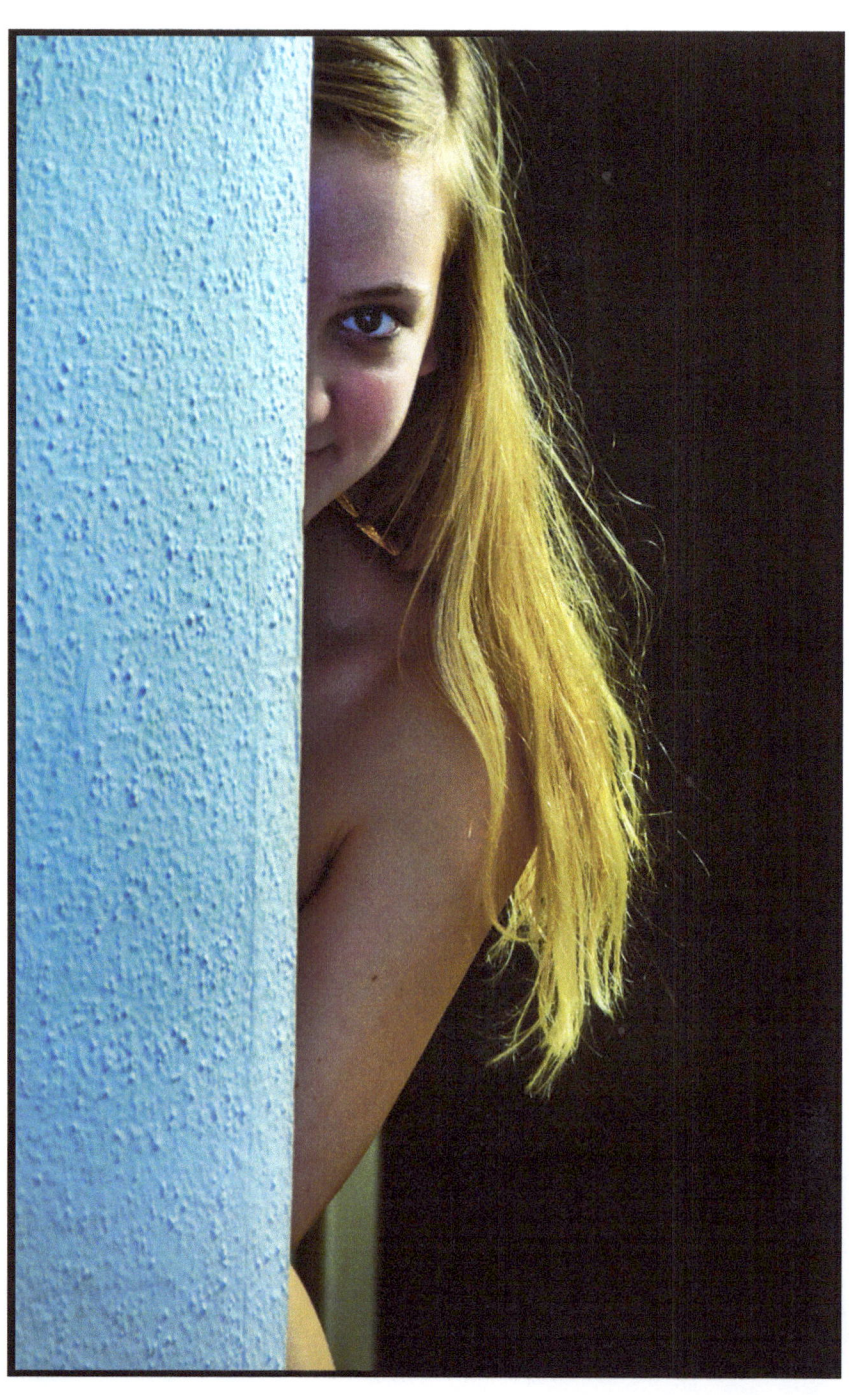

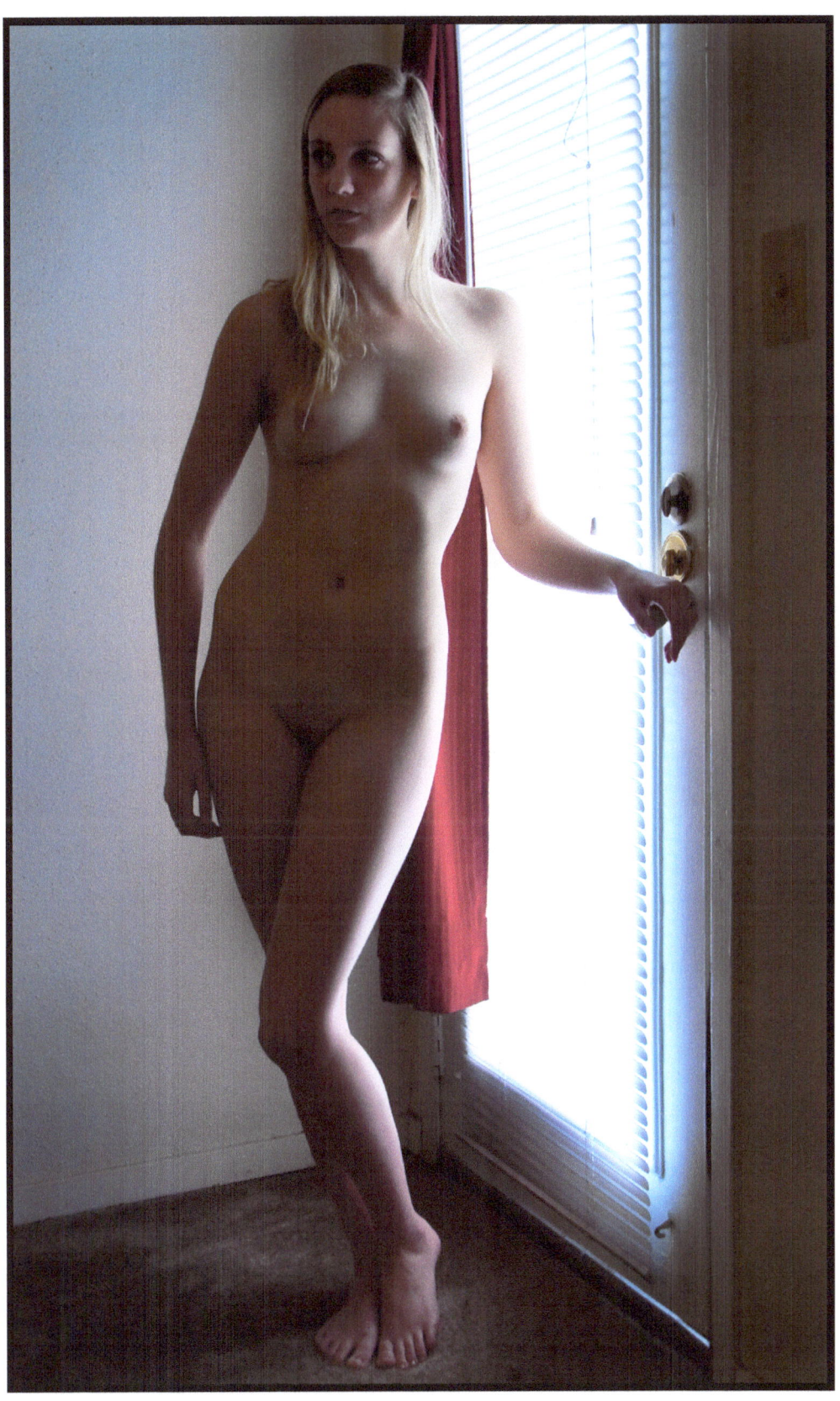

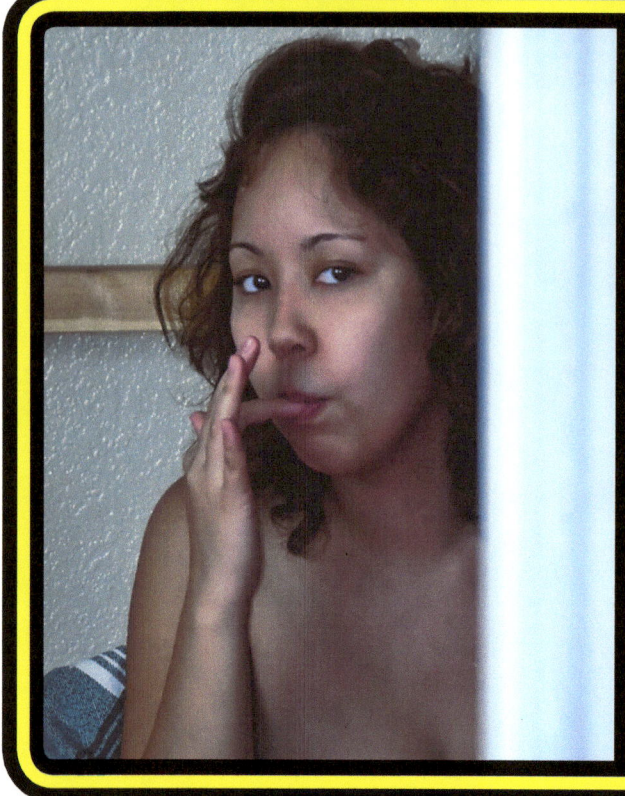

Jessica

♀♀♀♀♀♀♀♀♀

"I like who I am!"

While Jessica, 23, is a real sweetheart, she's also a no-nonsense, "take-no-prisoners" type of woman. Confident and strong, she'll impress you with her candor and wit.

I'd like to be famous - for what, I don't know exactly. The chances of that happening, realistically, are very slim - I do realize that. Maybe this book will be my chance!

♀♀♀♀♀♀♀♀♀

There was a lot of good and bad in my childhood. I do remember nice little things, like trips my parents took me on, going to amusement parks, birthday parties, Christmases...things like that. But sometimes I remember things I'd rather forget.

The thing about childhood, though, is that even the bad moments are pretty integral and important to who we become. I don't think I'd be who I am today without the bad...and I like who I am. Those experiences were a "necessary evil" in a way.

Let's just say that from my preteen years until I was a young adult - I didn't get along with my parents. There was a lot of disagreement with the way I chose to live my life: they didn't like my friends, my clothes, my music, etc. I didn't have any freedom - they wouldn't let me date, or just hang out with friends. Up until the time I moved out (at the age of 20), I was never allowed to do what I wanted or to stay out late.

There were so many issues with my parents - more than I care to talk about here. To this day, when some of these subjects come up in discussions, it angers me that they try to act like there was a good reason why things were said or done back then. You cannot convince me that there was, however. It's bad enough that they argue there was a need for it, but then it's another when they claim not to even remember some of the things they said or did.

♀♀♀♀♀♀♀♀♀

Growing up, I wanted to be a radio disc jockey, but was kind of talked out it by a school counselor with friends in that industry. She told me that the format at a radio station can change any day, or that someone can come in and buy your station at any time and you're fired. It's very cutthroat - lots of stations being bought out by the same companies, or you can get replaced by someone who's syndicated, or by automated music, etc.

I wanted to go to one of those broadcasting schools, but was told that most of those hired by stations actually had journalism degrees from universities.

Otherwise, I didn't really know what I wanted to be.

♀♀♀♀♀♀♀♀♀

My parents didn't let me have a say in what college I went to - they picked out a private women's college in Virginia for me, and that was that. When I moved out and started college, I was surprised at just how demanding it all was. They told us about it in high school, but I didn't expect it to be as tough as it was. The courses were hard - honors and advanced placement courses in high school don't really prepare you for them. Living on campus, not being familiar with the area, plus being around so many people I didn't know were are all new and stressful factors in my life.

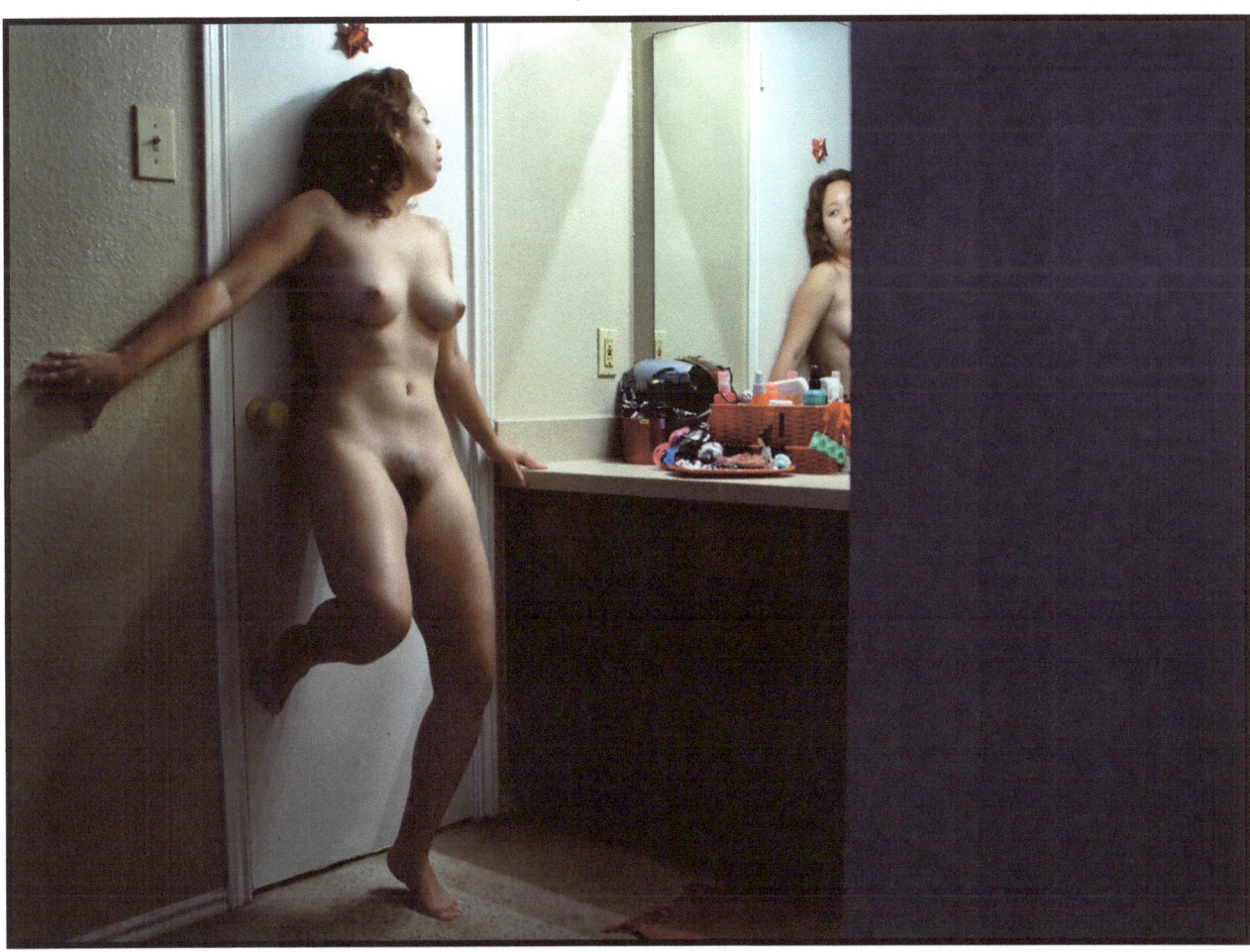

Just learning to live with someone who was not a family member for the first time in my life was hard. To this very day, I don't have any more room mates. I learned it was more trouble than it was worth.

I was used to having more assignments in each course, so that blowing one didn't affect your grade so much. In college, one bad paper or one messed up mid-term could lower your grade enough so that it was difficult to bring it back up. I wound up dropping out before the end of the first semester - it was just more than I could handle at the time.

♀♀♀♀♀♀♀♀♀

My next "rude awakening" was when I moved out in my early twenties to live on my own. I found you don't have much of a support system. People who you thought were good friends turned out not to be. Co-workers have a lot going on in their own lives and can't be there for you when you're having problems.

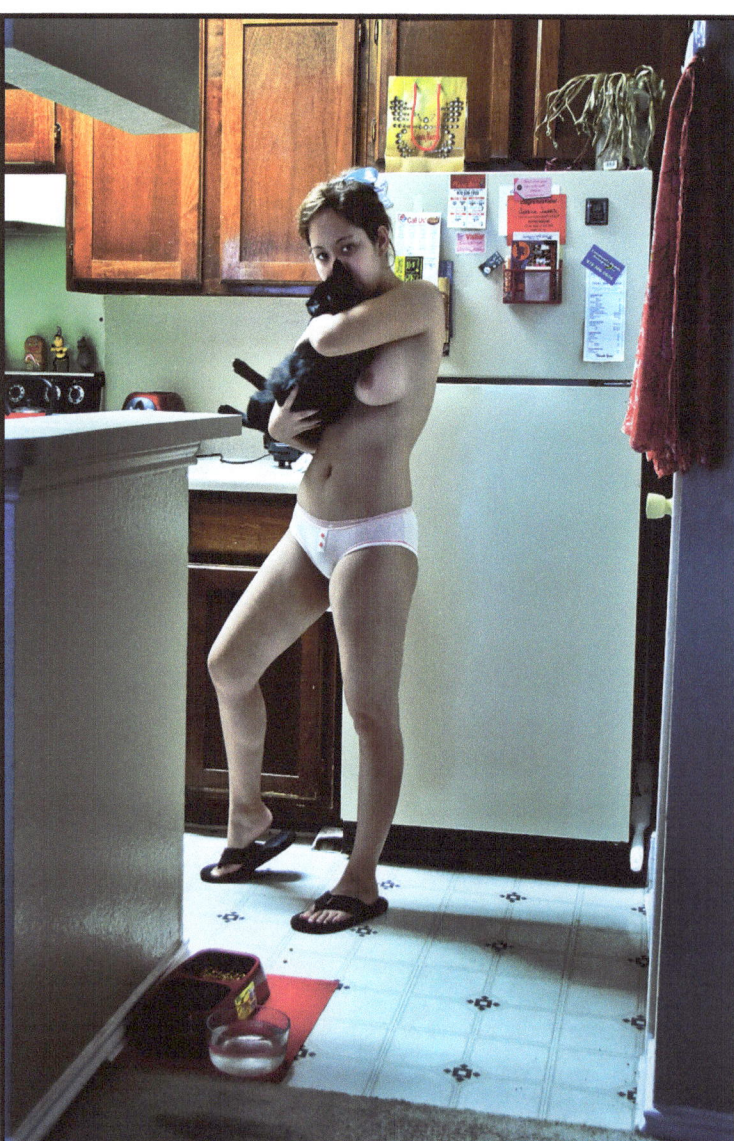

I won't say that people don't care, but most have plenty to deal with on their own plates.

I moved from Georgia, where I grew up, to Texas - knowing only a few people and having no relatives in the area. The sense of security I had at home - of knowing that I could always go to a friend's house, or call up a friend to talk when needed wasn't there any longer.

I learned about office politics, and was surprised to find how people can back-stab at even lowly hourly wage levels. It was the sort of thing I thought only existed at higher levels. I had been so sheltered growing up at home - it was all a shock to me.

If I had it to do over, I would have moved out on my own at 18 instead of 20. I think it would have given me a head start on learning about life - I think I'd be farther along my path.

♀♀♀♀♀♀♀♀♀

As a kid, I used to think that everything was like a sitcom on TV - that you always won the contest you entered, always got the gift you wanted, and your parents always said "yes". By the first or second grade in school when I learned that everything was not scripted like on TV - I was very disappointed.

♀♀♀♀♀♀♀♀♀

Most people don't know that I can draw pretty well. I used to draw all the time. They're also surprised when they find out I can cook. I've gotten pretty good with baking cakes and making casseroles and such!

♀♀♀♀♀♀♀♀♀

If I could go anywhere - I'd like to go to Europe. It would be cool to live there for three months and then come back. I'd like to visit the different societies and see what is tabu and what is acceptable. I'd like to see for myself if some of the differences you hear about really work, if they are better than what we have here. For example - should we adopt similar health care systems? Should we be less puritanical about sexual stuff here? Are some things better there, or is it just a case of "the grass is always greener"?

♀♀♀♀♀♀♀♀♀

People can be so judgmental about what you say sometimes (so I may catch a lot of flak about this), but I often wished I had just been "white" growing up. My father is Caucasian, and my mother is Asian. I was often made fun of and discriminated against because of that mixed heritage. If I had grown up in Hawaii or California - it might have been okay. But growing up in Georgia - it was definitely NOT okay. It was very hurtful, and it caused a lot of the insecurities I have now. It's been much better in Texas, where there's a more diverse population.

♀♀♀♀♀♀♀♀♀

There are times when I'm glad I'm a female. As a male, I wouldn't be able to get away with some of the things I do. I enjoy fashion and I do like to shop. But there are still a lot of double standards in our society, and a glass ceiling for women in most of the corporate arena.

I have been known to go outside my gender roles - for example, I have no problem going up to a guy and asking him out if I feel like it. Some guys are put off by that - they don't like a strong, aggressive, confident female. It bothers them and

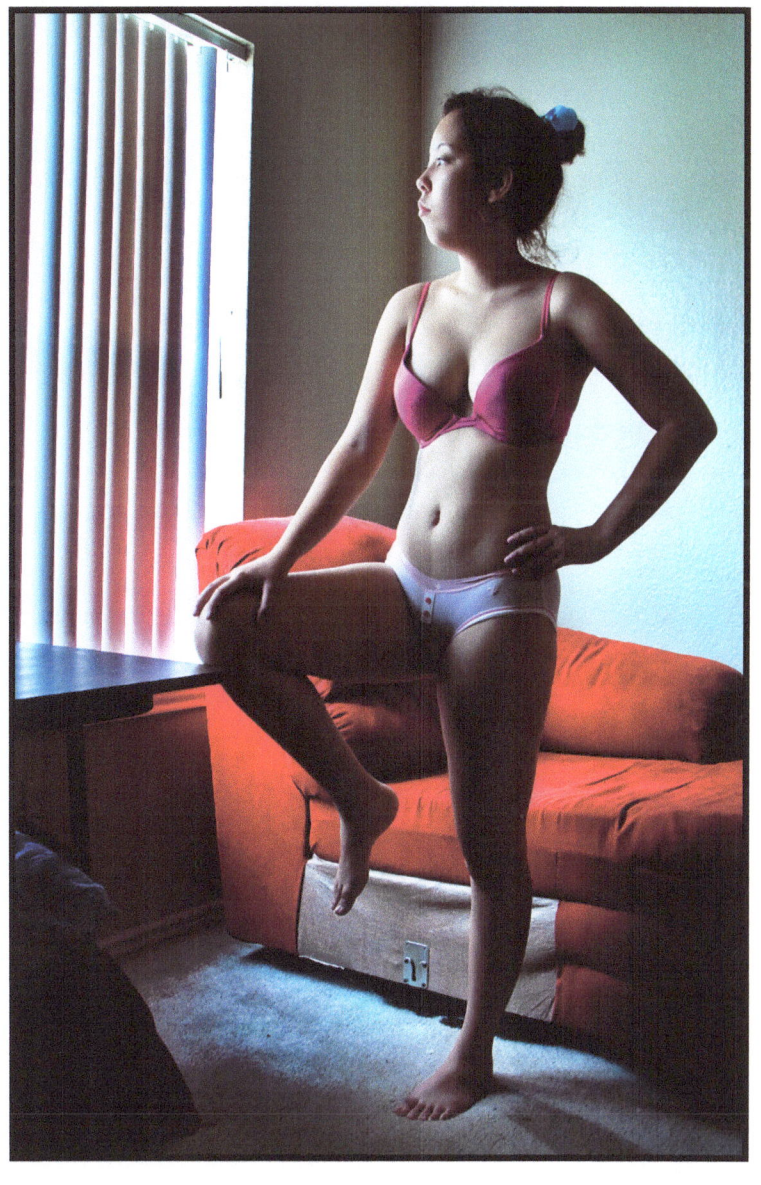

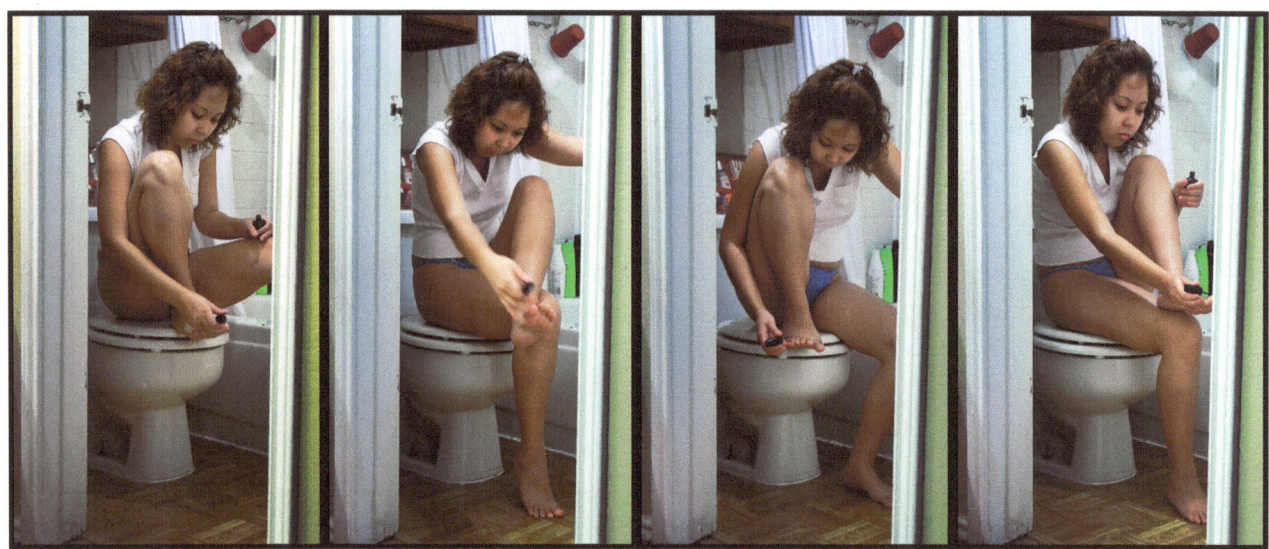

makes them insecure. In a relationship sense, it's hard to be female as opposed to a male. Sometimes, I think that if I had been born a male, I could have been more successful in the workplace, maybe met a serious, permanent significant other by now, and probably I'd have more money. I think I would have gone through life with less judgement passed on me. I have been sexually harassed in the workplace and I feel like that would have never happened if I had been a dude.

Having said all that - if I could magically change into a guy - I don't think I would. It might be interesting for a day, but I wouldn't be me if I weren't a woman, and I don't think I'd feel as sexy as a man.

♀♀♀♀♀♀♀♀♀

The best part of being a woman is that we have all the power in dating relationships, I think. My dad used to call it "using your feminine wiles" - meaning we use what we have to get what we want. I know it sounds manipulative, but dating is a big game and we have to use what we have in our arsenals to win it.

The worst part of being a woman comes from the unfortunate fact that there is still a lot of debate today about what women can and can't do with their own bodies. Men don't have to worry about becoming pregnant, or what they would do in that situation. And they don't have that "biological clock" ticking. They don't have all the "mother" issues we have to deal with. It's a lot of responsibility that we're the only ones who can actually give birth. Some women don't want to have children, but at the same time, we want to please everyone. Women have to sacrifice their careers and aspirations for children much more often than men do.

♀♀♀♀♀♀♀♀♀

This is going to sound really boring, but my favorite sexual position is the missionary. I like to be on the bottom - I'm very submissive. Oh, I'll get on top occasionally, and I'm cool with doggie style and other positions. But just as a spontaneous thing - if I'm in the mood, and the guy's in the mood, and he kind of puts the moves on me and I wind up on the bottom - I really like that. I don't know why - I just do! Some guys think missionary sounds boring - but if they tried it with me - they'd find out it wasn't boring at all!

♀♀♀♀♀♀♀♀♀

Sexual fantasies: sexy burglar breaking in, doing it with a vampire, or the UPS guy shows up and he's really good looking. I answer the door in just a towel or nothing at all and it just goes from there. Just anything where I would not expect it - someone shows up and it just happens!

I like a lot of role playing, so anything involving costumes is cool, too: naughty school girl, cheerleader, etc.

But really - someone showing up and giving me the business when I least expect it - that's pretty much it!

♀♀♀♀♀♀♀♀♀

My favorite comfort food used to be pasta, but now I've really grown to love mashed potatoes - like really loaded up with cheese, sour cream and bacon bits! I'll go to Applebee's and just order a double serving of their mashed potatoes. If I'm sick and don't feel like eating anything real solid - I ask people to bring me those tubs of Country Crock mashed potatoes already prepared so I only have to heat them up.

♀♀♀♀♀♀♀♀♀

The best day of my life was in August when I went to Vegas - everything was just so sparkly and pretty! There were slot machines in the airport. It was the nuttiest thing ever - you don't even have to leave the airport and it's like you're already at a party! The hotel on the strip was just beautiful. It was all so exciting - I wish I could live there for a few months. All the shows are so wonderful, and the hotel room had a TV in the bathroom mirror! I'm like brushing my teeth and watching TV - it's nuts. I had a view of the strip from my window that was really cool. The casinos are so nice, and the buffets were excellent! Everything was even better than you thought it would be. The first day there, my mouth was just hanging open all the time! I'd love to go back one day.

♀♀♀♀♀♀♀♀♀

The worst day of my life was when I was sexually assaulted by an ex-boyfriend - a guy I was even engaged to at one time. We had gotten together at my place to discuss the possibility of getting back together, when

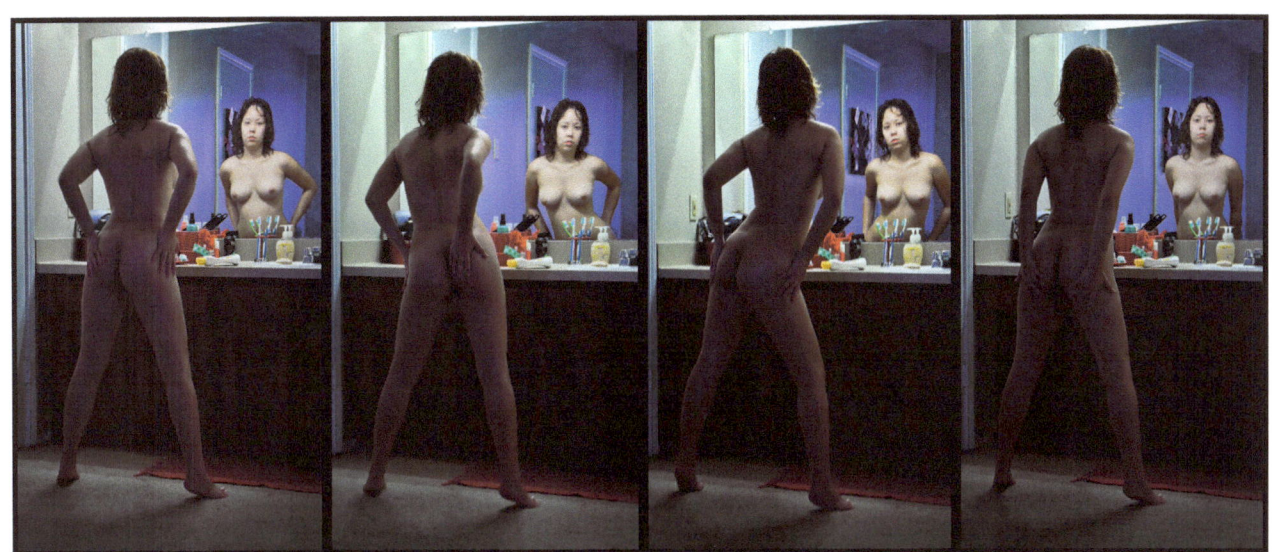

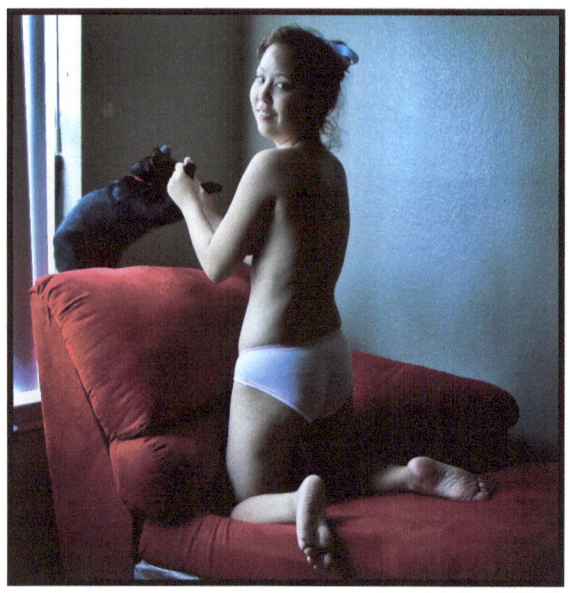

he became rude and strange out of nowhere. When he found out I had gone out with a customer from work, he went into a jealous rage. Before I knew what was happening, he pressed me against a wall, then dragged me to the bed where he pinned me down by my neck. He then sexually assaulted me in such a vicious way - it left me injured and stunned. I couldn't believe he was acting like he was - I didn't recognize him. Afterwards, he acted like he hadn't attacked me - he said something like "I love you, see you tomorrow," kissed me on my forehead and left like everything was normal. It just didn't make any sense. The whole thing was so unreal and so unlike him - it would have made more sense if a stranger had broken into my apartment and attacked me! I felt totally betrayed.

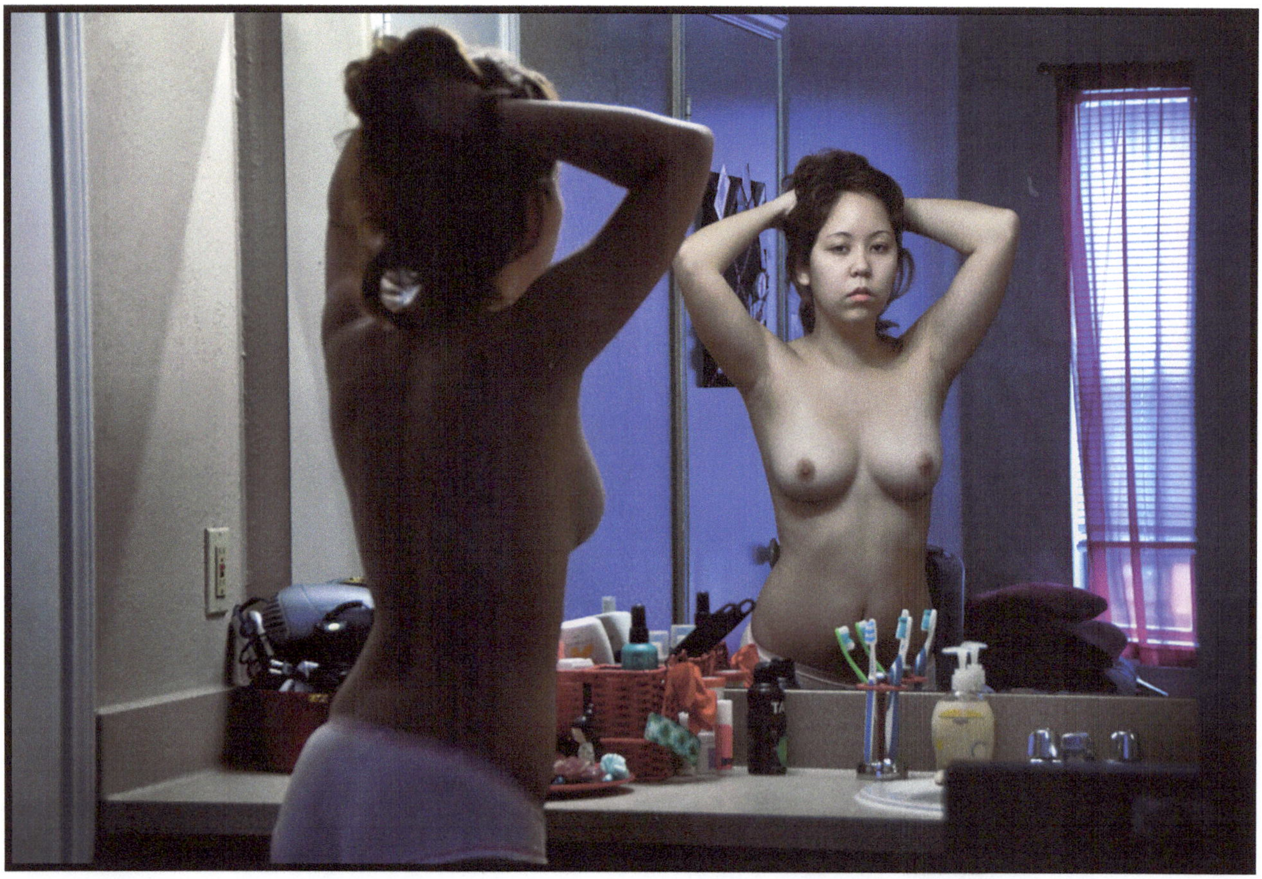

The attack happened at four AM, but it was around nine by the time my head cleared and I realized I had to report it to the police. It had been like an "out of body" experience - it was so unexpected. I even found myself wondering if it really happened - but my injuries were only too real. The police questioned me and took me to the hospital, where I was examined, poked and prodded. They asked me for my "emergency contact" - but that was the guy who attacked me. I had no family in the area - no one to hold my hand and tell me "it will be all right". The person who should have been comforting me was the person who attacked me. That was really the worst part - going through all that - while feeling so totally alone and vulnerable.

A lot of people have trouble bouncing back from something like that because they feel "damaged". I'm not sure why - but I didn't feel that way. But it was definitely my worst day, and I wouldn't wish it on my worst enemy!

♀♀♀♀♀♀♀♀♀

If I could be any animal, I'd be a cat - and not just because they're my favorite. I love how they're agile and graceful, and the way they run and jump. Cats are more independent and sophisticated. In a lot of ways, I'm already a lot like a cat - I like to just lay around! And I love my cat, Roxy - she's the best cat ever.

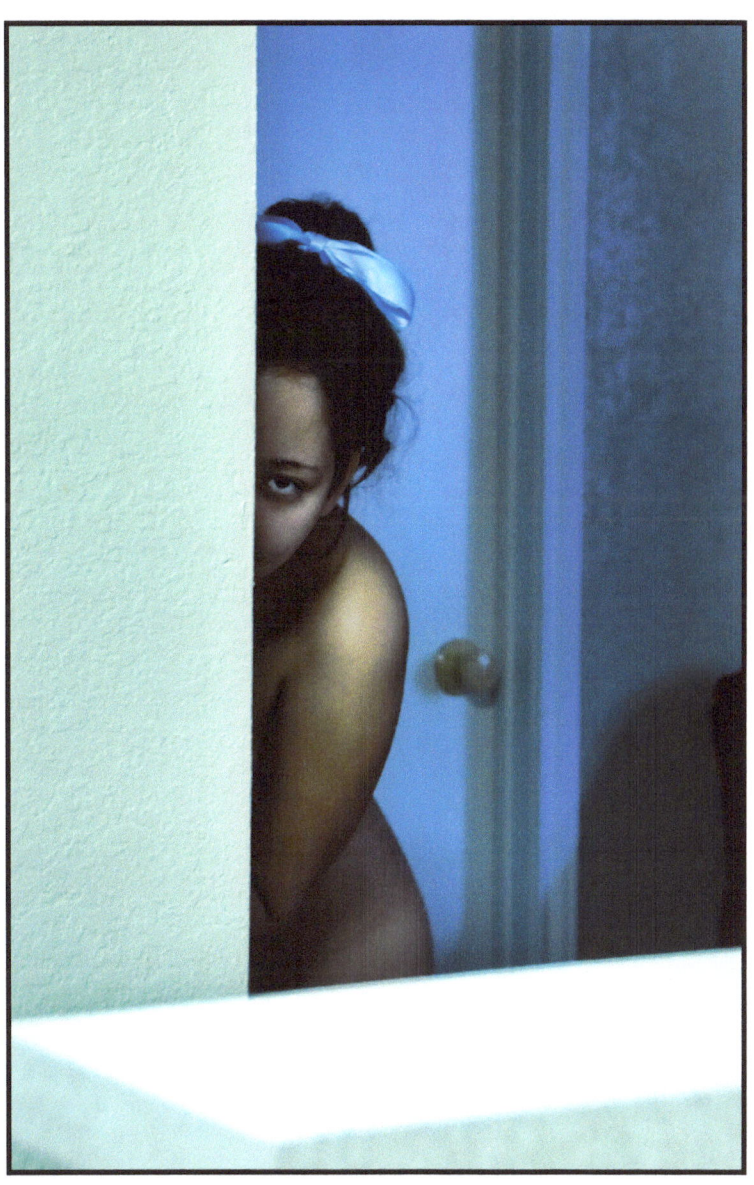

♀♀♀♀♀♀♀♀♀

I love rock music - something about it just excites me! It crosses over into the sexual parts of my life because I used to like to date guys who could play musical instruments - that was really a turn on for me. I really admire people like that. And I prefer concerts to clubs. I love going to concerts when I can afford it.

♀♀♀♀♀♀♀♀♀

I don't care much for most TV shows today, but my all-time favorite is definitely "Seinfeld". That show is like, what - 15 years old - yet the humor still seems so relevant today. That stuff was just too funny! So many people today seem to want humor that is just strange or twisted or offensive. My generation doesn't seem to get the subtle humor of "Seinfeld".

My favorite film is "Fast Times at Ridgemont High" - I'm really into 80's comedies. I'll watch that movie over and over. I know people will want to throw fruit or something at me for saying this, but I think that playing Jeff Spicoli was Sean Penn's greatest work ever!

♀♀♀♀♀♀♀♀♀

To win my heart, a guy's got to do something he wouldn't normally do - kind of like a sacrifice. I wanted my current boyfriend to take me to the state fair. I love going every year, but he hates it. He says it's too crowded, noisy and expensive. But he went ahead and took me. He acted like he was miserable at first, but at some point he actually began to enjoy it. That was a turn-on for me and he was definitely rewarded when we got home!

♀♀♀♀♀♀♀♀♀

I guess I'm an exhibitionist. There was a time when my mother would get mad at me because I would change clothes with the blinds open. It was no big deal to me. I don't have any real modesty about my body - I'm proud of it!

♀♀♀♀♀♀♀♀♀

It's slowly getting better to be a woman today, but it can still be a very oppressive thing sometimes. We're not allowed to be sexual unless it's to please guys. If we talk about what we like, then we're seen as sluts.

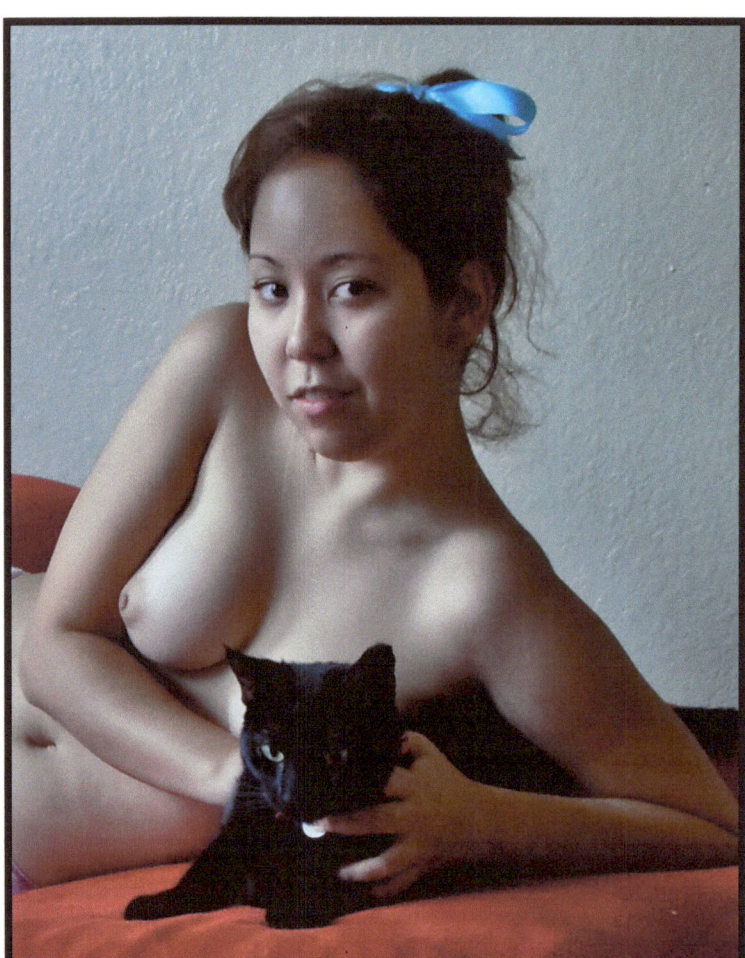

It's sad that some people still feel that way. I get branded as a slut sometimes because I like to flirt a lot. I get branded if I sleep with a guy that I just met a week before. 'Sorry - I didn't realize that there was a rule that says we have to wait "X" number of dates before sexual activity! If I were a dude, I wouldn't get crap over something like that.

There's a lot of pressure on us to look very thin, and very blonde, and very curvaceous, etc. It's difficult, but compared to 30 years ago we're better off. We do seem to be progressing slowly.

Jessica

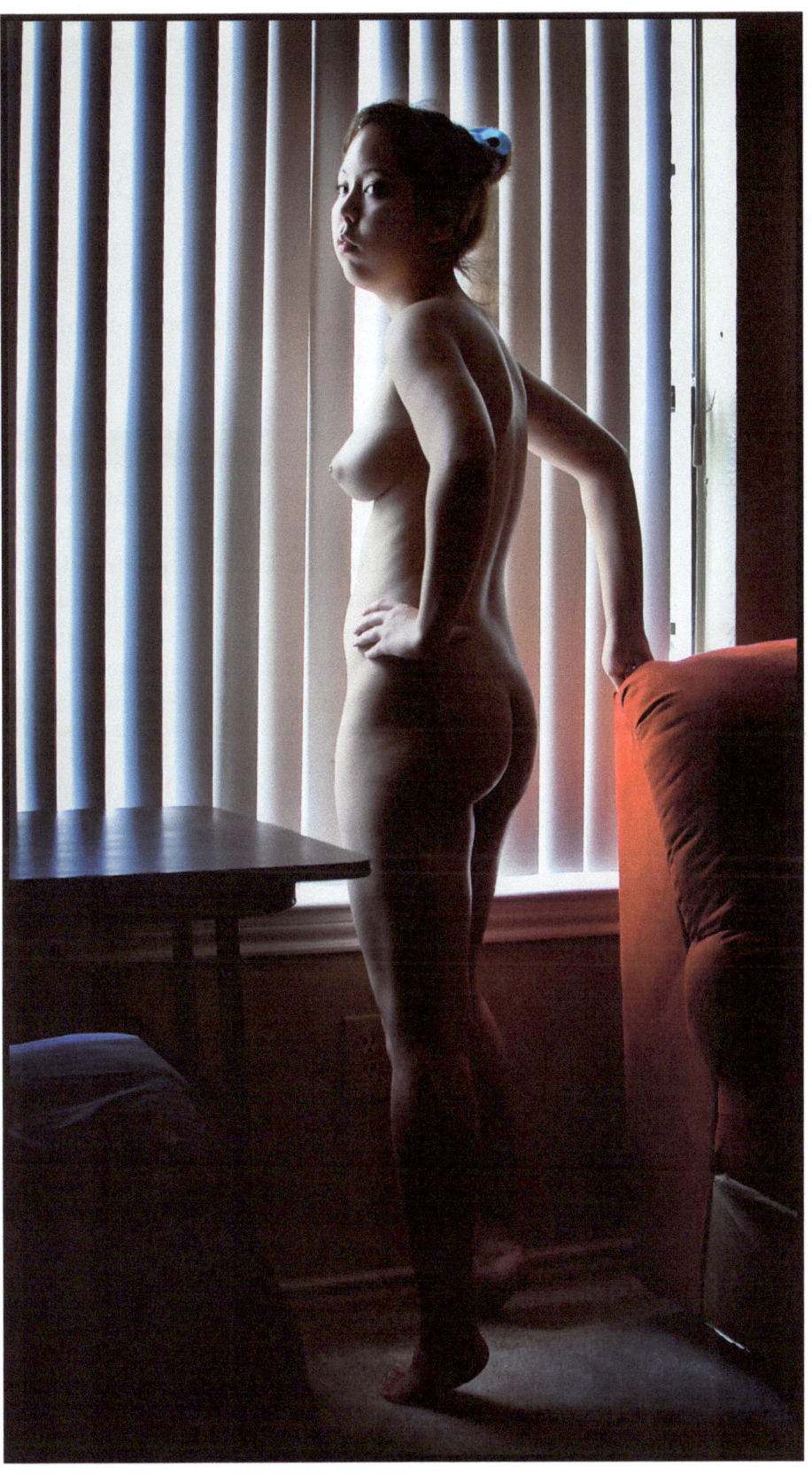

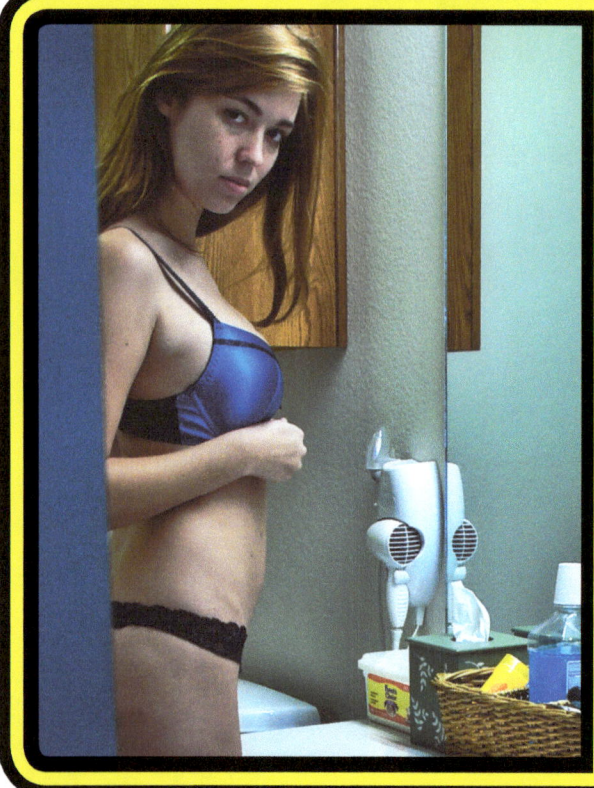

Jess

♀♀♀♀♀♀♀♀

"I'm not so unapproachable. Just come say 'hi!'"

Jess, 24, is a successful art and glamour model who has appeared in several Playboy Special Editions, among other publications. I was pleasantly surprised when the tall, natural beauty expressed an interest in being in my book.

As a kid, the first thing I distinctly remember dreaming about was being the first ballerina on the moon. When I tell people about that, they ask me if I'm disappointed that it never happened. I respond with "what do you mean?"

♀♀♀♀♀♀♀♀

I had a pretty normal childhood - it was actually pretty blissful. I was born in Portsmouth, Virginia, but only lived there a couple of years. My dad was in the navy, then later worked for the government - so we moved a lot. We lived in upstate New York, then Michigan, California, Texas, Illinois, and Louisiana - never for more than three years in one place, sometimes for as little as three months.

I remember living in a small town in Louisiana as a girl - it was the first time we had lived in the south. The family next door had a little girl my age and I went to swim with her in their pool. Her father came out, and the second thing out of his mouth (after "hi" I think) was "we're so glad you guys aren't black!". I was completely taken aback. It amazed my that someone could have that notion, and then voice it to a complete stranger who was their new neighbor. Living in that town was like being time warped back 50 years. At school I went to - it was like there was a line down the middle of the cafeteria, with one side for whites and one side for blacks.

In a way, the fact that my family moved so much gave me a broader perspective on everything. But in another, it was a hindrance to my development. I wasn't getting much reflection - feedback - from my peers. I was constantly making new friends, so it was not like growing up with the same people. It was kind of hard deciding how I should grow up in the absence of life long friendships.

By the seventh or eighth grade, I was as tall as I am today - five feet, eleven in my bare feet. I was rail thin and had this horrible haircut that was kind of short and lopsided. The concept of a blow dryer or a curling iron was totally lost on me. I mean - you just wash your hair, sleep on it and get up - right? I thought it looked like everyone else's - silky and straight - but of course it didn't. Looking back at pictures from that time, I looked very awkward: braces, glasses - and the idea of makeup was something I had never even considered. I saw all my friends wearing it, but it didn't occur to me that it was something I should do. When I finally did - I was so old it almost felt awkward to acknowledge that. There's a point in a girl's life when she either does or doesn't begin doing all these feminine things. I was so far down the "doesn't" path that to come over to the "does" side was really strange.

I didn't always feel that I was attractive. Sometimes, I like to say that I had "ugly duckling" syndrome - meaning I was required to develop a personality first. In high school, while I was pretty (I had all the same physical characteristics I have now) I didn't really know how to manifest that. I was like a "diamond in the

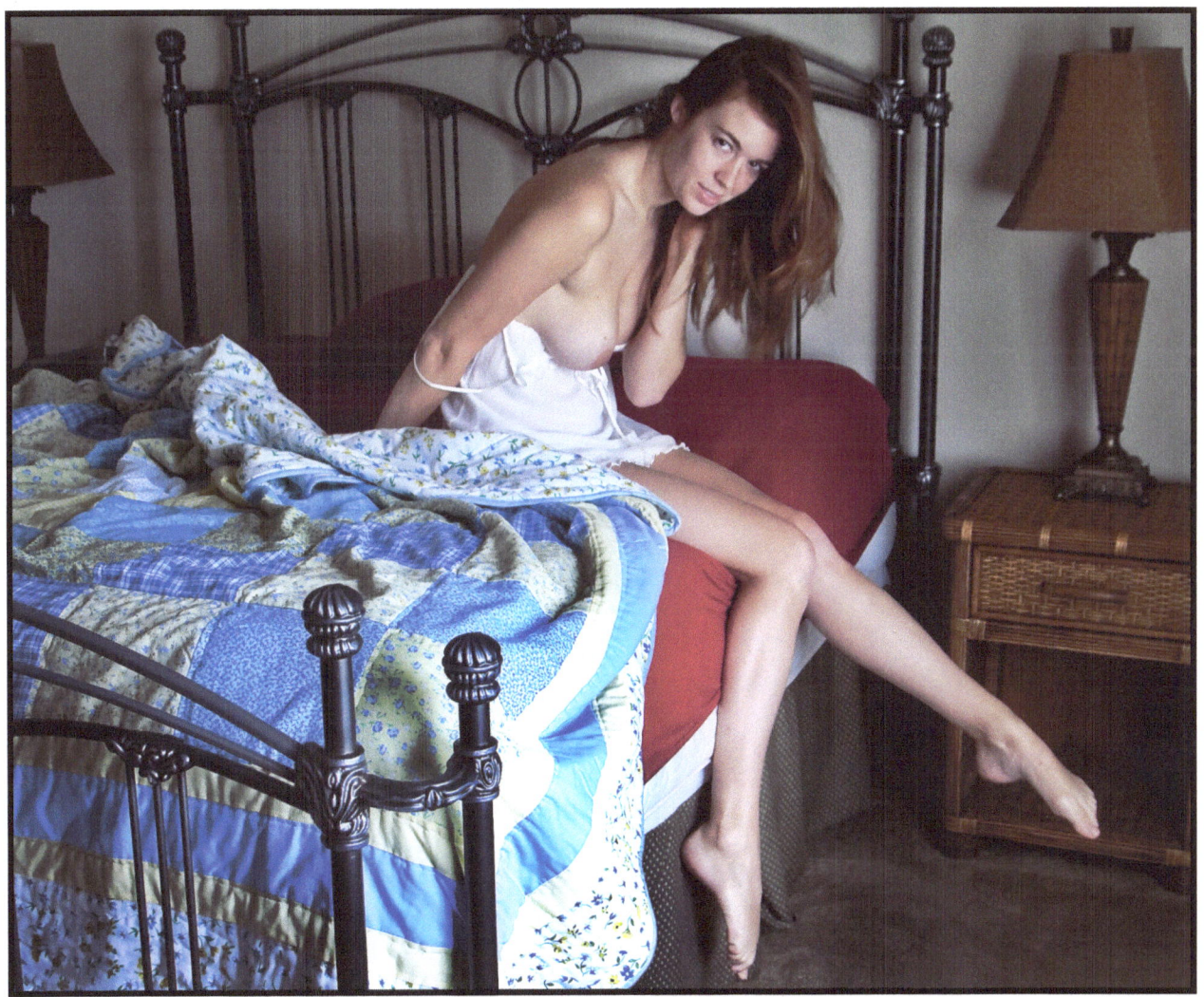

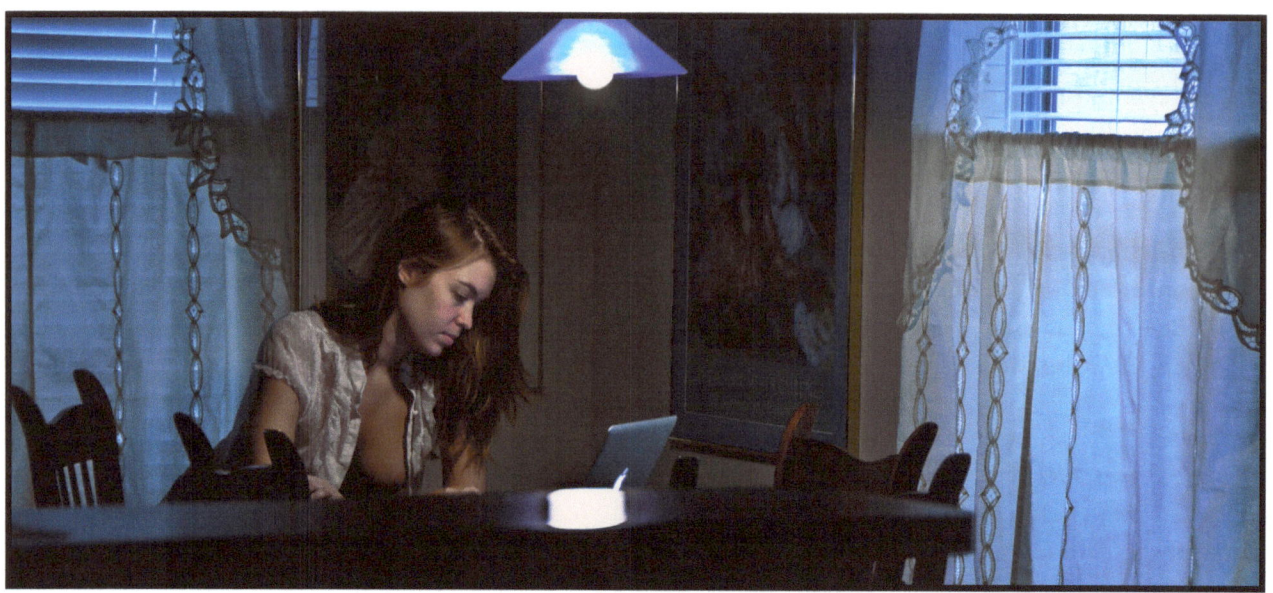

rough" that needed some "spit and polish" to really shine. Other things came first: intelligence, sense of humor, personality - which all kind of finally came together nicely to work with - well - beauty.

I actually moved between tenth and eleventh grade and I figured out a lot of stuff about that time. I had moved after eighth grade, so I did ninth and tenth grades in one place, with one group of people that were different from the ones that I had spent the earlier, terribly awkward times with. Then my last two years of high school, I decided it was going to be different, so I took everything that I had learned (but was too embarrassed to incorporate) and just started using it all. Everything sort of came together then.

So, I finally had brought my looks together - but still, I only had one boyfriend and pretty much no friends during those last two years. I didn't really do much of anything - didn't really participate in much during that time (for reasons I won't go into here). The bottom line was that I just couldn't wait to get out of high school!

♀♀♀♀♀♀♀♀♀

I don't know exactly what my perfect job would be - but it would be fast paced, and it would require critical thinking along with constant learning. It would probably be something high pressure. I do well under those circumstances.

♀♀♀♀♀♀♀♀♀

I'm a really good art model, but I'm mostly seen as a glamour model. I really love artistic projects and would like to be involved in more of them.

♀♀♀♀♀♀♀♀♀

My biggest regret would probably be moving in with a college boyfriend at 18, and living with him until I was 23. I didn't realize how much of myself I had sacrificed with that arrangement, because I didn't have a chance to develop myself. I hadn't noticed (until after we broke up and I had moved on) that there was a whole person in there that needed exposure to the world.

♀♀♀♀♀♀♀♀

If I could travel anywhere - I'd go home! I travel about two weeks out of every month for my modeling, so travel has gotten kind of old and has lost some of its luster for me. Then add to that the fact that plane rides more than three hours long tend to drive me crazy, and that limits where I'd be willing to go: maybe just North and Central America - though as I think about it, I guess I would like to visit a country somewhere in South America.

But, really - if I was going to take a trip for pleasure, it would be more about who I was going with, rather than where I was going.

♀♀♀♀♀♀♀♀

One of the harshest realities I've experienced as an adult is that I don't have a lot of friends. I make friends and they disappear for whatever reasons. When you're a kid, I think friendships are just something that happens. Kids want other kids to play with, and you're at school. As an adult, it's all too easy to become an island.

♀♀♀♀♀♀♀♀

One of the main problems of my early adulthood is that I don't have a lot of ambitions or dreams that I'm driven to accomplish. I go to school, but I don't put a whole lot into it. I'm 24 and I haven't graduated. I model because it's fun and I've learned a lot doing it - but I'm not doing it towards any end. I'm working on a bachelors degree in neuroscience - I have about 40 credit hours left to complete it. I've studied and tried a lot of things. I'm generally gifted at most of what I've attempted to do, but I really haven't found anything that really gets me out of bed every morning. I also have a bad habit

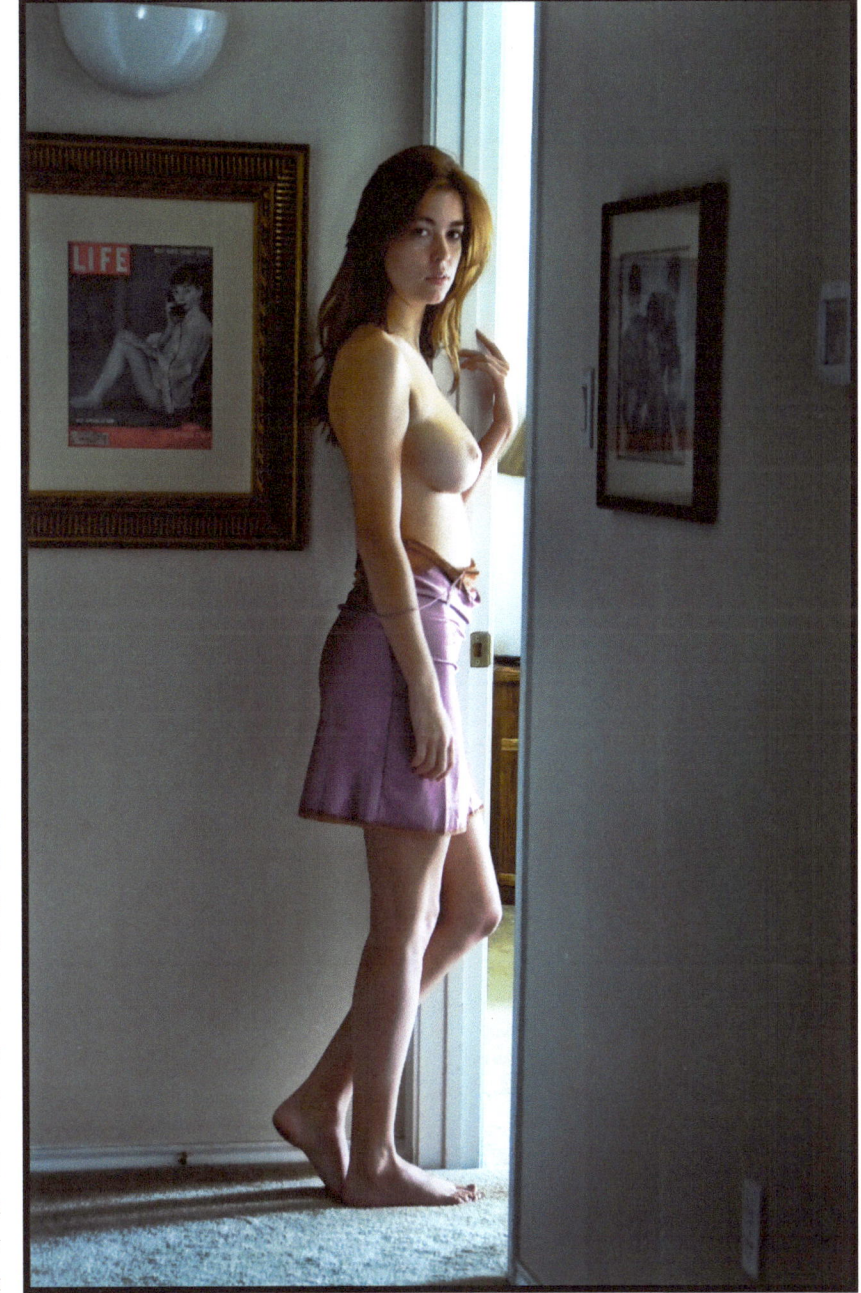

of not finishing a lot of what I start, especially with big projects. Mostly because I get bored before I finish.

♀♀♀♀♀♀♀♀♀

Best and worst qualities? I'm extremely intelligent, and I'm extremely lazy!

♀♀♀♀♀♀♀♀♀

Favorite sexual position? What day of the week is it?

♀♀♀♀♀♀♀♀♀

I don't like thunderstorms - they scare me. Well, it's wind really that I don't like, especially at night. A tornado hit my house about 3 years ago.

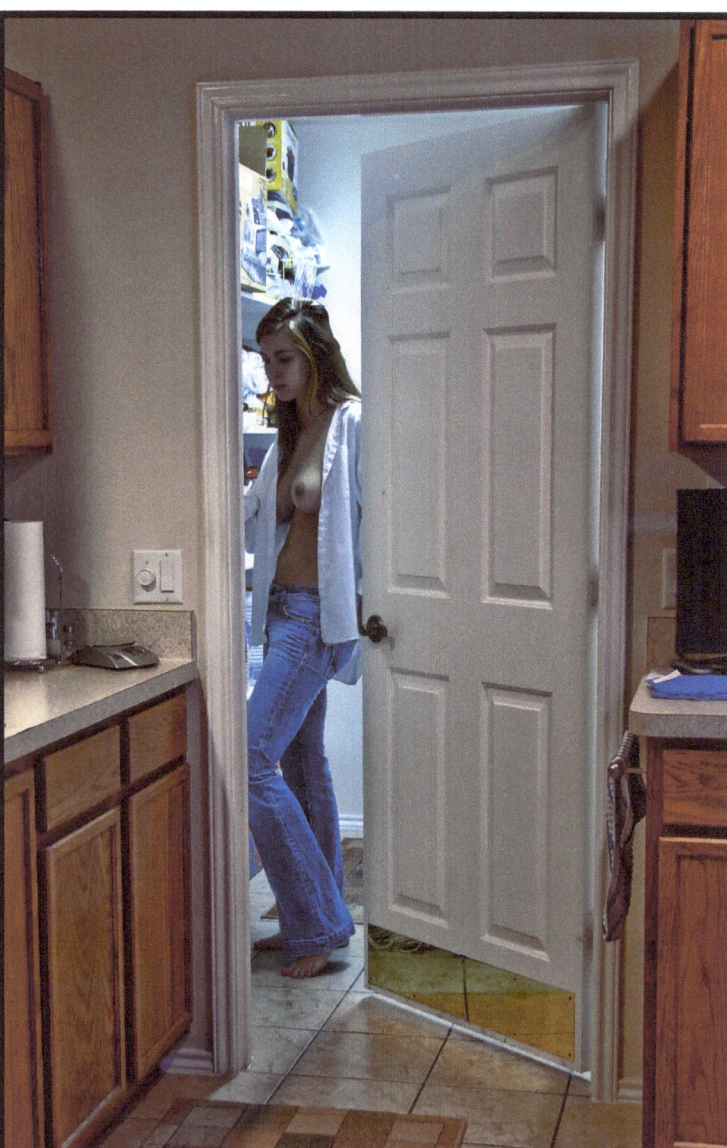

♀♀♀♀♀♀♀♀♀

For a man to win my heart, he has to have self-confidence - that is absolutely key. Just about anything else I can deal with, but no sniveling and no whining! They have to be confident - it's real easy!

♀♀♀♀♀♀♀♀♀

The best part of being a woman is - I don't know - being pretty? Being pretty is fun - guys don't get to be pretty.

The worst part of being a woman? I deal with a lot of constant sexualization of relationships. I don't have many relationships with people that aren't at least somewhat sexual. Oh, I guess it could be argued that all relationships are sexual to some extent, depending on your particular take on human psychology. But when it gets to the point of disabling the relationship - it's really sad!

I've had a lot of friends who eventually say we can no longer be friends because they have fallen in love with me. When I don't reciprocate - they're gone. This happens to a lot of women, and I think that's unfortunate.

♀♀♀♀♀♀♀♀♀

The thing about men, is that they don't

get interrupted in their lives as much as women do. If a man has some overreaching dream or ambition, he can pretty much pursue it, and still have relationships and families or whatever.

But women are kind of expected to be the "glue" and that option takes away from many other things that might be getting done. It takes a certain kind of woman to say "no, I'm going to go do this anyway" because that would be against the grain. For a man, however, the same thing would be "admirable"!

On the other hand, part of that very issue can work against men. They are expected to go forth and conquer, but maybe they don't want to do that. Maybe they just want to be happy in a simple life. "Did you get that job?" "Did you get that promotion?" Maybe they don't care about that.

♀♀♀♀♀♀♀♀♀

I've mellowed out a lot. I used to be very serious and very elitist. Now I've learned to take the good from people and not really focus too much on the bad (if it's not too bad) - just take whatever enjoyment I can take with whomever I can.

♀♀♀♀♀♀♀♀♀

If I could change anything about myself, I would be less jealous - I'm a very jealous person!

♀♀♀♀♀♀♀♀♀

I'm not so unapproachable - just come say "hi!"

♀♀♀♀♀♀♀♀♀

People being stupid for no reason drives me crazy. Like, have a reason for the things that you do, if they're extreme!

♀♀♀♀♀♀♀♀♀

My significant other should be honest, self-sufficient, and comfortable with themselves as an individual. And they have to love me!

♀♀♀♀♀♀♀♀♀

The best day I ever had? At the beginning of this year, I had a bunch of great days, and I said to myself - I'm going to make every day in 2009 a great day! I made it pretty far - I got two or three months in of great days, every day. It's definitely an attitude, a mind-set. And

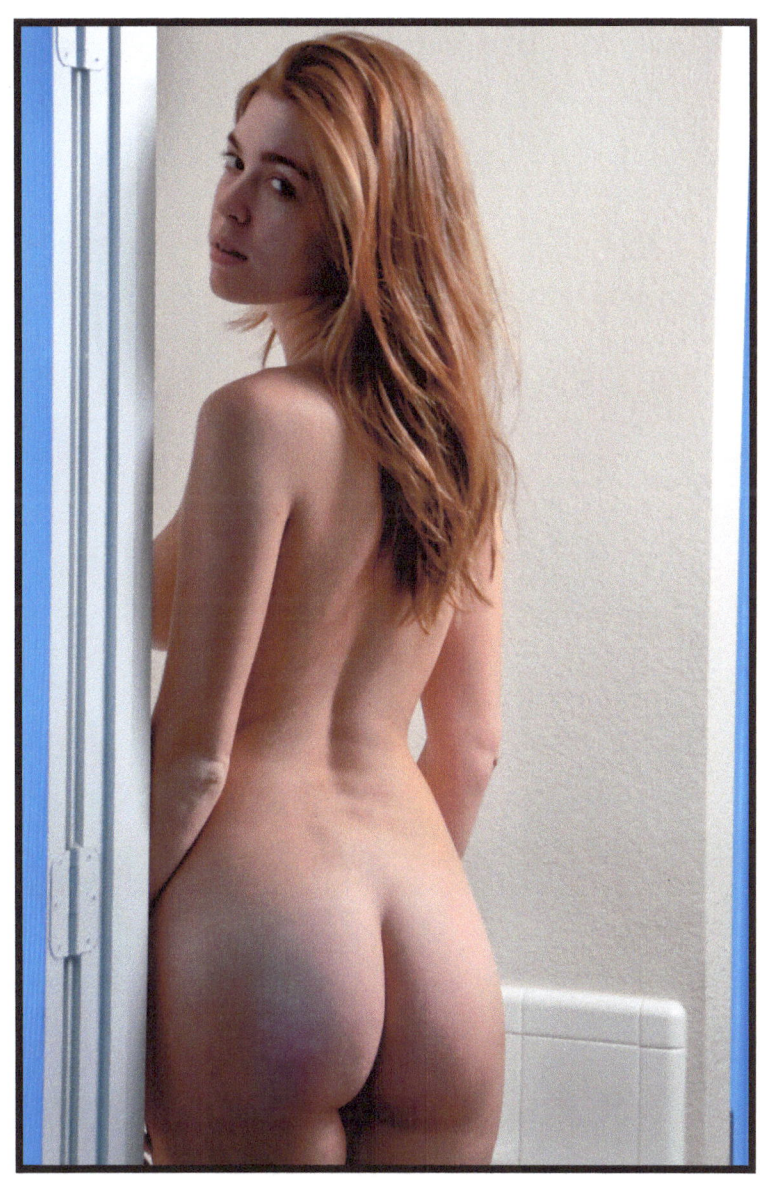

then one day just piled up and I couldn't make that day good, no matter what I did!

Worse day? Well, recently I had one doozy of a bad day! I flew into Sacramento for a photo shoot one morning really early. I was sick and I got to the rental car place and it was a huge problem. My phone died so I had to go back to the terminal to use a pay phone, because they didn't have one at the rental car terminal. I'm on the phone and my phone card runs out of minutes, so I call the phone card place and they're closed. I use what little change I have to call my boyfriend but he doesn't recognize the phone number, and he's real busy so he says "I'll call you back" and hangs up on me, so I lose all the change I have. I'm like crying at this point, and I go over to a concession stand and ask for change - and they say I have to buy something. So I buy something and they give me change - I go back to the pay phone and sort things out, get my rental car taken care of (got gouged on it big time). Then I drive for an hour and a half north of Sacramento where I'm meeting this guy - and he's not at the rendezvous place. I call him and email him, but I don't hear back from him. It's three in the afternoon by this time, so I decide to go ahead and get a hotel room and see what happens. The guy calls me at 6:30 the next morning and says he forgot his phone. So we wound up shooting anyway. But it was one really bad day!

♀♀♀♀♀♀♀♀♀

I'm cold almost all the time, so my favorite time of the year is summer.

♀♀♀♀♀♀♀♀♀

I've thought a lot about it, and for me, posing nude is self-actualization. To not do it would be limiting some part of myself. Like if I had a talent as a singer, but I didn't use it. So if I have a body perfect for art nudes and glamour, and I didn't pursue that - then that's shutting a little part of myself off. Why would I do that?

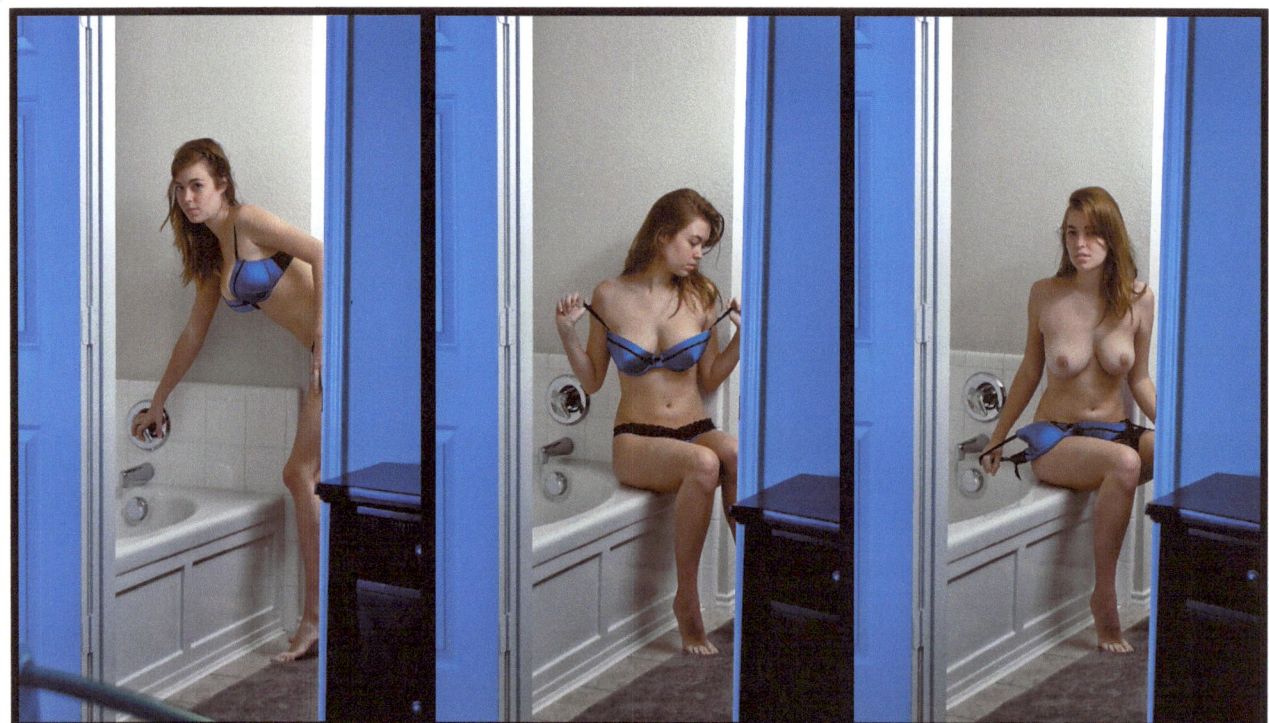

I have no religion, so I've had to carefully define my own morality. And I've done that based on reason - rational thought. When I came to thinking about morality and duty - I couldn't come up with any compelling reason to make posing nude immoral for my own sort of structure.

♀♀♀♀♀♀♀♀♀

I don't think I'm an exhibitionist, but everyone says I am - so maybe I am one. I think it's just a matter of me having a very casual attitude about nudity.

♀♀♀♀♀♀♀♀♀

Some favorites of mine:

Alcoholic drink: anything with tequila in it!

Non-alcoholic beverage: I've been drinking a lot of pink vitaminwater lately.

Comfort food: spaghetti

Color: green

Music: I don't listen to any kind of music!

Sport (to play): I played soccer for a long time when I was a kid, but I haven't played in a long time. I guess now it would be tennis.

Sport (to watch): basketball or hockey

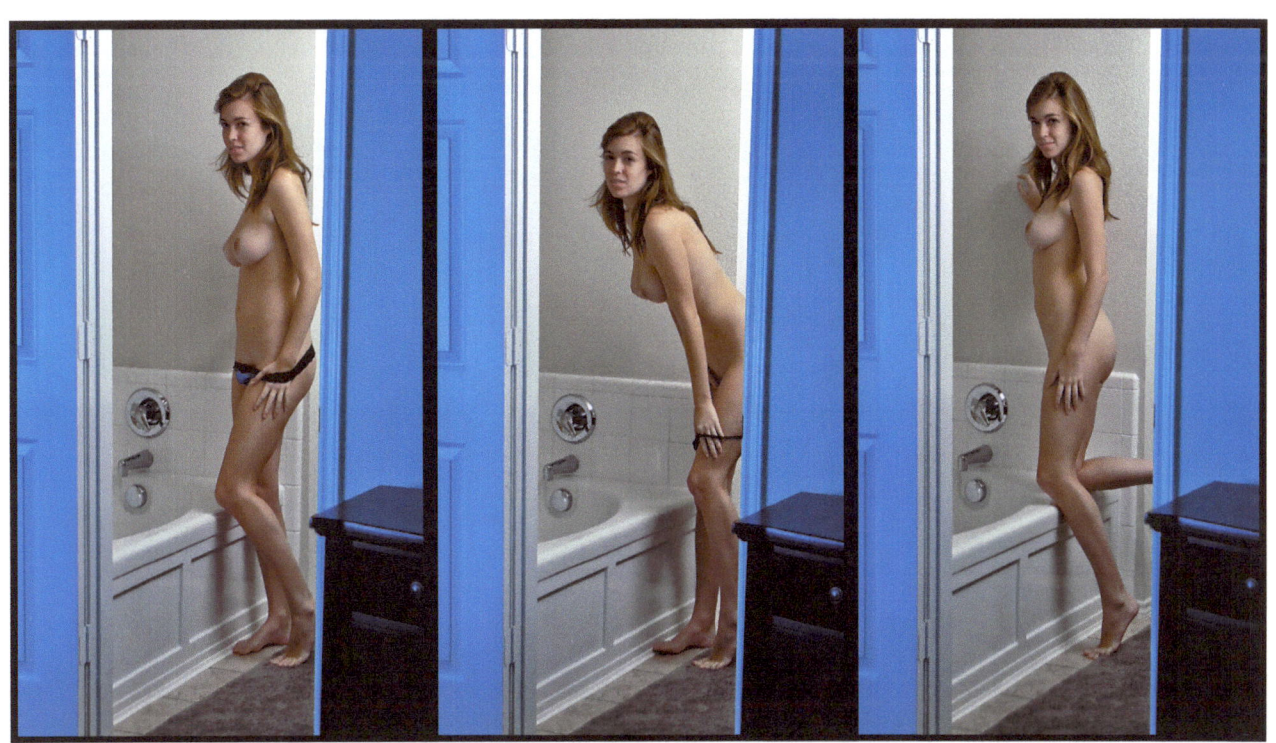

♀♀♀♀♀♀♀♀♀

People are generally pleased when they stumble upon success, so in that manner - I'm sure I would be too if I hit it really big. But I didn't get into modeling because it's something I've been dreaming of since I was four years old (it wasn't), or because I want to be the next Tila Tequila or whatever (I don't). Fame and fortune never motivated me. I am constantly employing myself at the very minimum required to support the very spartan lifestyle I live - and I don't know why that is. I model because it makes sense, and I happen to be lucky enough to be genetically inclined to do that. I don't do it because I'm chasing something grander.

Jess

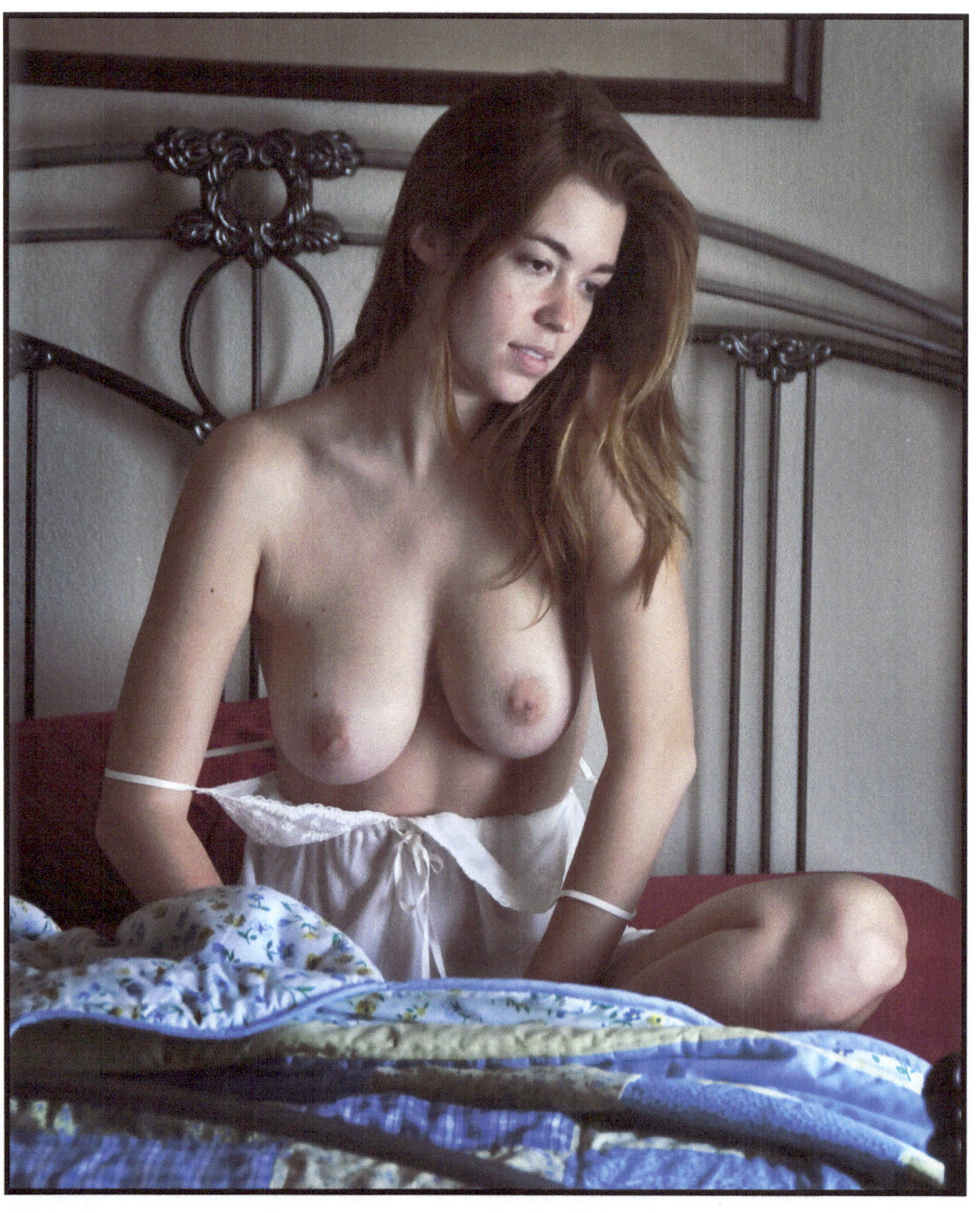

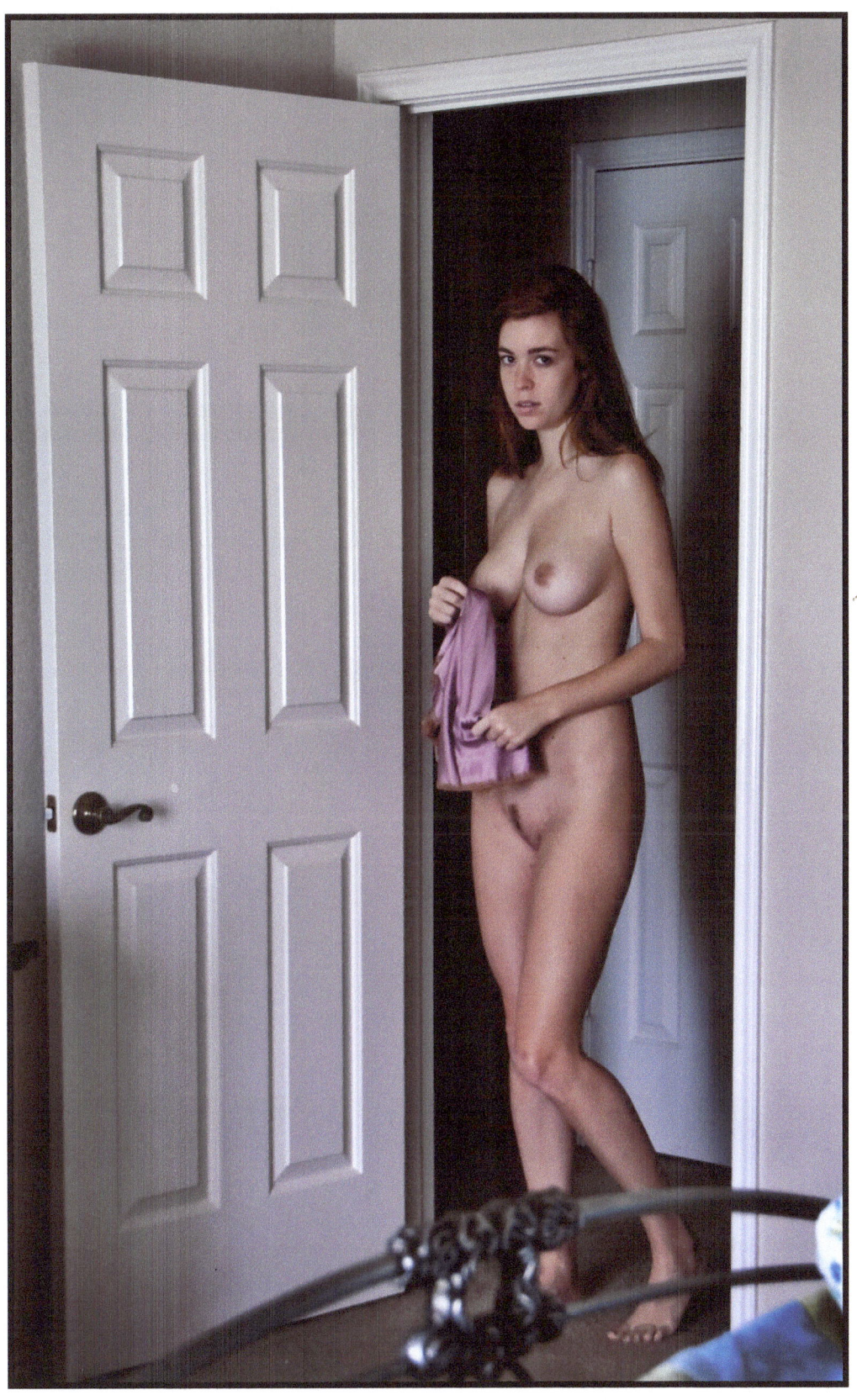

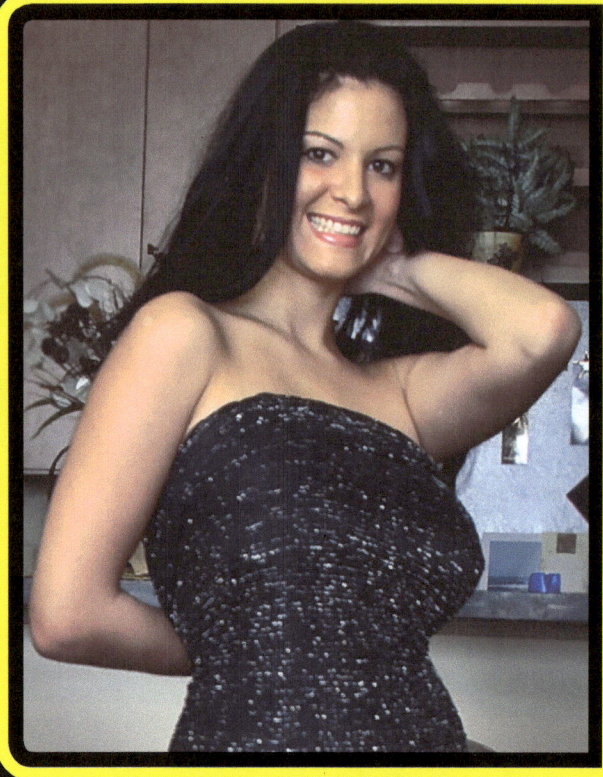

Marilyn

♀♀♀♀♀♀♀♀♀

"Every day of my life is an adventure!"

Marilyn, 27, is the "bombshell" of the group: very sexy - and very charming. She seems to be very upbeat and cheerful all the time.

I always wanted to be in entertainment - as an actress, singer or model. I wanted to be out in public, on-stage. It's always been a way for me to be myself - by being somebody else.

♀♀♀♀♀♀♀♀♀

My childhood was wonderful! I grew up with the usual stuff - just learning to be myself and accept myself. I have a great family - very close with lots and lots of love. They have always been very supportive of me in everything I've ever done.

I really enjoyed my time in high school. I was a drama major and performed in several plays. I was also a cheerleader and had lots of friends.

♀♀♀♀♀♀♀♀♀

I'm very lucky. If I could wave a magic wand and do anything I wanted, I would keep doing what I'm doing now, which is modeling. I love being a model.

♀♀♀♀♀♀♀♀♀

One of the toughest experiences I've had as an adult was the ending of my last serious relationship - something that happened just a short time ago.

Sometimes you don't plan on meeting someone or falling in love, but it just happens and it changes everything. I met and got involved with an executive for one of the companies in California that I've worked for. He's a great guy, but he didn't always want to understand about my work - even though he's in the same business. He sometimes tried to change me and that was hard. People who love you shouldn't do that - they should accept you and love you just as you are.

I've dated a few guys over the last few years, but he's the only one I really loved. We had our problems, but it was all that much tougher because of the distance involved: I live in Texas and he lives in California. We were only together for a few months - but a lot of that time was really great! Sometimes you don't know what you have until you lose it.

♀♀♀♀♀♀♀♀

When I'm not working, I like to work out at the gym, go to art galleries - stuff like that. I also love to read - history novels, biographies and mystery/crime novels. Lately I've been thinking that I'd really like to learn to play the guitar.

I'm pretty much an "artsy" person.

♀♀♀♀♀♀♀♀♀

Every day of my life is an adventure - I'm an adventurous kind of person. I like to rock climb, and I'd really like to try bungee jumping one of these days.

♀♀♀♀♀♀♀♀♀

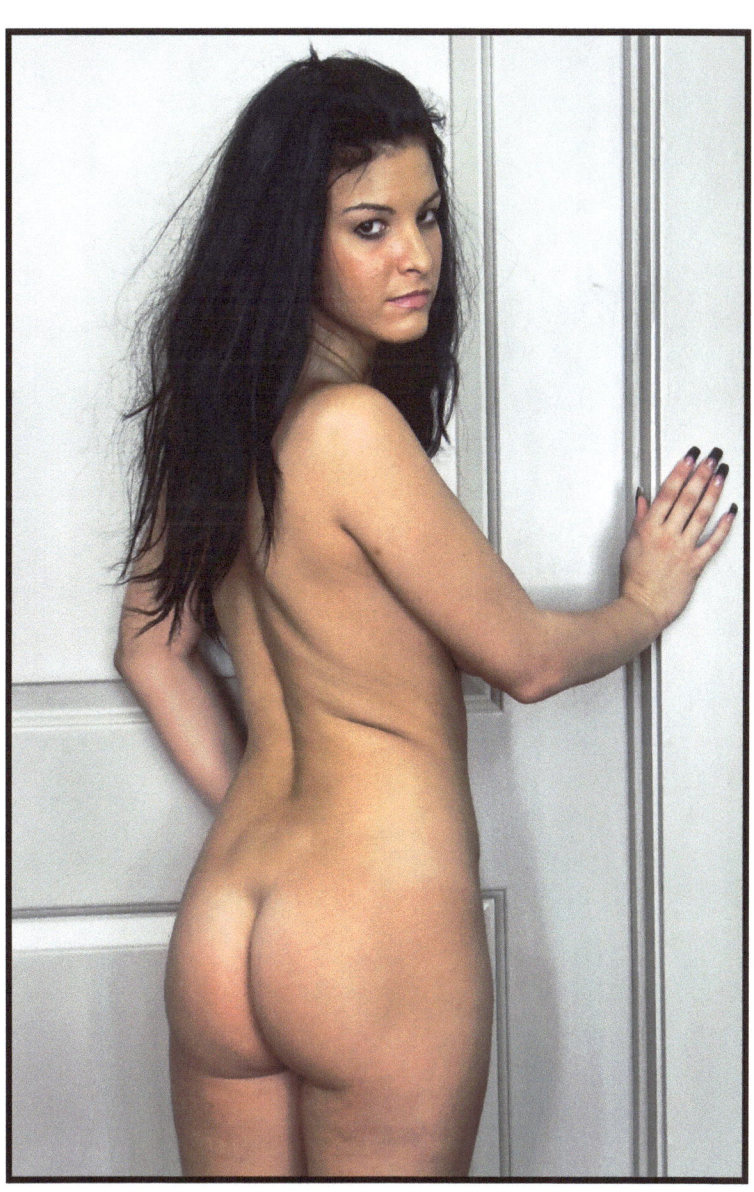

One of the greatest joys of my life was when my brother entered my life - when he was born. He's 12 years old now, and he has supplied a lot of joy for me in that short time. I don't have any children, so I enjoy spending time with him.

I'd like to have a family one day - a husband and children - but it's not a real high priority for me right now. I'm really into my career presently. I would have to meet just the totally right person.

♀♀♀♀♀♀♀♀♀

If I could go just anywhere at all, I'd love to go to Germany. That would be so cool - I love history! The place I'd like to see most after that would be Paris.

I've never been out of the United States, but I'd love to visit other countries one of these days.

♀♀♀♀♀♀♀♀♀

A lot of people don't know this about me, but I'm a good decorator. Really - I'm pretty good at it!

I'm a good listener, and I'm always there for my friends. I'm not shy at all when it comes to my work, but I'm a really shy person in my "real" life.

♀♀♀♀♀♀♀♀♀

I have some regrets about my life, I guess. You always think that you'd like to go back in time and re-do a lot of things, but you wouldn't be the person that you are today if you did. I wish I were more trusting of people, because my last relationship is my biggest regret. Sometimes you have to keep work as work and not mix it with your private life.

I'd like to have more time for more of the people in my life - friends and family - but I can't think of any

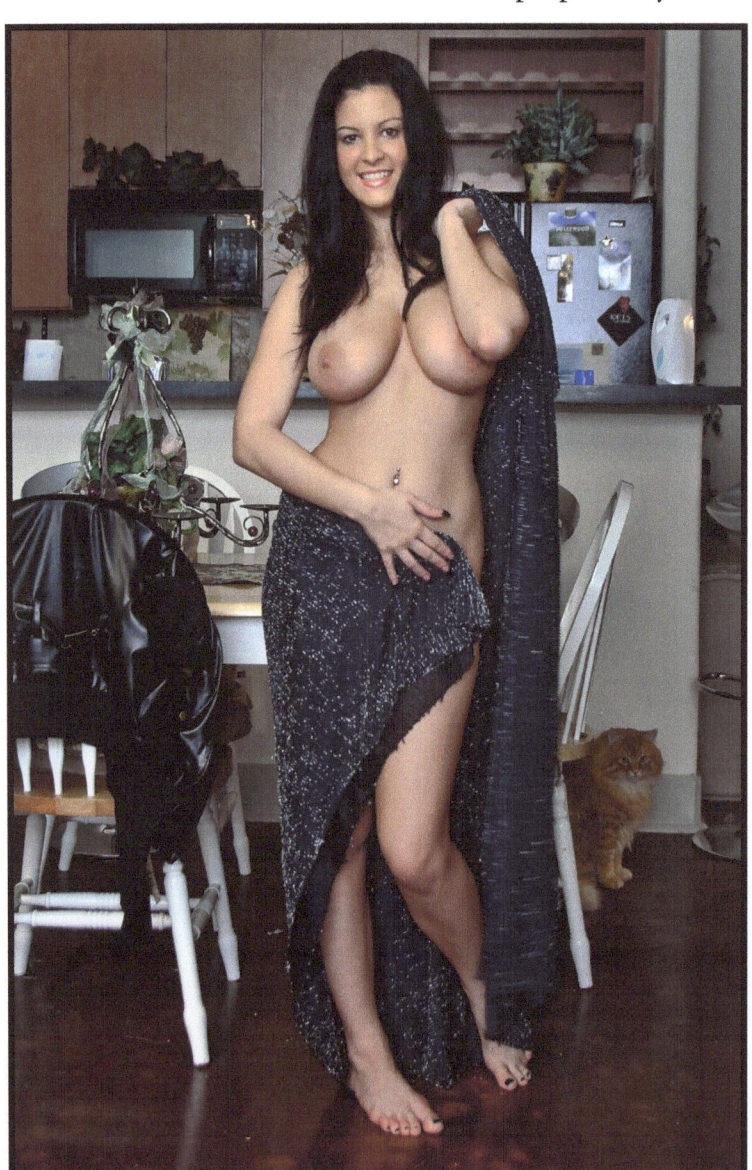

personal characteristics that I'd want to change about myself. Nobody's perfect, but I've been pretty happy with who I am.

♀♀♀♀♀♀♀♀♀

I'm really proud of a lot of the work I've done recently. It's cool to see myself in a magazine (I was in "LA" magazine not too long ago) - or to have friends see me in something and tell me about it. I've even gotten a couple of awards lately.

♀♀♀♀♀♀♀♀♀

I wouldn't want to be a man if I could magically change into one. Even with all the hard things we women have to deal with - a woman is a beautiful creature!

The best part of being a woman is all the feminine things. I don't know - just make-up and dressing up - guys don't get to experience all that!

The worst part of being a woman has definitely got to be PMS! Yeah, there's really nothing else compared to that! And I hate the double standard - like the way men can date lots of women and that's cool, but if a woman does that - she's a "playgirl."

♀♀♀♀♀♀♀♀♀

I've learned not to judge people so much. I've learned always to keep my wall up - never let it down. I've learned that some-times the best thing you can do is trust in yourself. You just have to be you - and if someone can't accept you, then "oh, well".

♀♀♀♀♀♀♀♀♀

I love cats - I have FOUR of them!

♀♀♀♀♀♀♀♀♀

My personality is my strongest asset. I'm a loving and caring person - I like to be there for people. I'm just very real.

I'm too nice for my own good some-times, though - and it lets people take advantage of me. I get taken for granted.

♀♀♀♀♀♀♀♀♀

Not much scares me - except for love. It can be a really great thing, but it can also be very frightening. Otherwise, I like scary things. Halloween is my favorite holiday!

♀♀♀♀♀♀♀♀♀

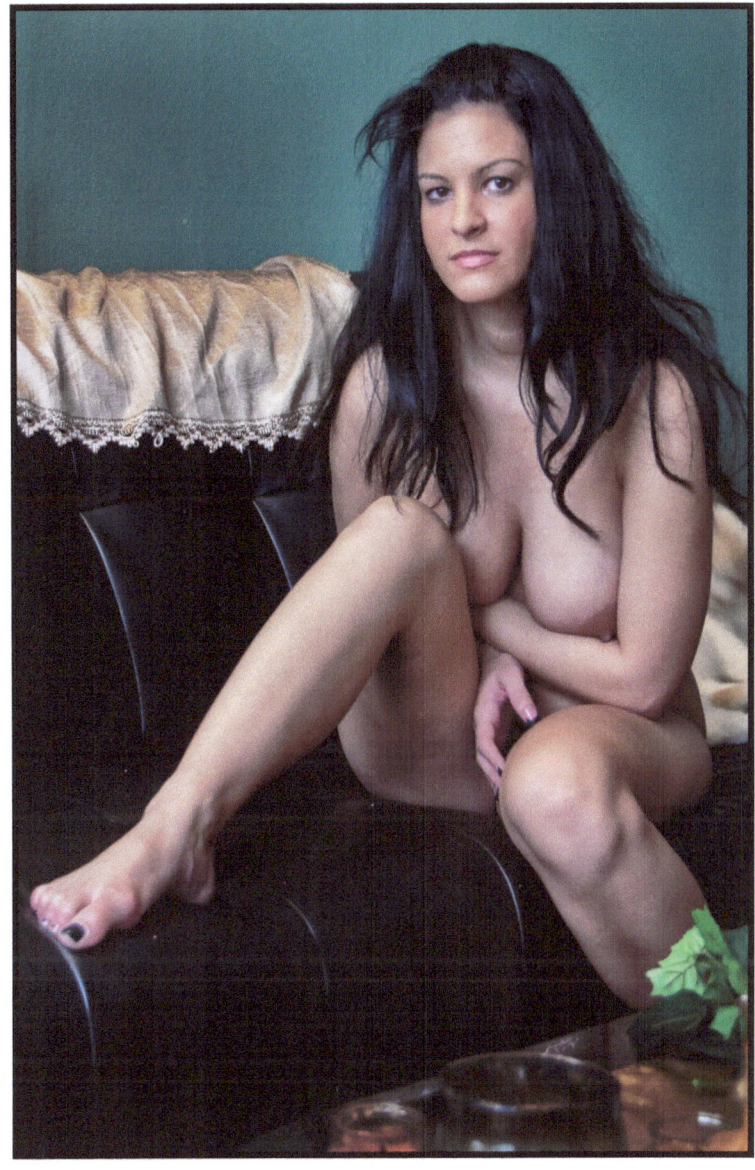

I was born in New Jersey and lived there until I was about four, when my parents moved to Texas. I used to go back and forth between here and New Jersey a lot, but now I mostly travel between here and California.

A lot of the work I do in Texas is in fashion, but I do more varied work in California. I've done some calendar work out there, and I've worked for some car companies - among other things. I typically make one or two California trips every month, working with a lot of the same people all the time.

I really like California. I think the people are more open, and of course - I love the beaches! I do more bikini wear photo shoots out there - which are always fun.

Everything is very different - I love just about everything about the place. I'd move out there - I've thought about it - but property is so much more expensive there than here. My family is here, and so that's a big

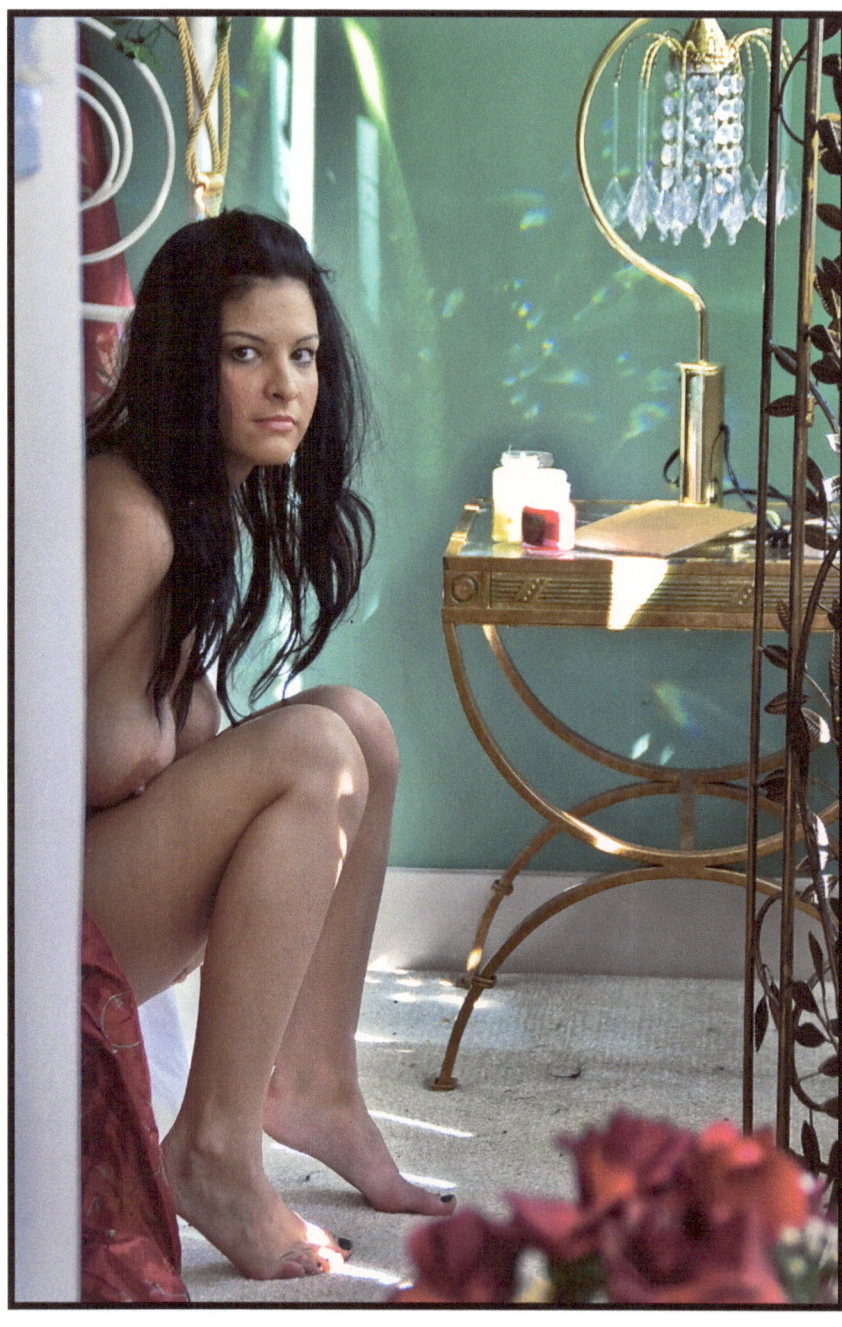

factor also. A part of me would really like to move, but I've been here for a long time. There's a lot to like about Texas as well!

♀♀♀♀♀♀♀♀♀

My favorite fairy tale is "Cinderella" because she finally meets the right guy, and she triumphs over evil.

♀♀♀♀♀♀♀♀♀

My favorite sexual position would have to be doggie style. I'm a real romantic (ha ha)!

♀♀♀♀♀♀♀♀♀

Fantasies? Oh, yeah - you always have to have the sexual fantasies! I think the whole "office sex" fantasy is real hot. You know - you go in for an interview and the guy is real sexy, and you just wind up doing it right there on the desk!

♀♀♀♀♀♀♀♀♀

I love sports. I love to ice skate and I love to work out a lot, too. I like to watch all kinds of sports - especially football, hockey, tennis and golf.

♀♀♀♀♀♀♀♀♀

I actually have a star crush on Eric Wareheim from the "Tim and Eric Awesome Show". I got to meet him in person not too long ago. That was totally cool!

♀♀♀♀♀♀♀♀♀

To win my heart, a guy has to be the person he was when I met him. He also has to be honest - not lie or cheat on me. He has to treat me right - spoil me really - and just be loving and real.

The qualities I look for in a significant other? Well, number one - he has to have a great personality and be a loving person. I guess looks and all that would rank below that for me.

♀♀♀♀♀♀♀♀♀

I'm passionate about work, family and love - and making lots of money!

♀♀♀♀♀♀♀♀♀

Some favorites of mine:

Comfort food: ice cream

Color: pink

Music: stuff from the 80's

Musical act: Madonna (I especially love her old stuff)

Movie: "Pretty in Pink" - and I LOVE Marilyn Monroe movies

Season: fall

TV Shows: "Californication" and "Tim and Eric Awesome Show"

♀♀♀♀♀♀♀♀♀

People who lie, people who are not consistent, and people who can't schedule anything really get on my nerves!

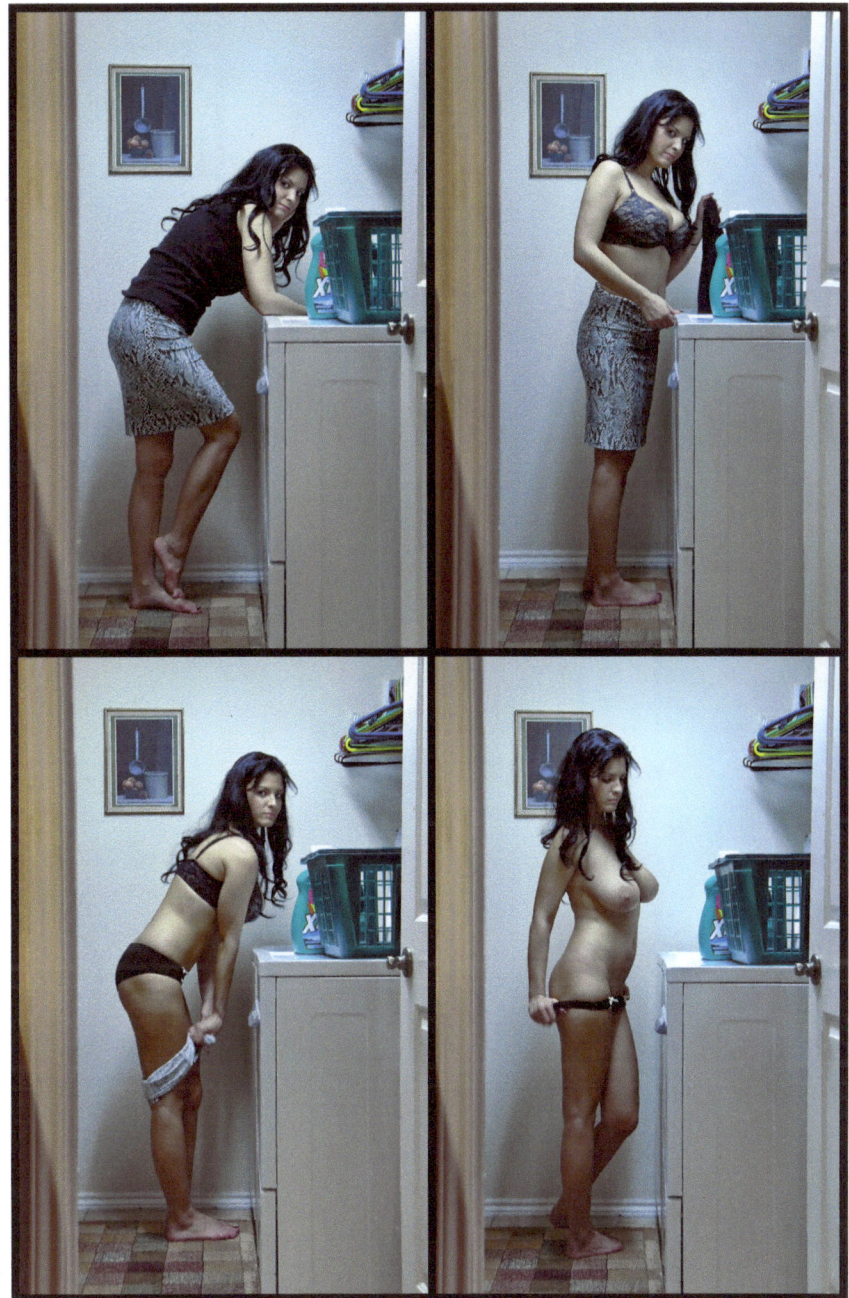

♀♀♀♀♀♀♀♀♀

I'm a pretty open person - I never have anything to hide. Lots of people do, though. If someone wants to know something about me, they should just ask me.

I don't know - sometimes I feel like my life is just an open book, which is mostly good - but can sometimes be bad.

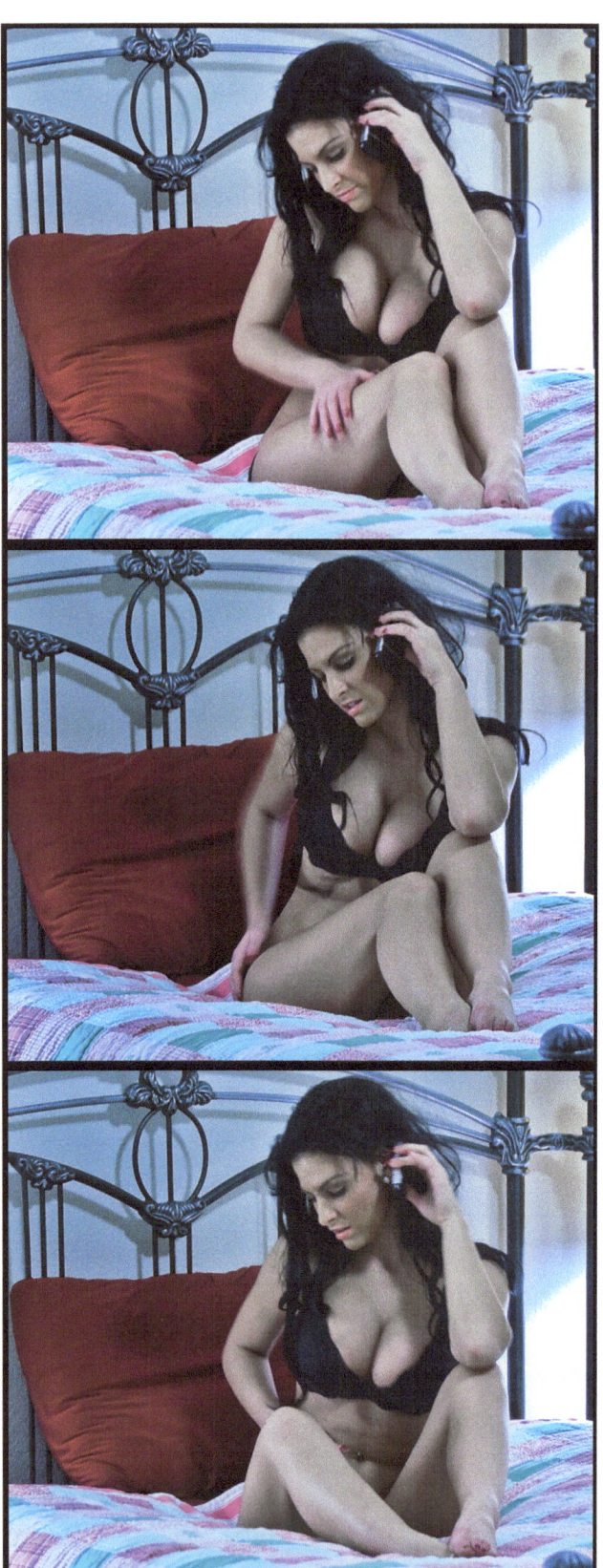

♀♀♀♀♀♀♀♀♀

My favorite subjects in school were history, science and literature. My least favorite was definitely math.

♀♀♀♀♀♀♀♀♀

The craziest, wildest thing I've ever done was going to California, by myself, without knowing anyone out there. I went out there saying "I'm going to a modeling agency", "I'm going to work as a model" and "I'm going to turn a job into a career" - and I did make all that happen. Most girls would have found that very difficult.

♀♀♀♀♀♀♀♀♀

The best day I've ever had was just this past summer on Venice Beach in California. I love the beach, but of course we don't have them here in north Texas. It was just time away from work, and seeing people and taking pictures of the beach. But especially - it was being with someone I truly loved and enjoyed being with. It was awesome!
The worst day of my life was probably the day I lost the love of my life. Sadly, my best day and my worst day both involved the same person!

The days I lost my grandmother and grandfather were pretty bad as well!

♀♀♀♀♀♀♀♀♀

My favorite alcoholic drink is Goldschlager. My favorite beverage is Coca Cola.

♀♀♀♀♀♀♀♀♀

My heroes? My dad would be one. My mom, my little 12-year-old brother - I love him so much!

Oh...and Marilyn Monroe.

♀♀♀♀♀♀♀♀♀

How I got into nude modeling was no big deal.

I've been around modeling most of my life, and I've always been comfortable being undressed. In college, I worked at Hooters, and all my girl friends said I should try nude modeling - because I had a nice body and could make good money. I was a pretty open person back then, like I am now. I did a lot of theater work, then I was a dancer for a couple of years, which I really enjoyed. That I enjoyed dancing surprised me, because I'd always been such a "goody-goody" kind of girl. Trying nude modeling was a pretty easy next step - I did it for several agencies.

I suppose I'm an exhibitionist - but in a good way. I mean, I wouldn't just go out and flash people - but I'm comfortable in my own skin, and comfortable being naked...some people just are. For example, I'm more comfortable sitting here - doing this interview naked - than I would be clothed. My friends don't understand that because I'm a really shy person normally.

♀♀♀♀♀♀♀♀♀

Being a woman in today's world is very difficult. I envy my mom and other woman in the past because I think they had it easier. Even though it was a little more of a man's world then - it was different: women were women. Now, guys really treat women terribly. They don't have any respect for us. So it's harder. And it's getting tougher to find old fashioned guys these days.

♀♀♀♀♀♀♀♀♀

Update: Just a couple of days before this book went to press (and several weeks after I did my interview for it), I took a trip to California. While I was there, I spent some time with the guy I had broken up with a while back (the guy who was part of both my "best" and "worst" days). We had been talking off and on for some time, but now we've decided to give our relationship another try.

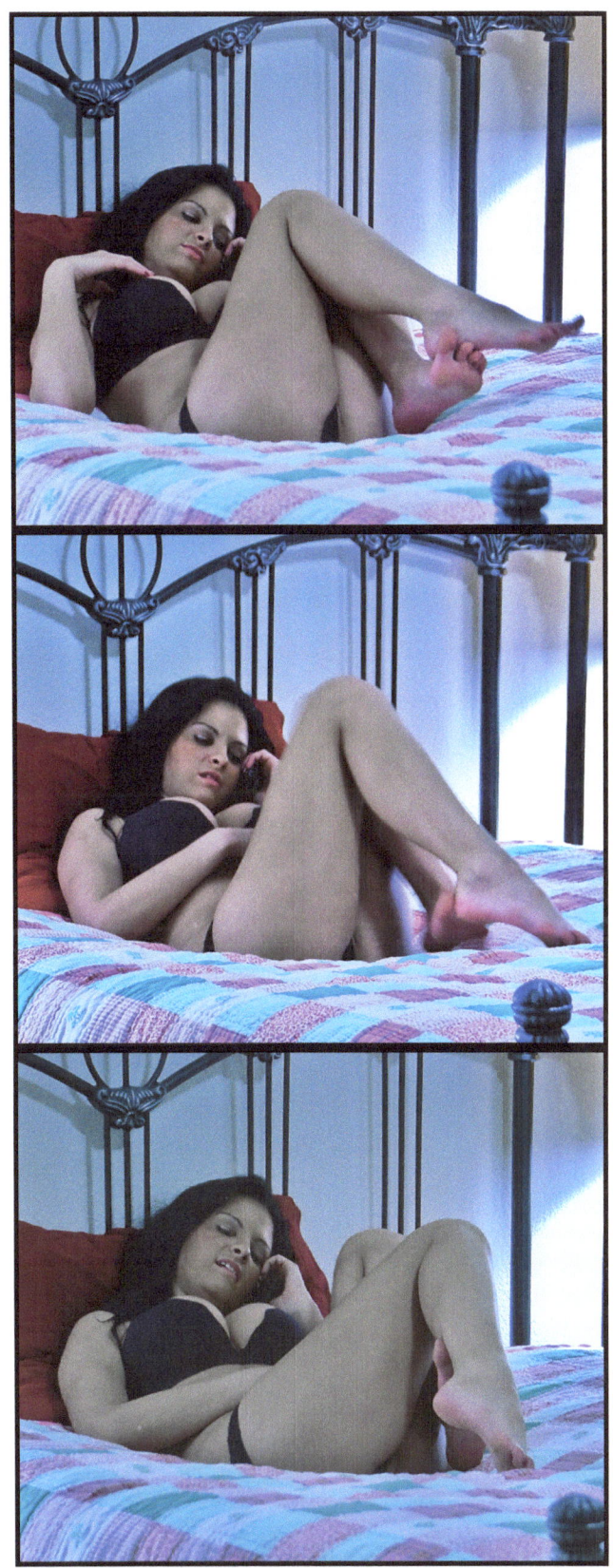

I've made some changes...he's made some changes - so now we're just "testing the waters" - slowly - to just see what happens. Some of the problems are still there - like we still live several states apart - but we think it's worth making an effort. The good times that we do have are REALLY good! We'll just have to wait and see what happens.

Marilyn

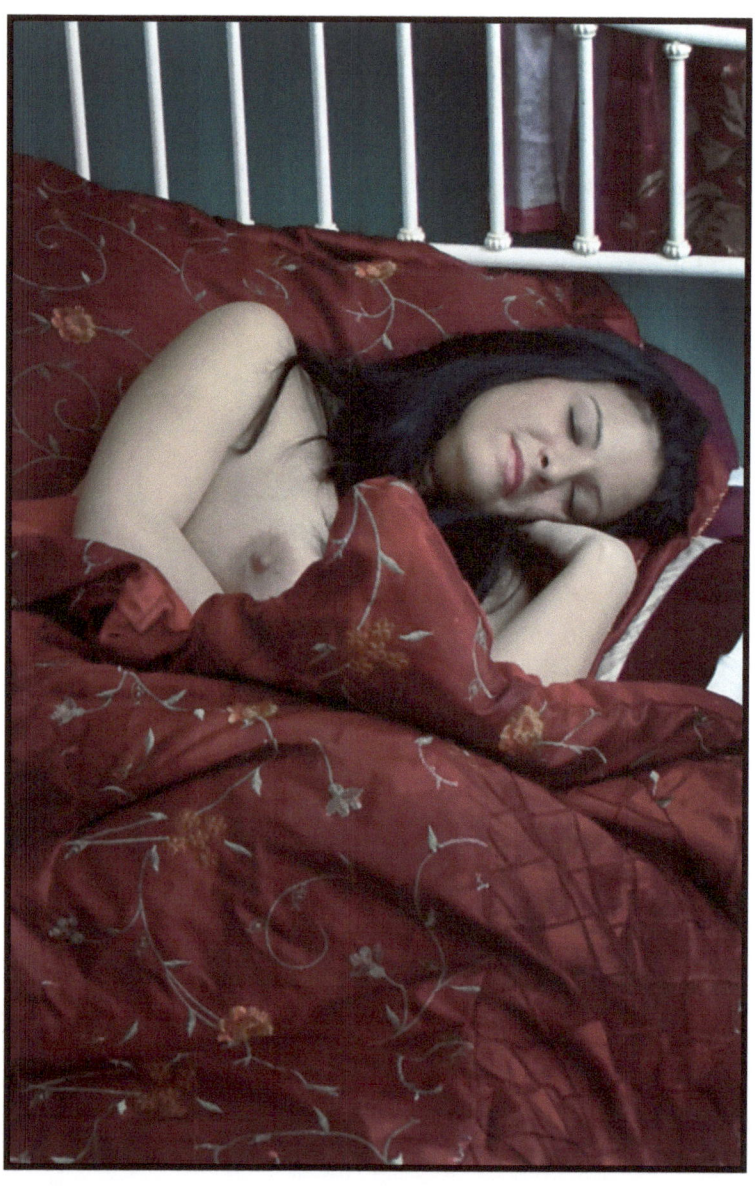

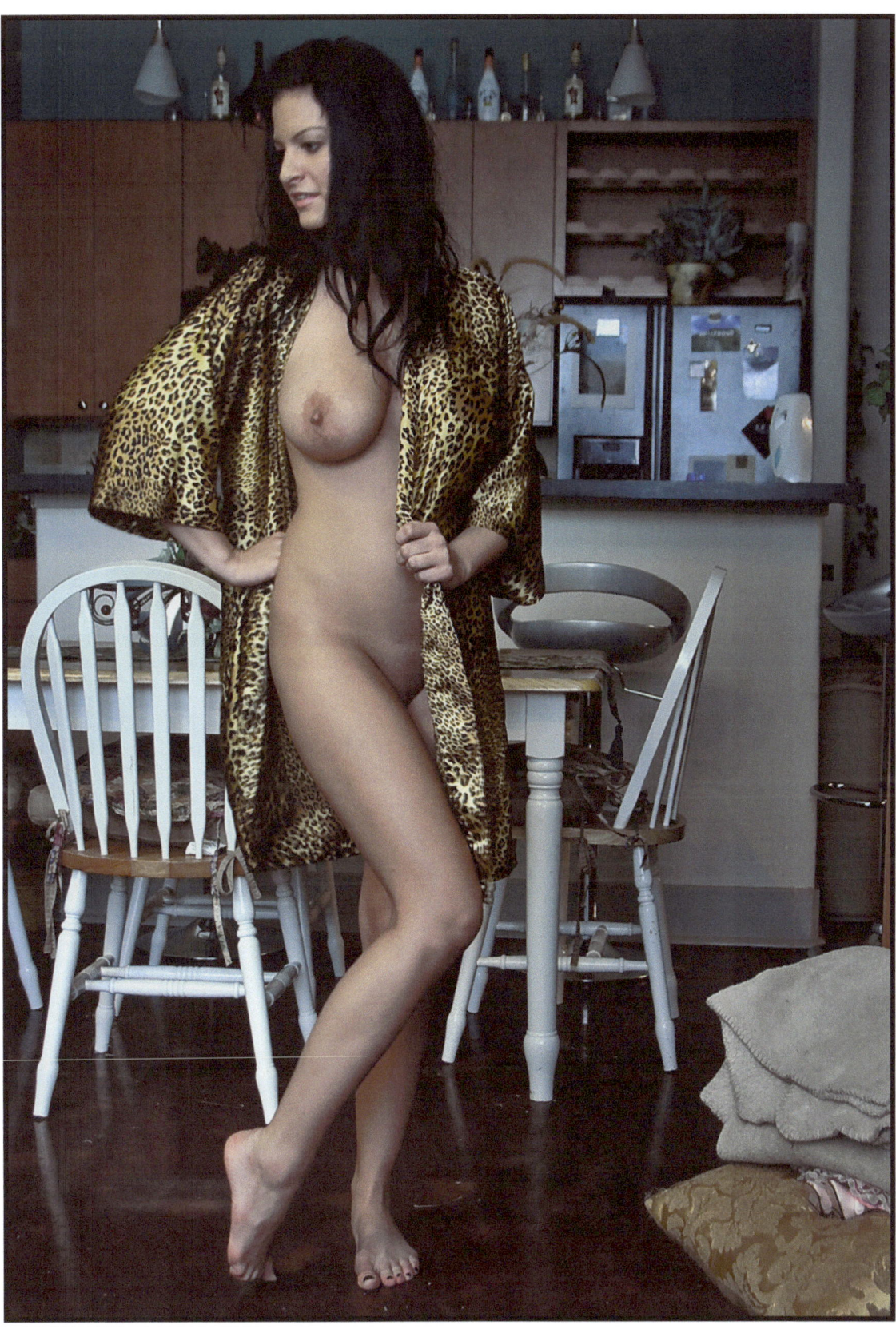

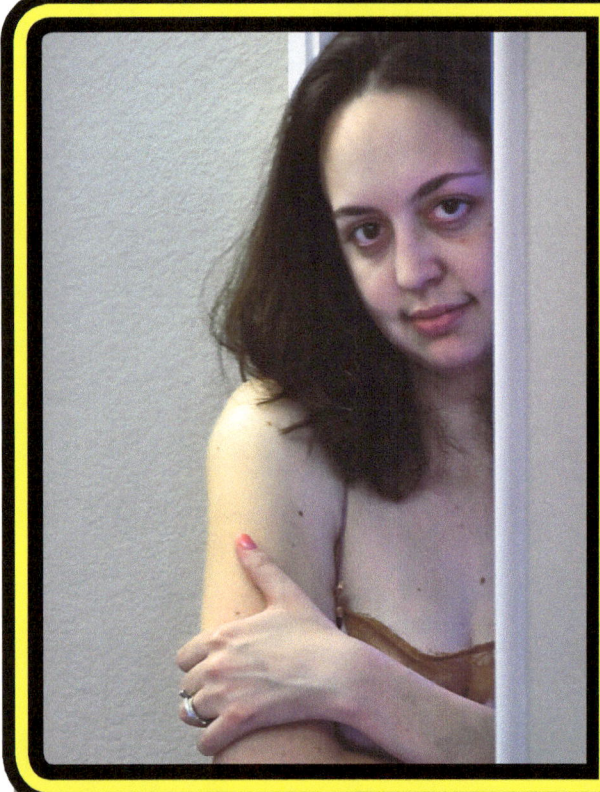

Roxy

♀♀♀♀♀♀♀♀♀

"I'm most passionate about being a mother."

A married, stay-at-home mom - Roxy, 26, models more for the art of it than money. She brought her artistic sensibilities to our photo shoot.

As a child, I didn't exactly know what I wanted to be when I grew up. I always thought it should be something that required a lot of thinking - something where I had to use my mind…maybe like a lawyer.

♀♀♀♀♀♀♀♀♀

I was born in Dallas, but mostly grew up in one of its northern suburbs. I think of my childhood as split into two parts: before my parents got divorced (when I was 13), and afterwards. Well, really my life changed a bit when I was eight, when my brother was born. I was an only child before that so I got all the parental attention. Once my brother was born, I had to learn to share my parents' attention - but that really wasn't bad at all.

I spent a lot of my childhood outside. I did a lot of things on my own - I really enjoyed exploring. I've never been the type of person who likes to stay at home all the time (even to this day). I loved to ride my bike on nearby trails, jump on my trampoline, swim, play softball - stuff like that.

When I was ten, we moved to Indonesia (my dad worked for an oil company at the time and he had to set up some projects there). That was more adventure for me - more exploring for me to do. I got to see what another culture was like - different foods - different everything really.

When I turned 13, we moved back to north Texas and my parents split up. That's when my life got a little more chaotic: two different parents in two different homes…so two different sets of rules. But those were my teenage years - whose teenage years weren't chaotic?

♀♀♀♀♀♀♀♀♀

One thing I learned fairly early on, is that there are people in this world who will try to bring you down no matter how perfect you are. There's always going to be a bully. Fortunately, I also learned early on that it doesn't really matter what that person says - because they're not important and they don't come from a good place.

As I came into adulthood, I hadn't realized that there were people out there who didn't need a reason not to like you - not until I met certain people (who will go unnamed here). I had always thought there had to be a reason why - maybe it was the way I looked, or the way I acted - something I said to them, or something I did. But you know what - there are people who don't care about anything but the fact that they don't like you. It's part of their personality - they can't help it. They want to make you feel bad.

♀♀♀♀♀♀♀♀♀

I'd love to go to South America. I've never been there, never been to that part of the world. I'd also like to go to Europe - places like Italy, France, and Germany.

♀♀♀♀♀♀♀♀♀

I've traveled around the world and seen a lot of different places. Besides Indonesia, I've been to Australia, Japan, Thailand, Singapore, Iran and all over the US. When people hear that about me, they're like "wow - I would have never guessed you've been to all those places."

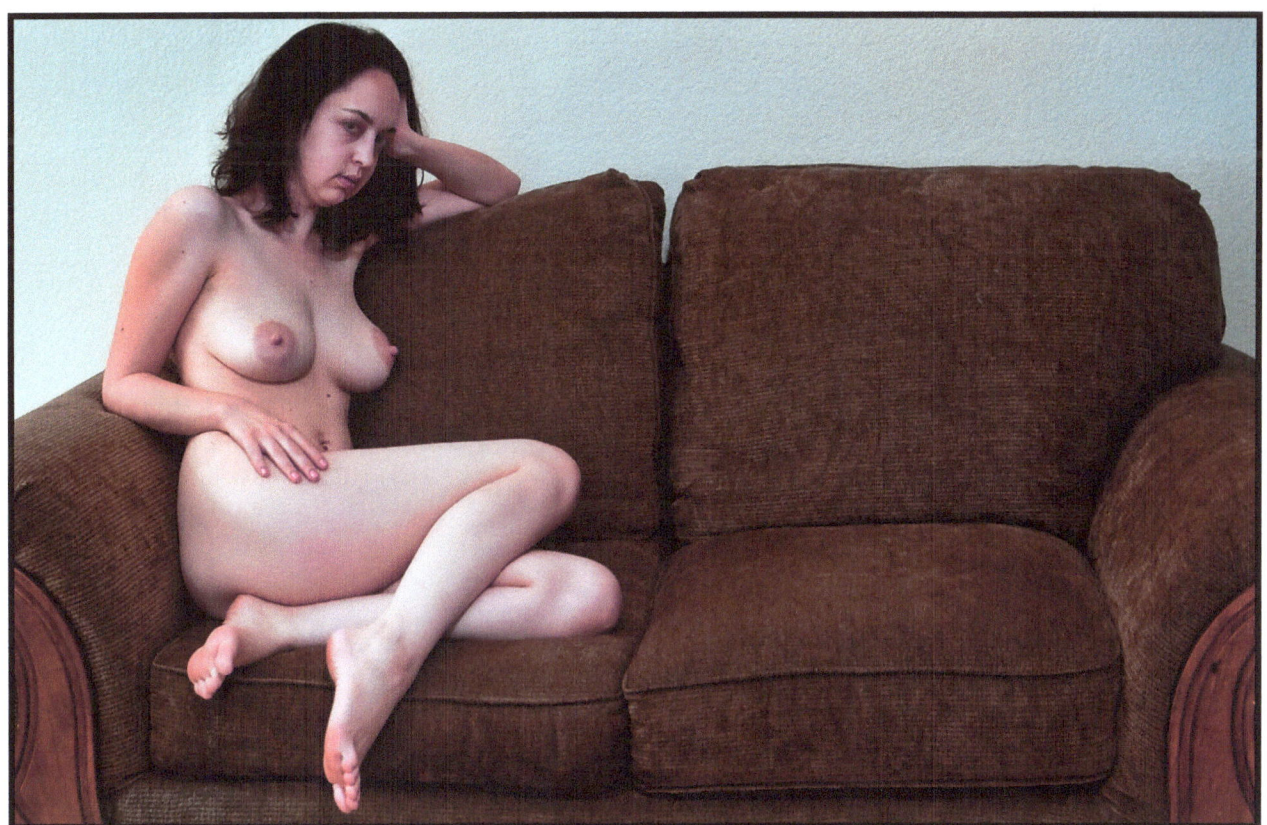

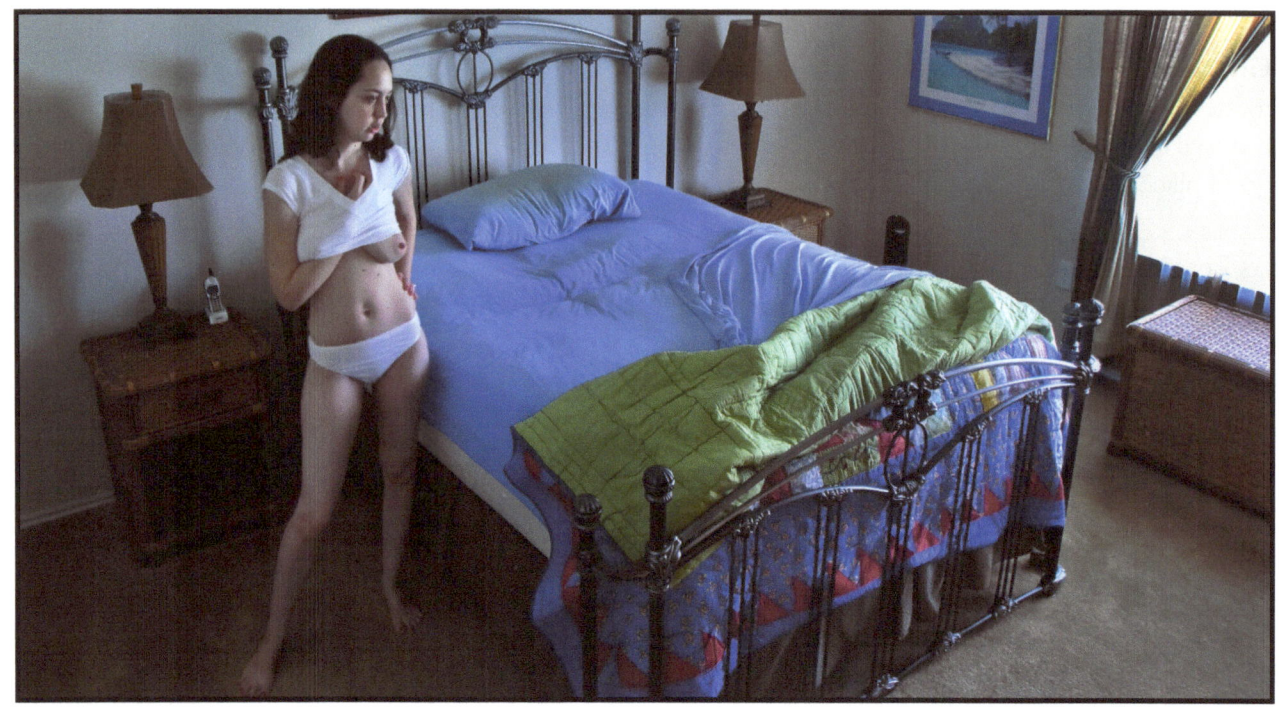

♀♀♀♀♀♀♀♀♀

If I could do anything, I'd like to adopt a whole bunch of children. If I had the resources, I'd open a school or something similar where children with no parents could go. I wouldn't call it an orphanage, because they wouldn't be looking for parents. It would be a place where they could go to just be kids and have fun.

♀♀♀♀♀♀♀♀♀

If I could change anything about myself, I'd probably change my feelings towards cleaning. I really don't like to clean. If it takes too much time, I just don't find value in doing it. I do like to have a clean house, though.

My laziness - that would be what I'd like to change.

♀♀♀♀♀♀♀♀♀

My proudest achievement would definitely be my children: a one year old and a three year old. Having my children and being able to stay home with them is something I never would have thought that I'd have the patience for. I knew for a long time that I was a nurturing type of person, but I never thought I'd have enough love and patience for one child, let alone two.

♀♀♀♀♀♀♀♀♀

I'm glad I'm a woman and would certainly never want to be a man, even if I could magically change into one. Being a woman allows me to, I guess, be taken care of. I feel like men are expected to work harder and do more for their family - whereas women (at least in our traditional family lifestyle) don't have to go out and worry about making a paycheck, or about having certain skills. All I have to do is just be with my children, and play with them, and teach them - which is a job I'm well suited for. As a man, I don't think I would take to the pressure of providing very well.

And that's the best part of being a woman (for me): having the opportunity to be nurturing - taking care of my children. But another wonderful part of being a woman, is that we are just more beautiful than men! I know that sounds silly, but it's true and I don't know how else to explain it.

The worst part of being a woman (though I guess this is more about being a housewife than just about being a woman) is that sometimes I don't feel like I have any control over certain situations, because I don't make the money. For example, if we have a bill that needs to be paid - I can't just go out and work for it, I have to depend on my husband. The lifestyle I chose - to be a housewife - means I have to stay at home with the kids. It also means that I have to depend on him to do the work and make the money. I just don't always like having to depend on others.

♀♀♀♀♀♀♀♀♀

In a lot of situations, men aren't allowed to be emotional (and I don't really think that's a good thing). A lot of men are taught that they have to be strong - that they have to be the ones to keep it together. I think some men may react to a situation in a more violent or dramatic way, compared to how they might react if they were allowed to just sit down and cry - you know what I mean? Sometimes, the way society makes men feel causes them to act out differently than they should. That's just a theory I have - I certainly can't prove it.

♀♀♀♀♀♀♀♀♀

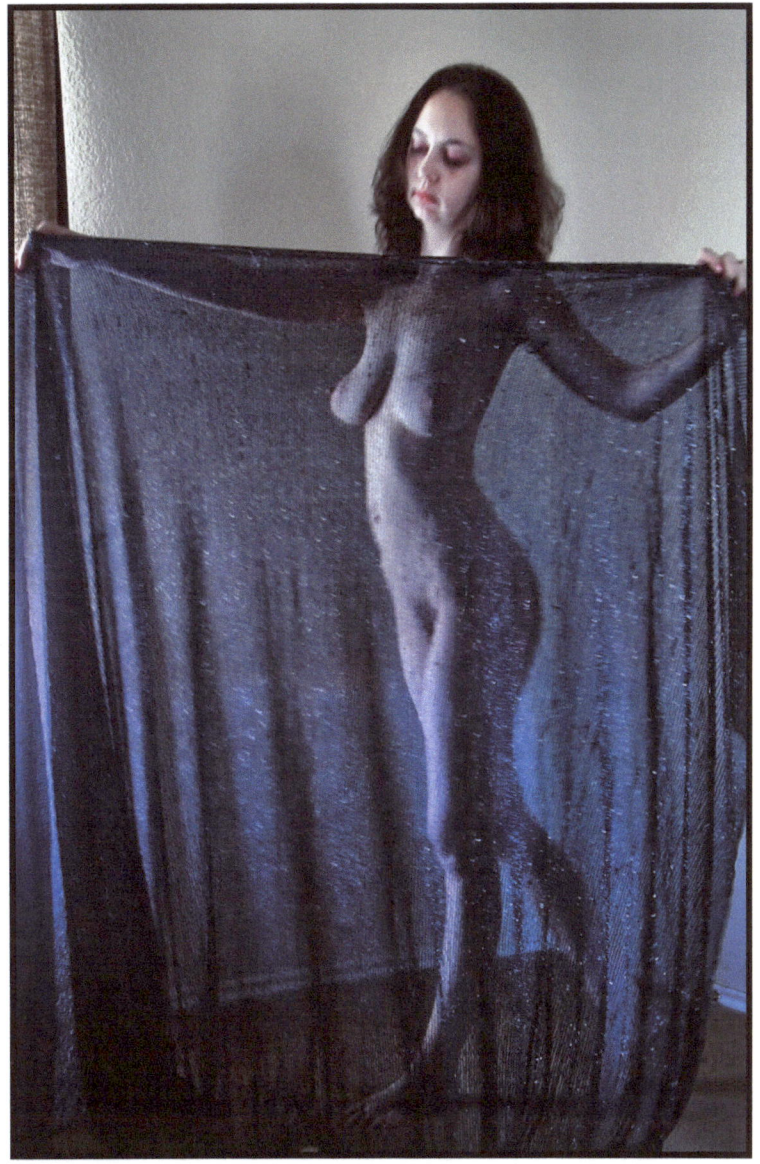

My general thoughts on sex? I hadn't really thought about it much before. I haven't been with a whole lot of people. I got married when I was 21, and in fact, I've been with my husband since I was 18.

I view myself as "normal." I guess I'm open to try anything once (mostly anything anyway). As long as it doesn't hurt, then who knows what I'd be missing out on. That's how I live my life, too - I don't want to miss out on anything. There was a time in the past when I used sex as I way to validate my worth, but I learned that I don't need that validation to be happy with myself. I actually don't have to be accepted by anyone to be happy.

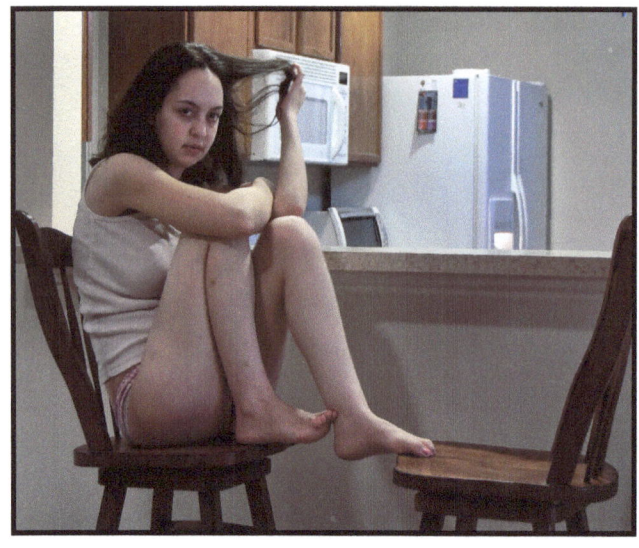

Sex, to me, is the most fun and exciting thing to do with your partner. I have learned, however, that the value of sex can be diluted and quality is worth much more than quantity.

Sex is supposed to be fun…to be an escape. I could probably have sex every day if I had someone that could keep up. I long for the passion and desire that every girl wants. When every day is not possible, I can live with having it less often - because when it does happen, it's totally worth it!

♀♀♀♀♀♀♀♀♀

If I could be any animal, I think I'd like to be a cat. Cats are independent - they only rely on you for certain things, but they can be left alone and be pretty happy. They don't need a whole lot of interaction.

♀♀♀♀♀♀♀♀♀

I get told a lot that I'm a good listener. People can tell me things without worrying about me judging them. I think it's because I've seen a lot of different cultures, and because of the way I view things with a "well, if it works for you" kind of attitude. I think more about why they might have done something, or what led them to do it - rather than about judging them.

I can definitely be lazy, though. If I don't feel like doing it - it's not going to get done. Some call it ADD, but I just call it laziness.

♀♀♀♀♀♀♀♀♀

Not a lot scares me, but as a parent, I worry about making mistakes that could hurt my kids down the line. We try to make decisions that are best for our children, but often we don't know right away if we're making a mistake.

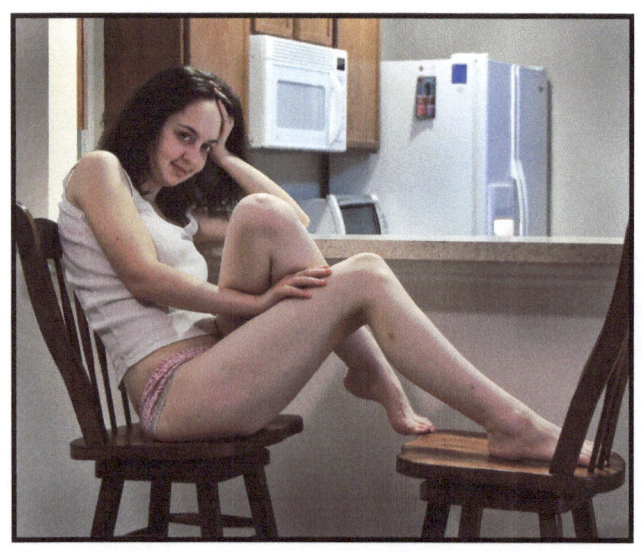

You can agonize over decisions - you can sit and wonder "if I do option A, how's that going to play out…but if I do option B, what will the result be?" You can't always know what will happen. I fear making a wrong choice without even realizing it.

♀♀♀♀♀♀♀♀♀

My favorite sport to play is baseball. It's really boring to watch, but when you're playing it and actually running the bases, it's kind of a strategy game. You have to think about how far you think you can get around the diamond.

My favorite sport to watch is hockey, though I'm

not exactly sure why. I like the ice skating aspect of it, and for me - it's easier to understand than football.

♀♀♀♀♀♀♀♀♀

Comedies are my favorite kind of movies…not slapstick, but stuff like "Seinfeld" where "situations" arise - and they turn out to be hilarious.

♀♀♀♀♀♀♀♀♀

To win my heart, a man would have to do something really different or exciting - something that captures my attention - 'cause I get bored kind of easily. I like men who are creative.

♀♀♀♀♀♀♀♀♀

Most important qualities for a significant other to have? He has to be really true and honest, and want to do things for me because he wants to - not because it's going to get him somewhere with me. I don't want to have to wonder what he's thinking, or what his true intentions are.

♀♀♀♀♀♀♀♀♀

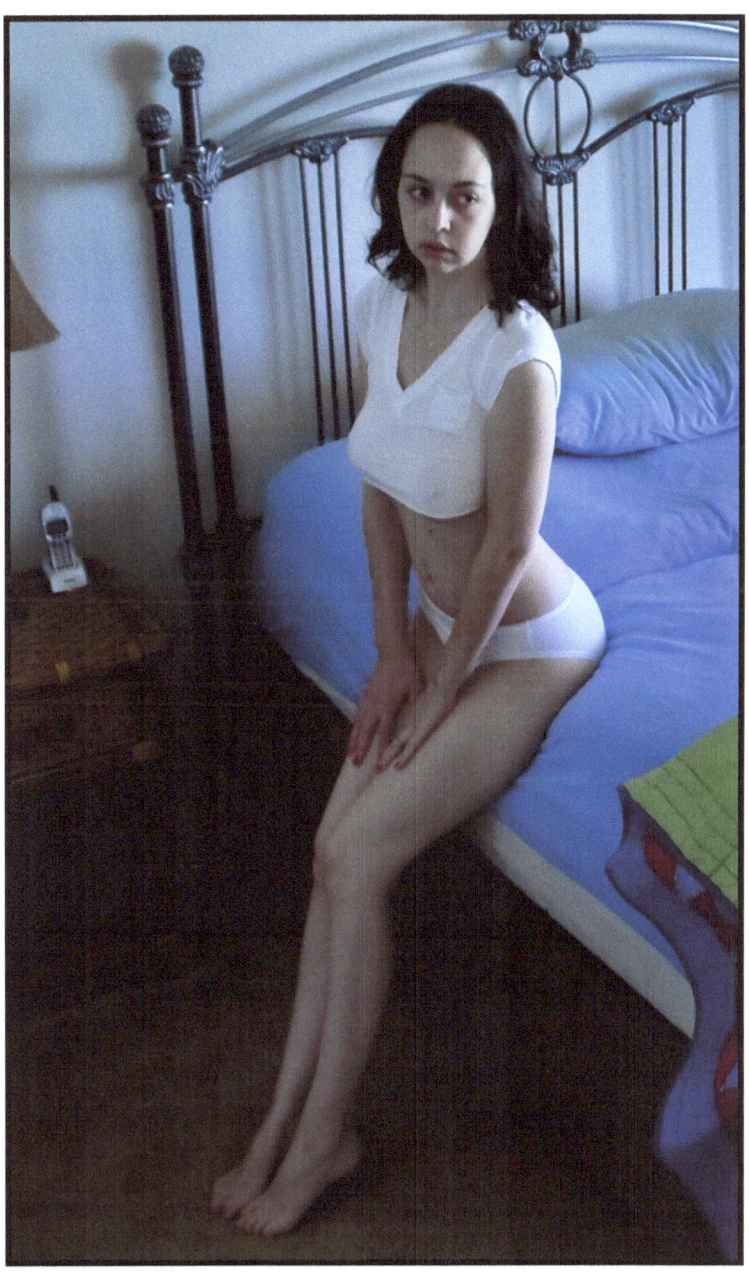

My favorite subjects in school were art (I've always loved art) and history. My least favorites were math and science.

♀♀♀♀♀♀♀♀♀

I'm most passionate about being a mother - I think - and about being a caregiver. I'm also passionate about art and my artistic ventures and projects.

♀♀♀♀♀♀♀♀♀

I really hate it when people don't pay attention and I have to repeat myself and be continually asked the same thing over and over again. And liars…they really irritate me.

♀♀♀♀♀♀♀♀♀

Most people probably don't know that I spend a lot of my time doing research and gaining knowledge. Usually when I'm talking about something - it's not just some random stuff I heard from one place, or that I'm just making up. I've actually done a bunch of research, and spent a lot of time looking in different books and other sources. I often actually know what I'm talking about.

♀♀♀♀♀♀♀♀♀

Some of my favorites:

Season - summer, because I hate the cold!

Comfort food - Cheese fries with ranch dressing

Color - purple

Music - I like all sorts of music, anything that's fast anyway - I don't like music that's too slow.

Musical group - Green Day

TV show - I love "The Office" and "Lost"

Movie - "Superbad", and movies like that.

♀♀♀♀♀♀♀♀♀

The craziest, wildest thing I've ever done? I can't really think of anything…and I say that because if it's really crazy or wild, I wouldn't have done it. I'm really not that kind of person. If I've done it, I wouldn't call it crazy…and if I haven't done it, it's probably because I thought it was crazy.

My husband and I moved away from the Dallas area to a small town in east Texas (where there were no opportunities) and started a business a few years ago - that was pretty crazy!
But I guess the craziest thing I've ever done is given birth without drugs. It actually isn't all that crazy, in fact, it's very natural. A lot of people see it as this crazy, wild, insane idea. It's really not, though - I've done it twice.

♀♀♀♀♀♀♀♀♀

My best day was the day my son was born. It was a very quick, natural water birth - it was beautiful and

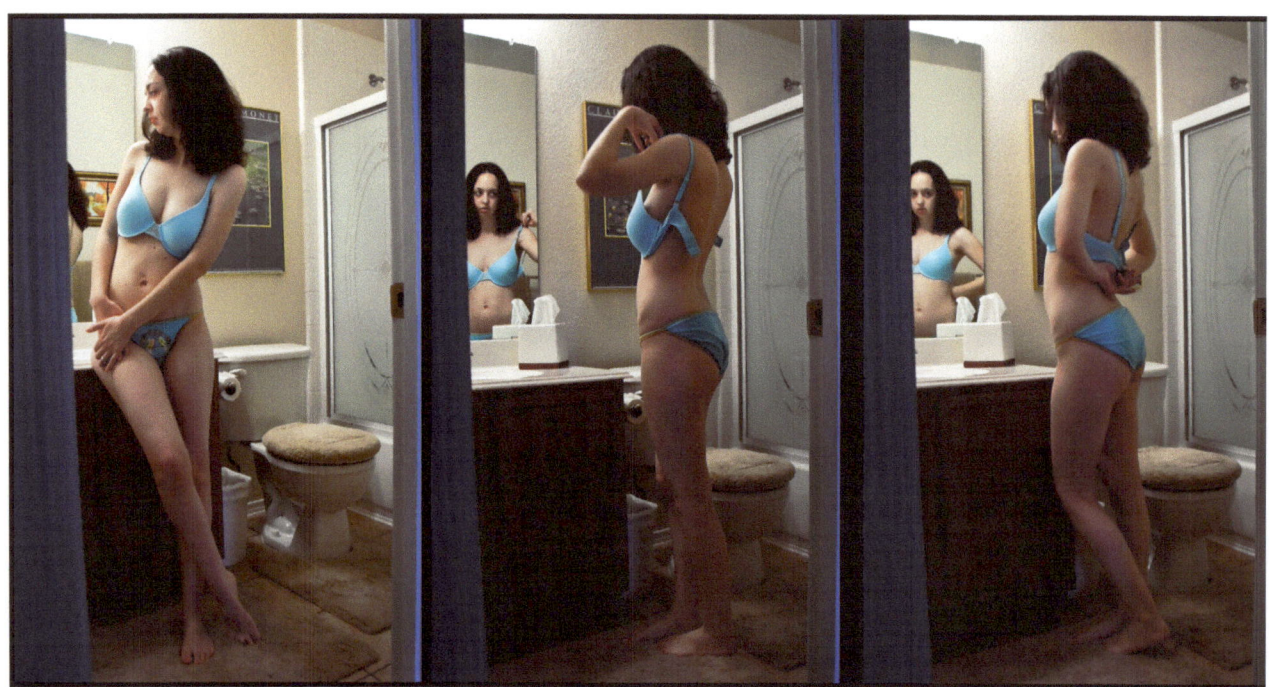

just the most wonderful moment because I didn't have a whole lot of stress in that childbirth. It was very easy for me.

I've had a bunch of bad days - probably the worst is when I've been in pain with the kidney stone that I have.

♀♀♀♀♀♀♀♀

Favorite alcoholic drink - anything with vodka, I'm not really picky. My favorite non-alcoholic beverage is just water.

♀♀♀♀♀♀♀♀

I guess I'm late more often that I'm early. I do try to be early - it just usually doesn't happen.

♀♀♀♀♀♀♀♀

Because of my modeling - I've been asked before if I'm an exhibitionist. I don't consider myself to be one really. I don't like to show off at all, or be the center of attention. Of course, that fact makes modeling very hard for me sometimes.

The reason I started modeling a few years ago was to learn more about photography (something I've found to be a wonderful outlet for me). By networking with photographers and working for them - even as a model - I've learned a lot.

I didn't do any nude modeling until about a year and a half ago. I wasn't interested in doing that when I started out because I really didn't feel comfortable with it. I thought it would be too easy for someone to take advantage of me, or use my images in ways that I didn't want them to. I felt like I wasn't quite ready for it. I wasn't confident, and didn't feel I was very good.

Finally, though, I decided to do it anyway - just for myself. I was able to find a photographer who wouldn't

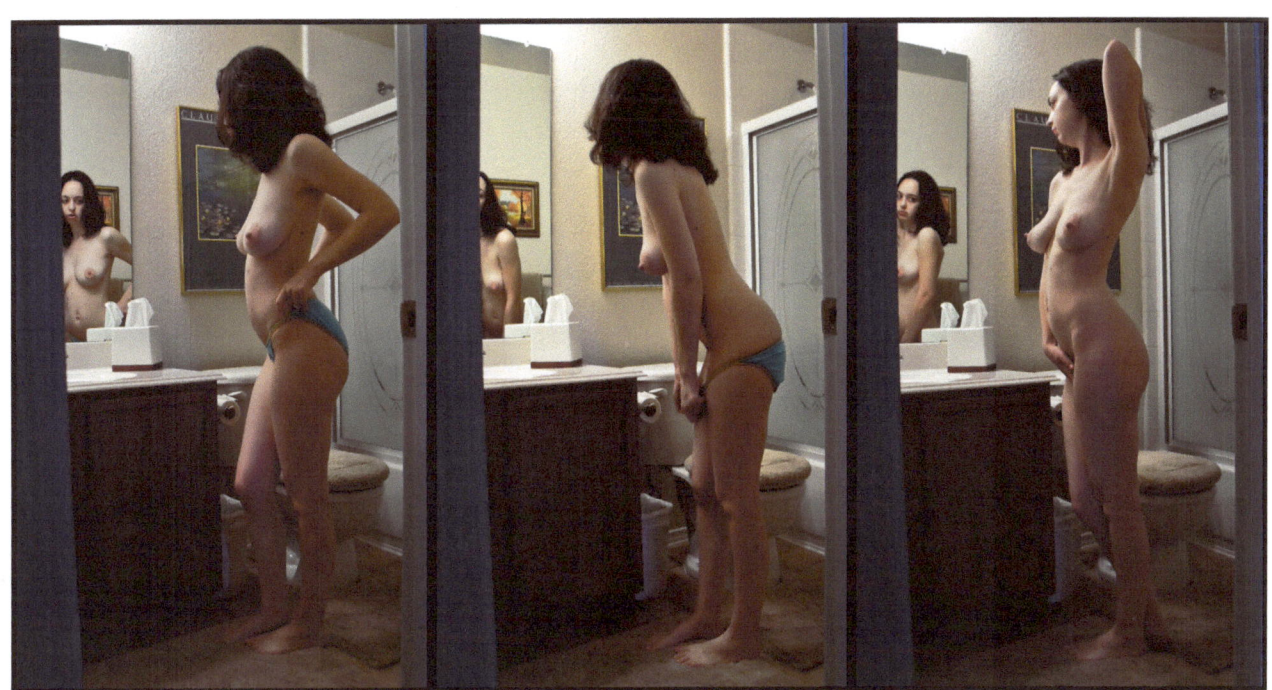

show or post the photos, then I "traded" with him. I posed for some lingerie shots for him in exchange for the photos I wanted him to take for me. When I saw them, I was so impressed - I was so happy with them - that I thought "why wouldn't I do this?"

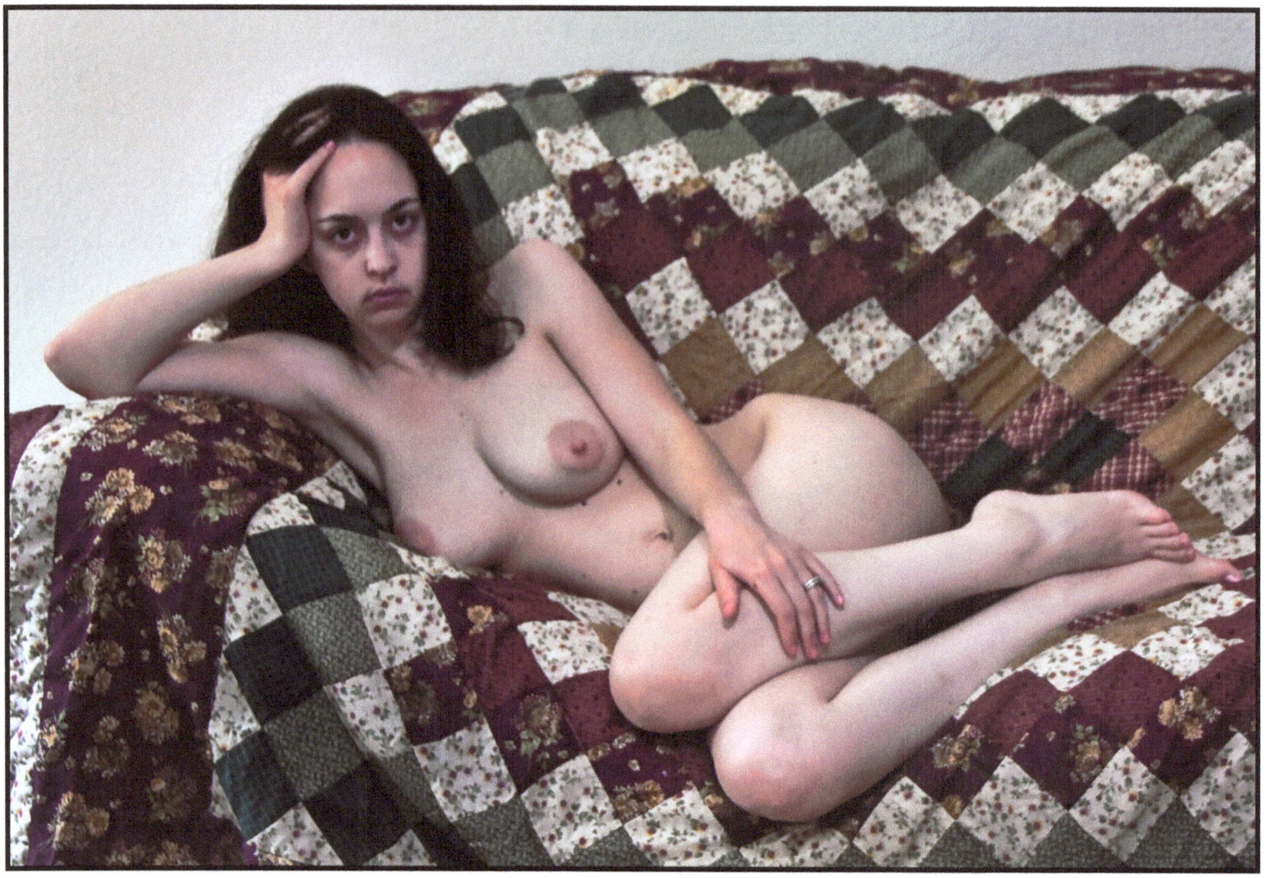

It was a good way to learn more about photography - especially since this was a field of photography I wanted to do myself. It makes sense to me - to be the subject of the kind of photos I want to take so that I'll understand it from their point of view.

I'm totally comfortable with posing nude now. Anyone who can't accept that about me probably shouldn't be my friend anyway. In the beginning, I wasn't really afraid of what other people thought, so it actually helped me filter out some people I didn't want in my life.

♀♀♀♀♀♀♀♀♀

What's it like to be a woman in today's world? I think it can be anything that you want it to be. These days - it's not uncommon for women to be in the workforce, or to be a mother, or to be involved in sports. I think you can be whatever you want.

Roxy

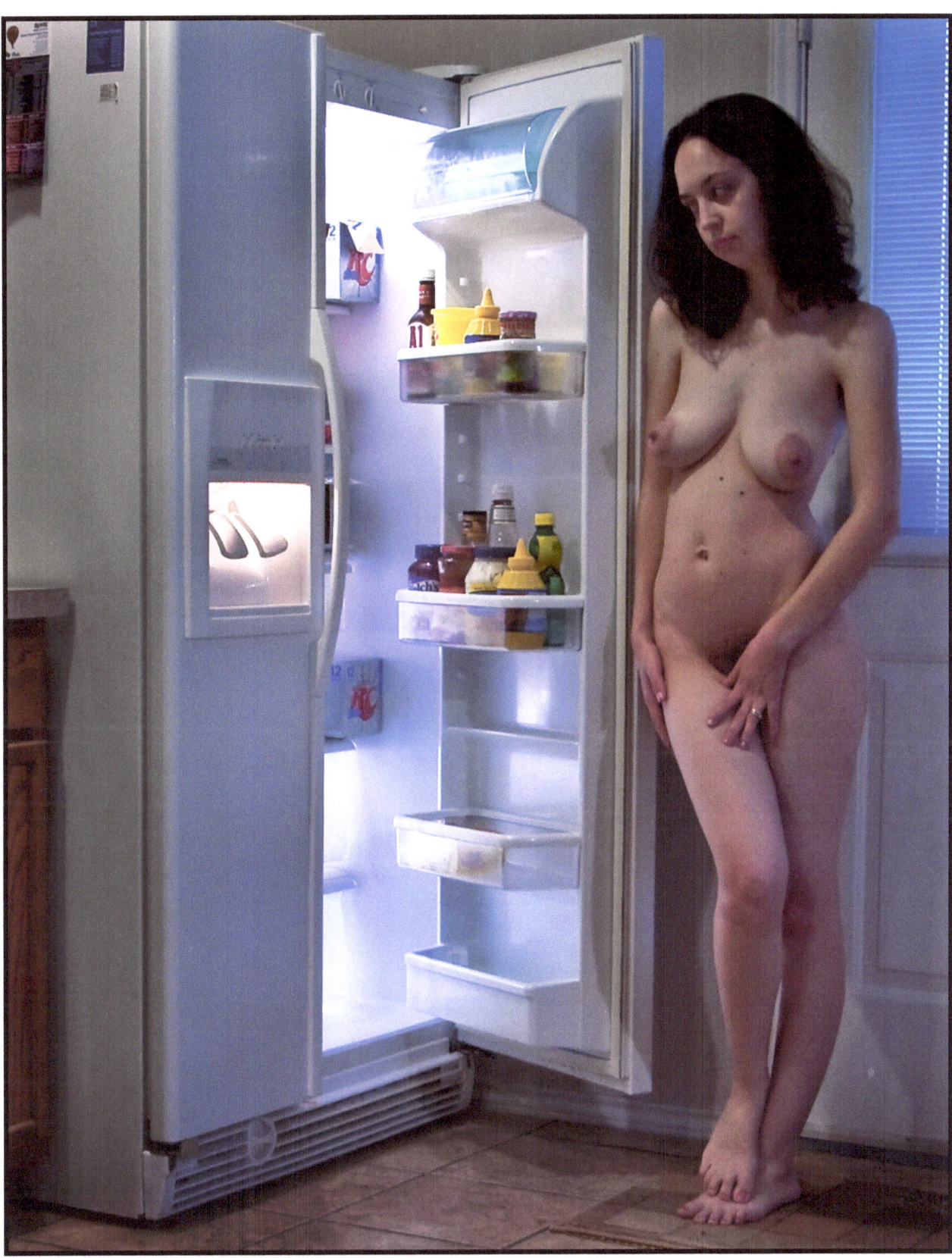

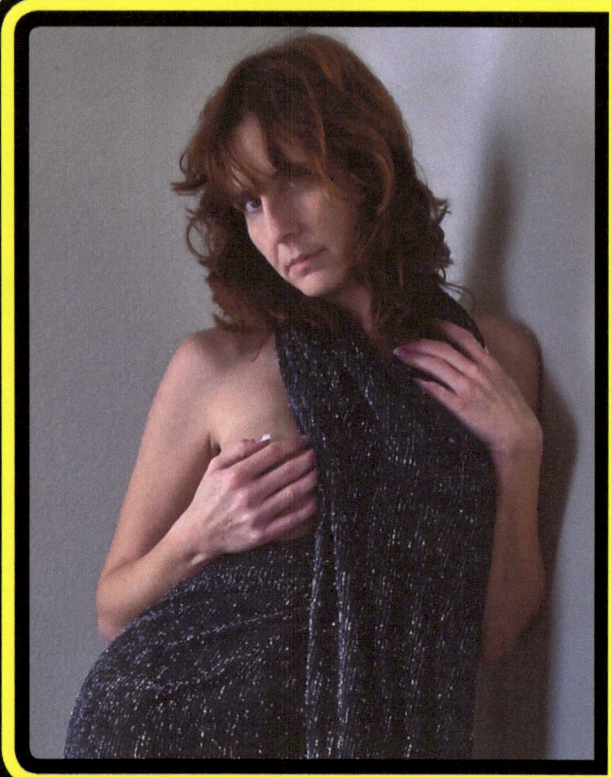

Rashell

♀♀♀♀♀♀♀♀♀

"Failure doesn't exist if you learn from it."

Rashell, 38, is a mom...and quite the cut-up. She was a lot of fun to work with. She has no problems expressing her viewpoints on most any subject, and can be quite entertaining in the process.

When I was growing up, I wanted to be a country and western singer like Dolly Parton - but I also wanted to be a horse trainer. There was a time when I wanted to be an acrobat - but I also wanted to be a farmer just like my granddad. I wanted to have six kids, live on a farm and drive a tractor to work...weird things like that. There was a whole plethora of dreams I had as a kid. Most of them were more country oriented - family oriented.

♀♀♀♀♀♀♀♀♀

I was born in Colorado Springs and grew up on a farm just outside Pueblo, Colorado with my parents, my grandparents, my two older brothers and four younger sisters (my grandparents lived maybe two miles away, but I spent a lot of time with them, including every summer). We raised chickens, cows, ducks, peacocks, turkeys, horses, sheep, goats, pigs and pigeons. We raised peacocks because my uncle liked them - he'd bring them out to my grandparent's farm. I gathered eggs from under the hens, I've been chased by geese, stepped on by a horse and bucked off a horse. I've been pinned by cows and helped them give birth. I've done the whole branding thing. I've given immunization shots and I've been stuck with the cow needles.

I was actually raised by a whole community. Besides my mom, dad and grandparents - there was my Aunt Linda, Uncle Larry, and my other Uncle Larry. They say it takes a village to raise a child and it really did. My dad called me his wild child, because I didn't follow the norm - he said I was "headstrong." I was the tomboy, always running, always getting into trouble. I had so much fun growing up: getting on grandpa's tractor and riding horses and cows (I think I even rode a couple of goats). I had a great childhood. There were some moments that weren't so good - like when I'd get into trouble. My brother and I called the sheriff one time because we thought someone had broken into the house. It turned out that it was my mom and grandmother moving stuff around in the house. I got whipped for that!

It was good being raised by both my parents and my grandparents - and having the freedom to explore - to find what I wanted with my life when I was a kid. It was very happy-go-lucky.

When I was still little, we moved to Texas, then to Kansas, back to Colorado and finally back to Texas again (when I was 11). I've been here too damn long now. If I could go back home to Colorado - I would!

♀♀♀♀♀♀♀♀♀

And if I could have any job in the world now - I'd like to work on a farm, training horses. I've always wanted to do that!

♀♀♀♀♀♀♀♀♀

The hardest thing I had to learn as an adult was that you can't always protect the ones you love. Sometimes you make a wrong choice, and by making that wrong choice - you hurt the people you care about the most. I wake up in the morning and look at my children and realize that I've made choices that have affected

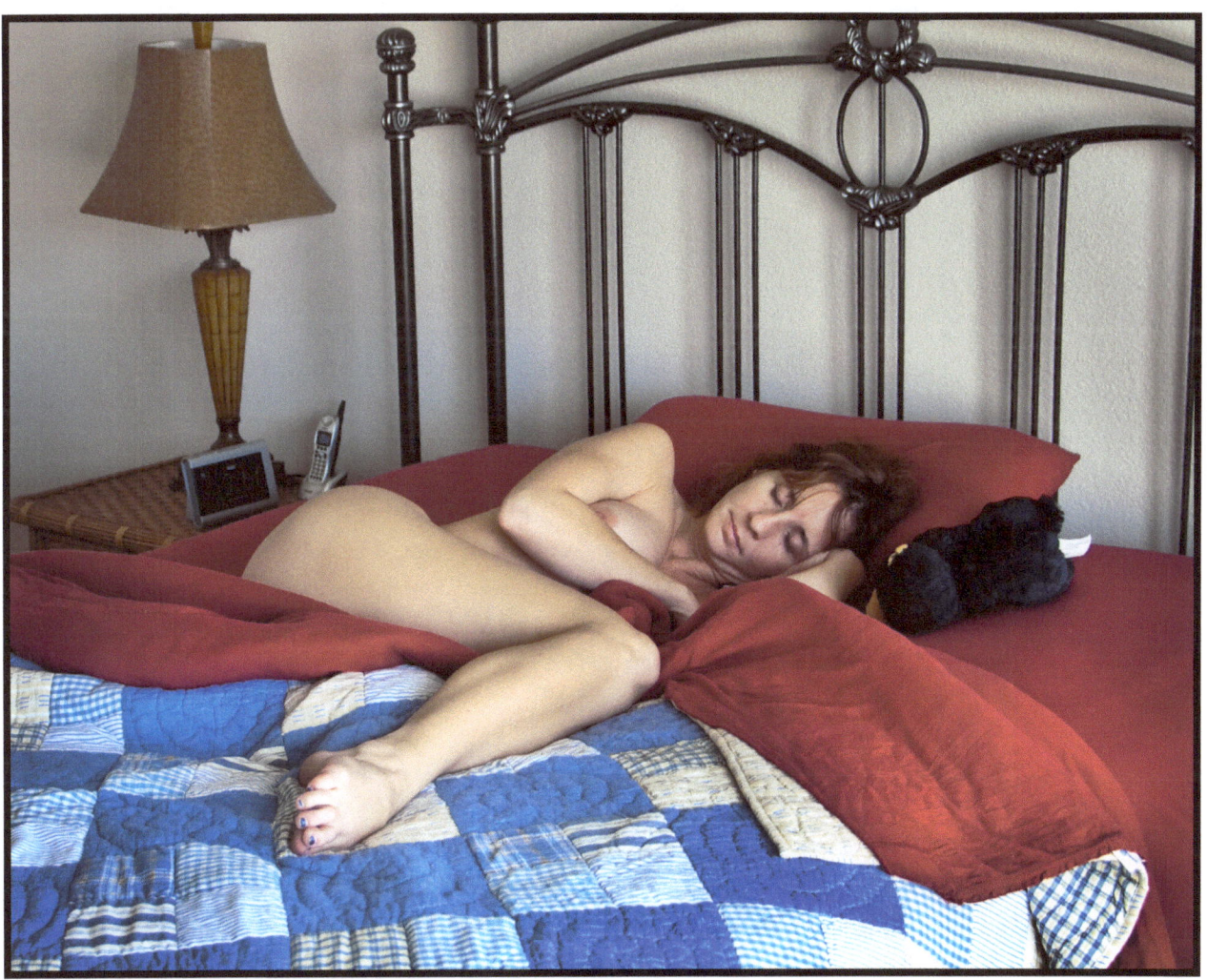

their lives - and not always for the best. I thought that when I raised my kids, I would do my very best for them - but there have been times when I let my own selfishness blind me.

The people I was raised around didn't lie - they were as honest as the day was long. The people I eventually married - that's all they did was lie. Because of them, I became a liar, too. I try hard to teach my kids not to lie. If I had known then what I know now - I probably wouldn't have made those mistakes, and life would have been better. I have to say, though, that I don't regret any of those mistakes - not one. If I did regret them, I wouldn't be the person I am now. You just have to learn from your mistakes. Failure doesn't exist if you learn something from it.

♀♀♀♀♀♀♀♀♀

I've been married and divorced twice, and have five wonderful kids as a result: three that I gave birth to, one that I adopted, plus one step son. My oldest is 21. She's in college, working on a double major with a 3.6 GPA. She's incredibly smart - even speaks three languages. I adopted her when she was 15 and she is just amazing. The second oldest is 19 and she's strong and incredibly brave. She's going to start college

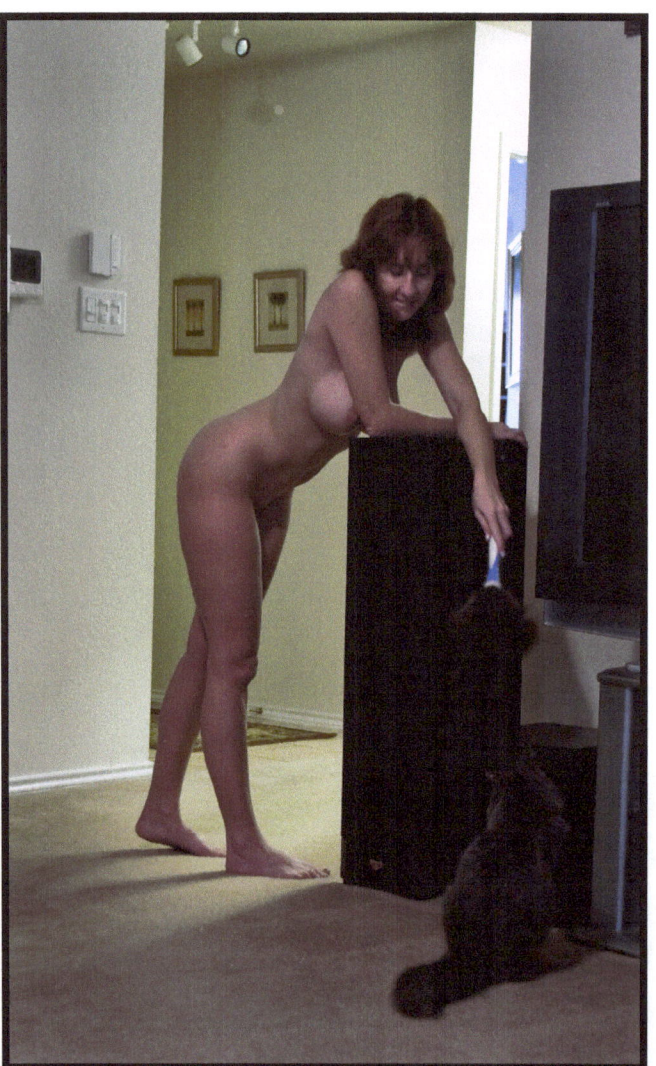

soon - probably at a community college just to get her core classes. She's tall and beautiful and everything I always hoped she would be - and more. Then there's my 17-year-old stepson - he's really smart. He lives in Florida with his mom. Next, there's my 16-year-old son who's a junior in high school. He's so funny - I can be in the worst mood ever and he will do nothing but make me laugh. He's really sensitive and giving and fun to be around - I don't know that I could go through life without that comic relief. I look at him and think "I've actually raised a good man." I hope that he will follow in the footsteps of my grandfathers and my father. Finally, there's my 14-year-old daughter who's energetic, smart, bubbly and bouncy. She has the most likeable personality. You can't help but love her, she's just so cuddly. She's an eighth grade cheerleader.

I see myself in all of them - all the best parts of me. They're my best achievement. I could leave this earth right now and know that they are the best things I leave behind - they are my legacy.

♀♀♀♀♀♀♀♀♀

I would love to go to Ireland and Scotland one day - I've always dreamed of going to the homeland. I'm Irish, Scottish, English, German and

American Indian. I didn't find out I was German until about a year ago. I was like - oh my God, I'm German! We've researched our lineage back to the 1300's - and found we originally came from Scotland. I've always been attracted to that portion of my family lineage - the heritage, you know. When my youngest graduates, we're going to take a family vacation and all go to Ireland or Scotland. It'll be just me and my kids - we'll all go to a pub and have a pint together. We'll just see the greenery and enjoy following in the footsteps of our ancestors.

My 16-year-old son…he wants to go to Paris, France. He says to me "Mom - we don't have to take the girls - it'll be just you and me. We'll take a mother/son trip". I told him "Okay - but you're paying!"

♀♀♀♀♀♀♀♀♀

If I could change anything about myself, I wouldn't change a thing - not one damn thing! There are things that I could improve on - like housecleaning - I could definitely improve on that. But I don't regret anything about myself, and I don't want to change anything about myself. If I changed the things that I've gone through, or the things that I will go through - I wouldn't be me, and I really like me. My way

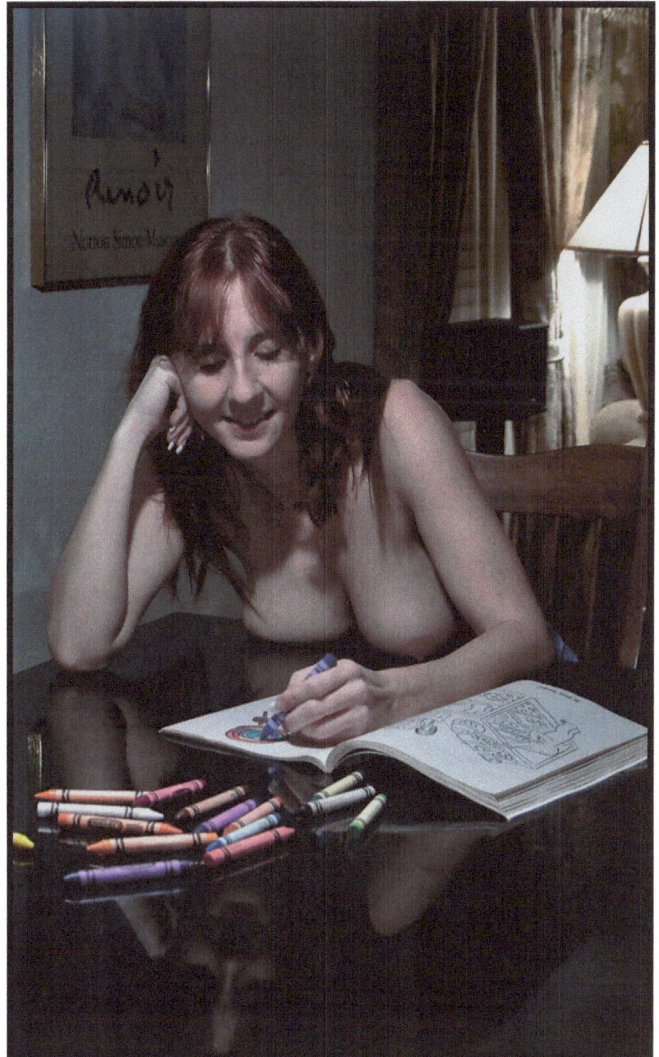

of thinking is that if other people don't like me - then to hell with them! What they think of me doesn't really matter to me in the grand scheme of things. Everybody wants to be liked, but if it comes down to "you have to change this thing or I'm not going to like you" - then don't like me. I am who I am for a reason. I'm exactly the way God wanted me to be. He's the one working on me.

♀♀♀♀♀♀♀♀♀

I love being a woman: it's powerful. I can do things that men can't: give birth, nurse, be the nurturer, be comforting. Women are the softer side. God made us that way for a reason. He made men hard and women soft to complement each other. I don't think I'd want to be a man even if I could magically change into one.

I love everything about being a woman except for the period thing (why did God do that to us?). It's the only time I wish that I wasn't a woman… well, maybe during childbirth, too! I wish more men could experience that, I really do. We'd probably have less of a population explosion. I think that if I could change anything about being a woman, I'd like to not be so emotionally haywire - especially during PMS. I have to take a step back and ask myself "am I really feeling that

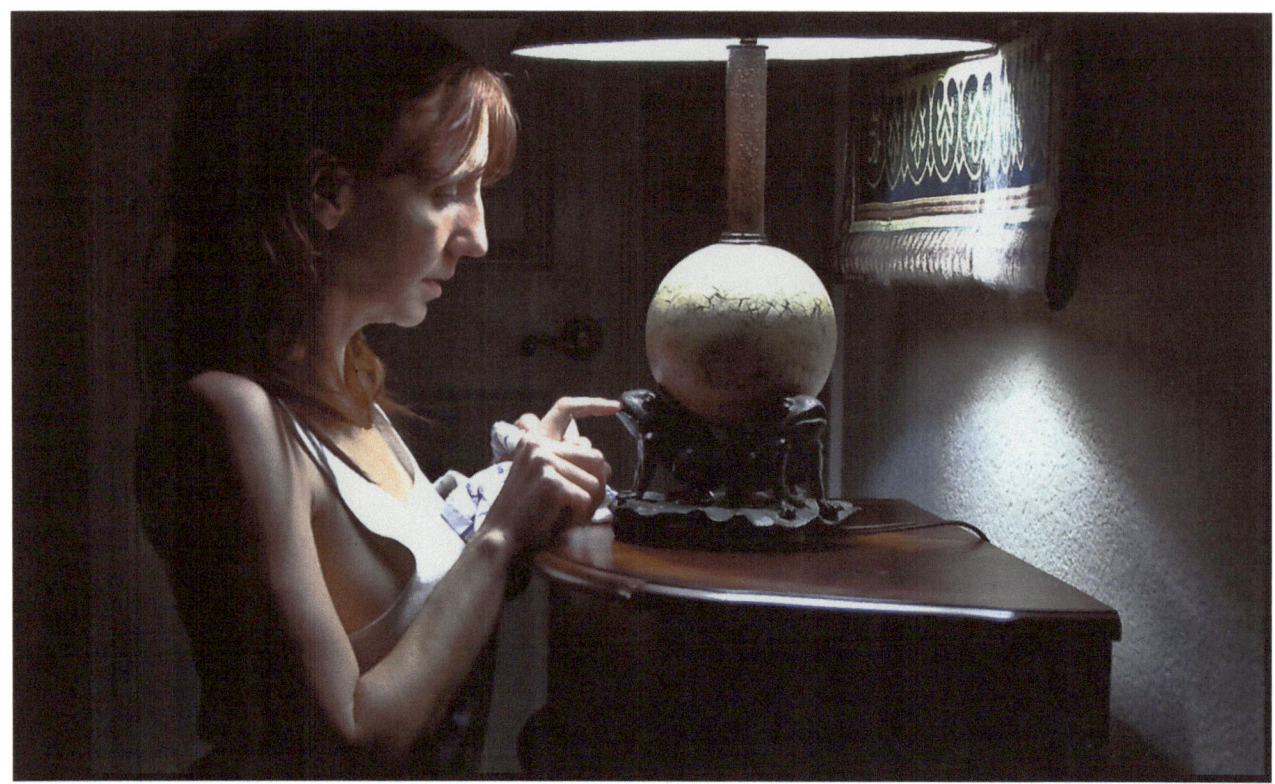

way, or is that just the hormones"?

I think that if I could change into a man for just one day - I would. I've always wanted to know what it's like to have a penis. Would I pee out of it standing up or sitting down…would I play with it? It's the weirdest thing - I've always wanted to ask men: do you even notice it, you know, when you're walking? Do you realize that it's there? Men are so enamored of our boobs - they're like "I just want to play with those - oh my God." I don't have "penis envy," but I have wondered what it's like to be built with one. Would I sit on my balls - do men do that all the time? What would it be like to masturbate as a man? Would I walk differently? Would I become mentally more manly? But, no - I don't want to change into a man. I kind of like my gender…as crazy as we are.

♀♀♀♀♀♀♀♀♀

Speaking of periods! You never know when those stupid things are coming, and you're always surprised when they do. It amazes me that something that bleeds that much doesn't die! Sometimes I feel like I'm a deer that got hit by a car. When I was younger and I was more sexually active (not that I'm not now… ok, I'm not) back before my kids were born - blood was symbology for me…like "yes - I'm not pregnant!"

♀♀♀♀♀♀♀♀♀

The double standard pisses me off. If a man messes around with other women while being in a relation-ship - I think that's wrong. But, when men do it - they're considered studs by their peers. If a woman does the same thing - she's considered a slut. It's kind of like men are all about how many women they *can sleep with*, while women are more about how many men they *don't have to sleep with*. I've heard the term "she who has the pussy, has the power", but it seems more like it's usually "he who gets it, has the power". I don't want to be "got". I'd like for the men in my life to be more than just "a second head." I want a man to be a man - but not the kind of man that people can't trust. I don't want him to be in control of me - I want him to be equal with me. There will be times when I'm going to be weak and he's going to be strong, and times when the opposite will be true. I want him to complement my life - not cause consequences to it.

♀♀♀♀♀♀♀♀♀

Still - I think that men are often misunderstood. We make excuses for them, like "he doesn't talk to me - it must be the way his mommy treated him". We make excuses when they don't share - "but they're not supposed to." I think that men should be more understood, and less examined. We women should just try to understand more. I don't want to examine someone like they're under a microscope. I just want to have a basic understanding of how being a man really works - why they do the things that they do. I pity the way men are treated by some women. They're used, abused and then pushed to the side…just like we are. Some people would call that fair…but it's not. We should treat all people with consideration, whether they're male or female.

♀♀♀♀♀♀♀♀♀

Do I have any "star crushes"? Well, I know he's older - but Sam Elliott has always been so much of what I want in a man. He's definitely a man's man. In every movie I've seen him in, he's always protecting the woman he's with, the woman he loves. He stands up for himself, for what he believes in. He's rugged…and just sexy - oh my God! He is definitely one of those men who I'd definitely drop my drawers for! I wouldn't care if he were 70 years old!

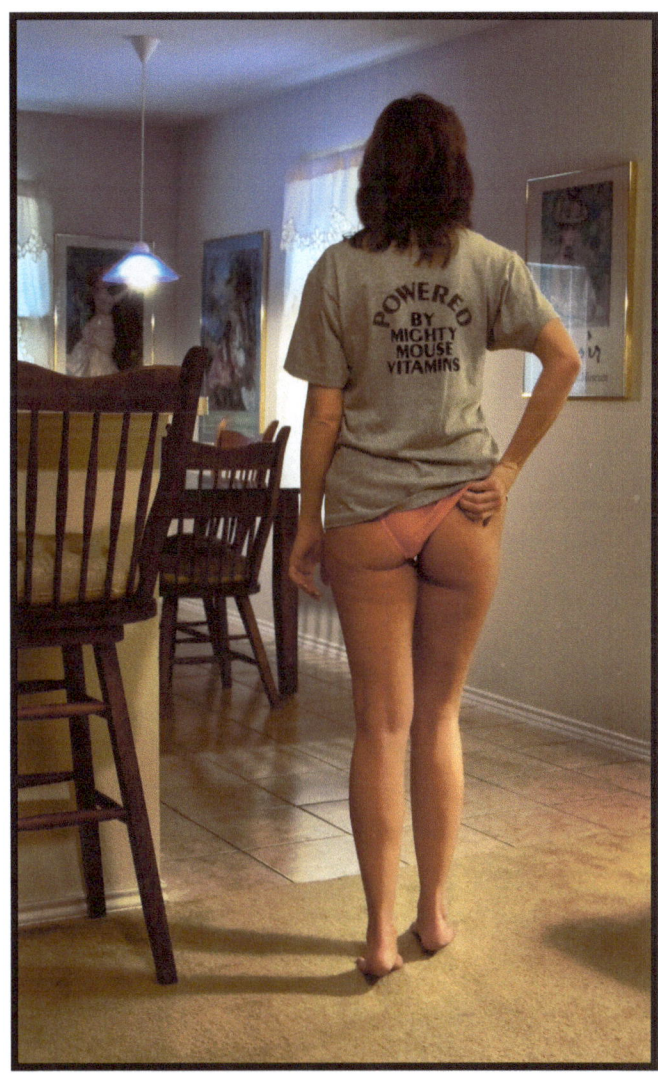

♀♀♀♀♀♀♀♀♀

Some of my favorites:

Comfort food - chocolate cake, ice cream, chocolate chip cookies, Ferrero Rocher candies. Anything sickeningly sweet - that's what I like.

Color - green.

Music - everything! I like everything from classical to opera all the way to death metal, heavy metal, country music - I like it all. I'm very eclectic in my musical tastes. I can't sing opera, I can't sing the heavy metal, but I like to head bang - I'm a child of the 70's and 80's.

Musical group - I love Heart, Patsy Cline, Etta James, David Bowie, Elton John, Poison, Def

Leppard, Men at Work, Journey, Aerosmith, the Beatles, James Taylor, John Michael Montgomery, Johnny Cash, Merle Haggard, Lorretta Lynn, Carrie Underwood, Reba McEntyre and Mindy McCready. I like Tchaikovsky, Bach and Beethoven. I love opera - ever since I saw "Phantom of the Opera."

TV show - anything on the Crime TV, True TV…"Forensic Files", "Cold Case Files", "Law and Order SVU." I love those - love watching them, because you can't commit the perfect crime - forensics will always figure it out. May take 'em some time, but they always figure it out. I like that, I like the puzzles.

Movie - "Seven Brides for Seven Brothers", anything 1940's musical - anything: Fred Astaire, Ginger Rogers, Gene Kelly, Ethel Merman, Marilyn Monroe…40's/50's musicals - love those - "Pollyanna" with Haley Mills, western movies - "The Good, The Bad and The Ugly."

Season - I like them all, but I guess if I was forced to pick one, it would be winter. I like the way the snow falls (I don't like Texas winters - they suck…it's cold and wet). Colorado winters are white and pure and beautiful, and the air is so crisp. It smells so clean - you breath in and you feel it. When you walk through

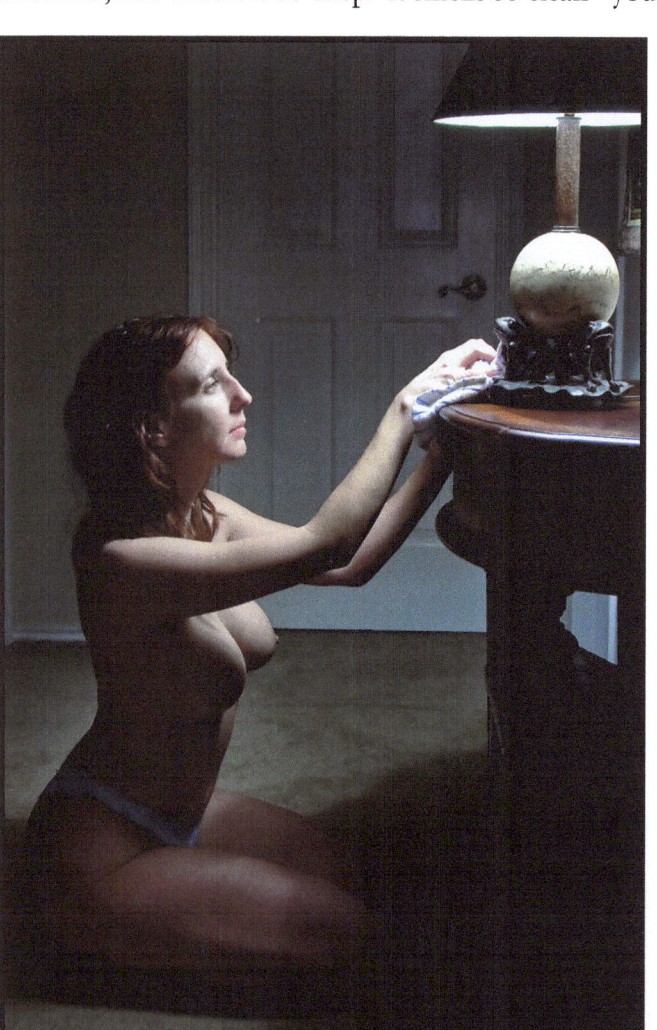

the snow and hear that crunch under your boots, and you lay down and make snow angels…I love winter. But then I don't like being cold - so go figure.

Alcoholic drink - Three Wise Men, Jagermeister and Rumple Minze…I love tequila and anything sweet.

♀♀♀♀♀♀♀♀

If I could be any animal - I'd want to be a horse. I wouldn't want to be a dog. I don't want to crap in the yard where people can see me! To be a horse would be absolute freedom. They're powerful, strong, beautiful, graceful and elegant. There's no weakness in a horse.

♀♀♀♀♀♀♀♀

My favorite sexual position? Oh my God - there's too many to count. I like 'em all! I've never been afraid to try anything. Let's see - favorite position…either I'm on top cowgirl position, or doggie style - those are my two favorites. And anything in-between those two - I'm good with those, too. How can you not just like all of them? You have to enjoy sex - God made it that way - read the Song of Solomon. Oral sex is even spoken of: "…come north winds to my southern gardens…" North winds/southern gardens…hello?! Oral sex! What is there not to like about sex? I like the hot, sweaty, monkey sex swinging from the chandeliers - or the slow comfortable sex between two people who have been together for quite a while. Sex is a way to know you're not growing old! If you can still do it - you're not too old. There's just certain ways you shouldn't do it when you get older, though…like you shouldn't put your feet behind your head - you'll throw out your back!

♀♀♀♀♀♀♀♀♀

Sexual fantasies? Sex on the beach! I don't really want sand in my ass crack…but sex on a beach…or just to go through a whole romantic night (something I've never had). You know: like going out to a really nice restaurant, then slow dancing under little twinkling lights in a gazebo - to music only he and I

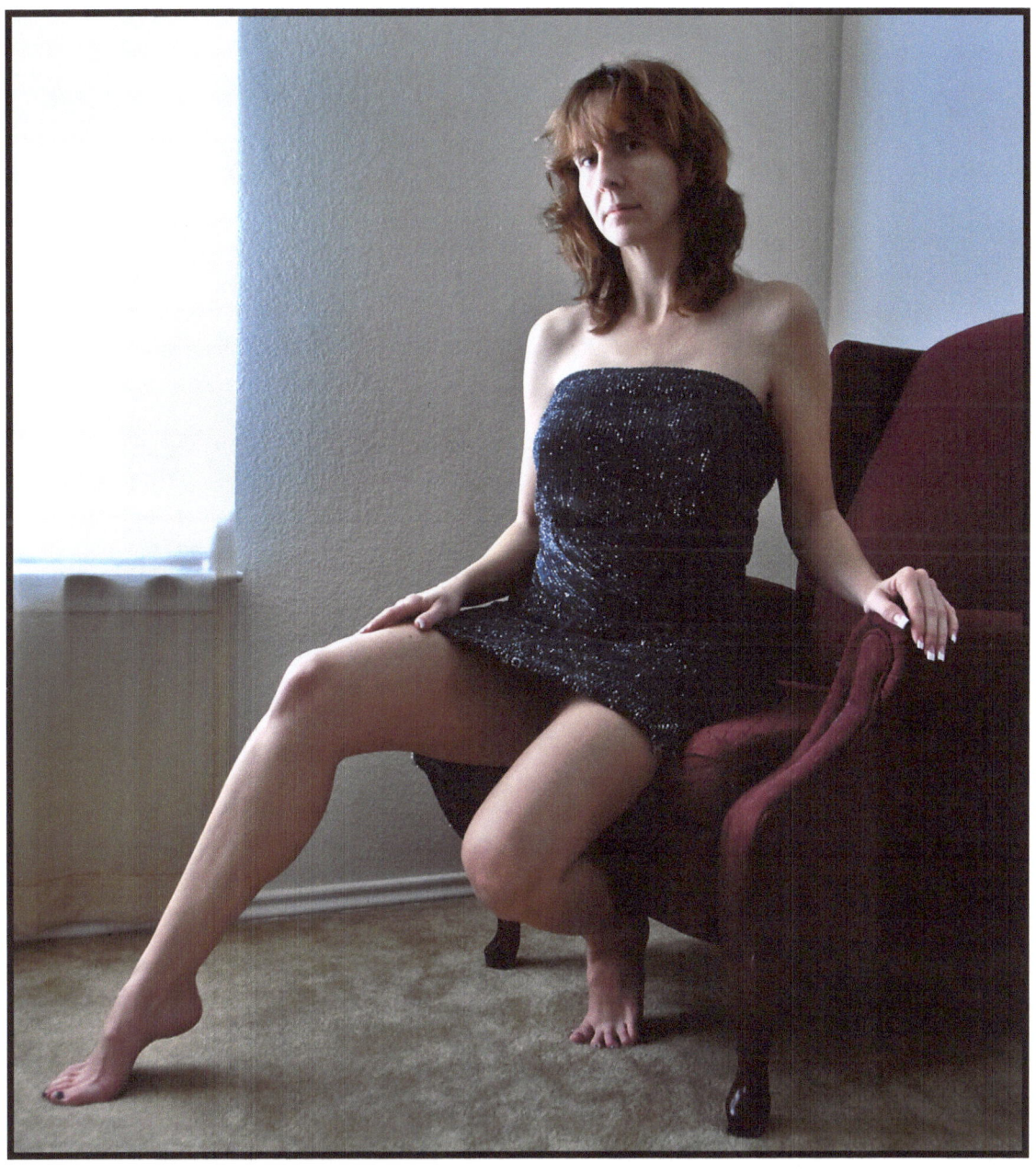

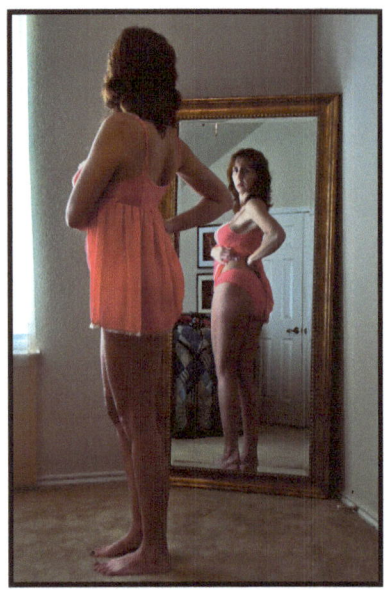

can hear. Afterwards, going home and the room has a sweet romantic scent, maybe candles. Finally making long, slow, passionate love for hours (and not necessarily on a bed).

Another fantasy would be to have the night I just described, starting out slow...but then you rip off each other's clothes 'cause you just can't wait to do it. You want it to last all night - and you wind up bleeding, broken, bruised and sweating (now THAT, I've had!). Don't hit me, but make me know that I will definitely remember it the next day - because I'll be walking funny.

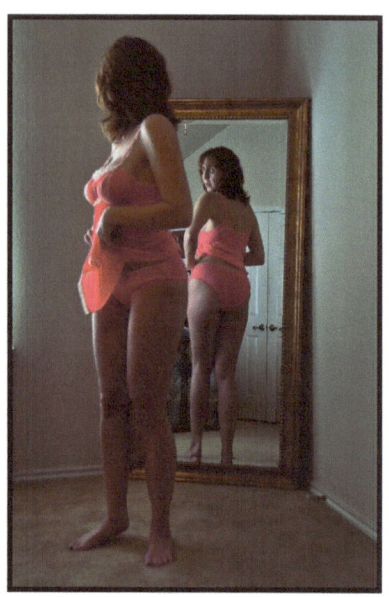

A lot of women have rape fantasies, but they're too scared to talk about it. The fantasy where he's in control - that's always good. Not brutal - 'cause I've been there, done that - had that happen. I don't want to go through that crap again. Just where he's the aggressor...he's in control - but then he lets me take the lead and I'm the aggressor (and he may not get up when it's over because he'll be walking funny).

♀♀♀♀♀♀♀♀♀

I love to swim. I taught my kids at a really young age, when they were still babies - under six months old. I always liked racing them in the pool. I like softball...I even played softball when I was pregnant - running...no, waddling to the bases - tripping over my own feet because I couldn't see them. I fell and landed on my elbows - avoided hitting my stomach. "Oh no - are you okay?" "I'm good!"

♀♀♀♀♀♀♀♀♀

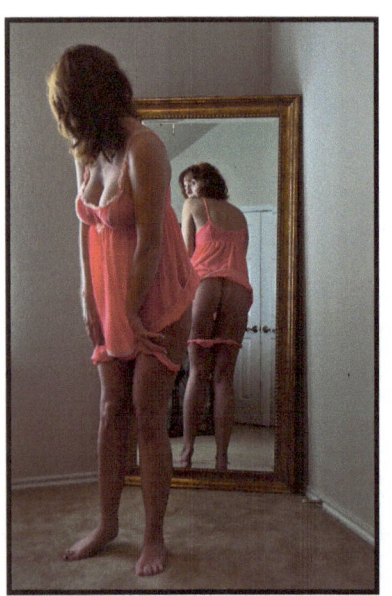

I love to watch hockey. I like watching football, too - I understand football. I hate basketball. I like baseball. Golf sucks - the most boring sport known to man. But I love hockey - LOVE the fights - I think that's what I love the most. Boxing...ehhh...just too powerhouse dudes beating the crap out of each other. There's nothing fun about that...but boy - watching hockey, I'm thinking "how many teeth are flying across the floor?" Love it! I don't want to get hit in the head with a puck...but it's fun to watch when they do a slap shot that hits the glass and it doesn't

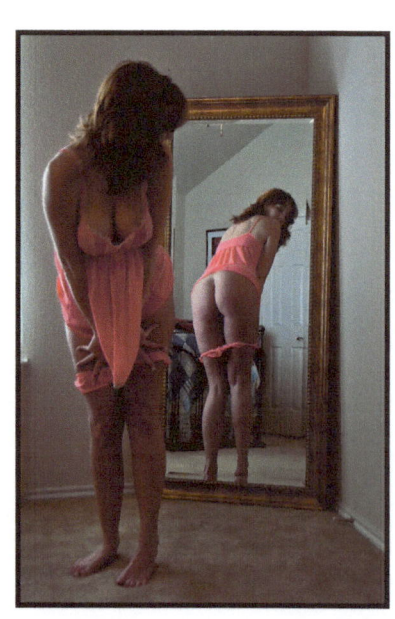

break. They go about 70 to 90 miles an hour, if not more - and I love that, I love the fast pace. It's a rush.

♀♀♀♀♀♀♀♀♀

The craziest, wildest thing I've ever done is when I got breast implants. I didn't tell anybody how I got them, or why I was getting them until the last week and a half before my surgery. I didn't want anyone to know. I just wanted to go "hey - I finally hit puberty!" I was on a web site called myfreeimplants.com and I made friends with people…who donated $7,000 for me to get implants! That's how I got them.

I've done a lot of crazy things, and a lot of stupid things. Everybody's done the generic skinny dipping, driving naked, having sex in weird places…been there, done that. Crazy/wild signifies fun and enjoyment.

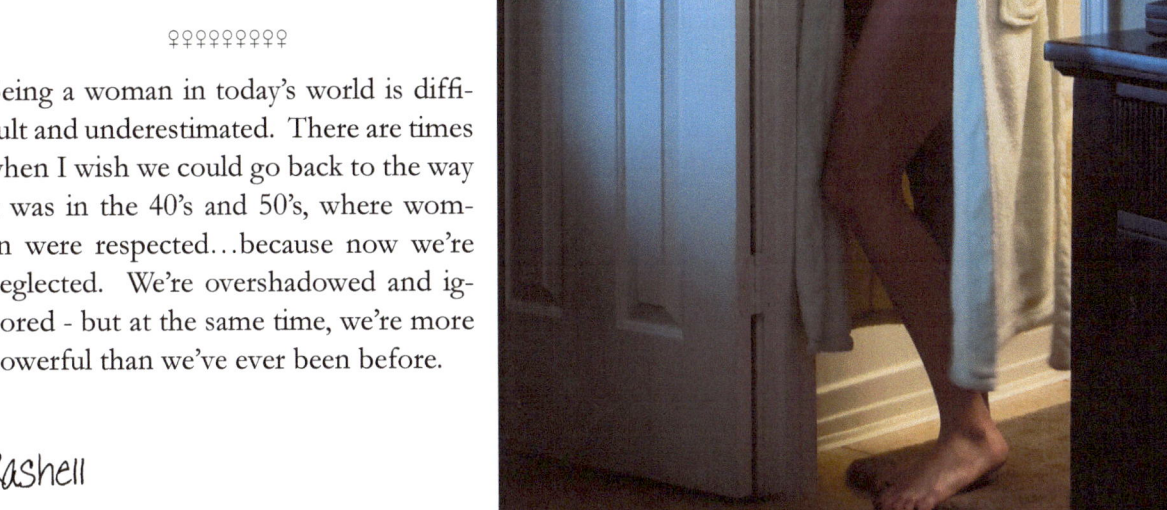

Crazy/stupid - now that's probably another question. Crazy/stupid…I was a drug addict - I'm seven years clean now. But those years - crazy/stupid is what that was. I don't regret that time - because it made me stronger. It made me know what I wanted…and didn't want in my life.

Crazy/wild and crazy/stupid I've done - and I'll probably continue to do both. Crazy/wild (and probably a little stupid): don't ride a horse bareback, naked, doing anything more than trotting. Number one, you get hair in your "hoo-ha" and a sore pubic bone. I thought it would be fun to try out what Lady Godiva did, but…good chocolate, bad idea.

♀♀♀♀♀♀♀♀♀

Being a woman in today's world is difficult and underestimated. There are times when I wish we could go back to the way it was in the 40's and 50's, where women were respected…because now we're neglected. We're overshadowed and ignored - but at the same time, we're more powerful than we've ever been before.

Rashell

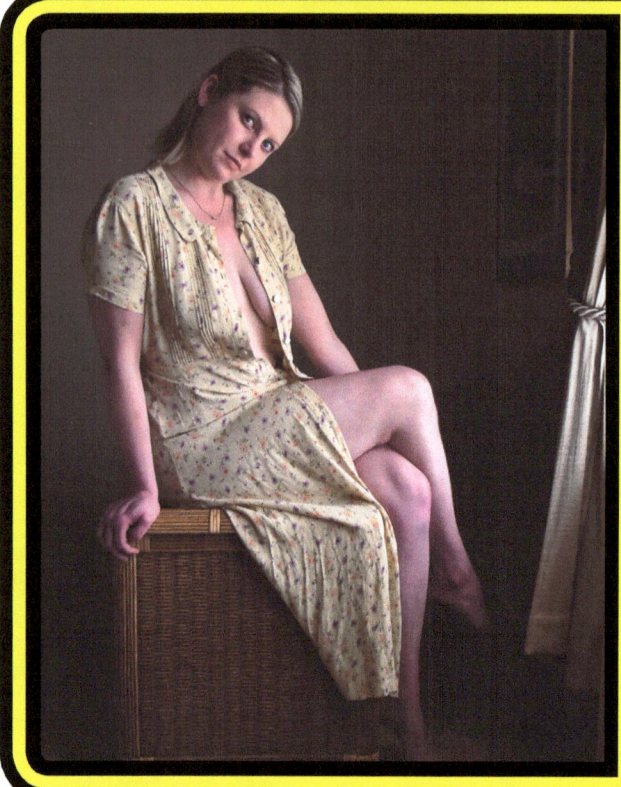

Joelle

♀♀♀♀♀♀♀♀♀

"I'd like people to know that I'm not as naive as I look."

Joelle, 29, is a housewife and mother who occasionally does some nude modeling to satisfy her artistic side. I really enjoyed working with her.

Growing up, I wanted to be a dancer - a ballet dancer. I was in ballet for years - absolutely loved the music and the rhythm. I was pretty good, but I quit. I really did want to grow up to be a famous ballerina!

♀♀♀♀♀♀♀♀♀

I was born in El Paso, Texas where I lived until I was 19. About that time, I moved to Austin to attend college, at Texas State University in San Marcos (which is just a few miles south of Austin).

I had a wonderful childhood. I was an only child and I was very, very close to both my mother and father (sadly, my father passed away earlier this year). I really couldn't ask for a better childhood. Oh, I went through the typical kid stuff - being rejected, being the last one chosen for a game - but nothing out of the ordinary.

My high school experience was fantastic. I was pretty popular - had a lot of friends. I wasn't part of a clique or anything but I had a lot of good fun, and did an awful lot of laughing. I had a pretty care free spirit. I made good grades and was very excited about going to college.

College turned out to be a very different story for me than high school, though. I struggled at so many different levels. I had no confidence. I loved learning and studying, but I changed my major five times. I really didn't know what I wanted to do with my life. Did I want to be a nurse, or be in business, or study art...it was such a confusing time. I ended up dropping out just a year short of graduation, and of course now I regret that. After all that work, all those credits and all those years, I pretty much lost my education.

Now I have to start all over. Seven years later - I'm currently registered to go back to college. So maybe it is never too late to go back, but it is going to be harder this time around - being a wife, a full time mother of two, AND a full time student. Wish me luck!

♀♀♀♀♀♀♀♀♀

I guess the toughest thing I've found about being an adult is having a family, knowing that bills have to be paid...just the pressures of everyday life, like being consistent in keeping jobs and making sure there's enough money to go around.

♀♀♀♀♀♀♀♀♀

If I could be anything, though - I'd love to be an actor.

♀♀♀♀♀♀♀♀♀

I'd love to travel to Greenland or Iceland or Fiji. I'd love to travel and see the world. My biggest regret is that I didn't travel more before I had children.

♀♀♀♀♀♀♀♀♀

If I could change anything about yourself, I would be more patient.

♀♀♀♀♀♀♀♀♀

My proudest achievement would be having my children - they are my most precious gifts. I have two wonderful, spirited little boys: one is four and a half, and the other is 15 months.

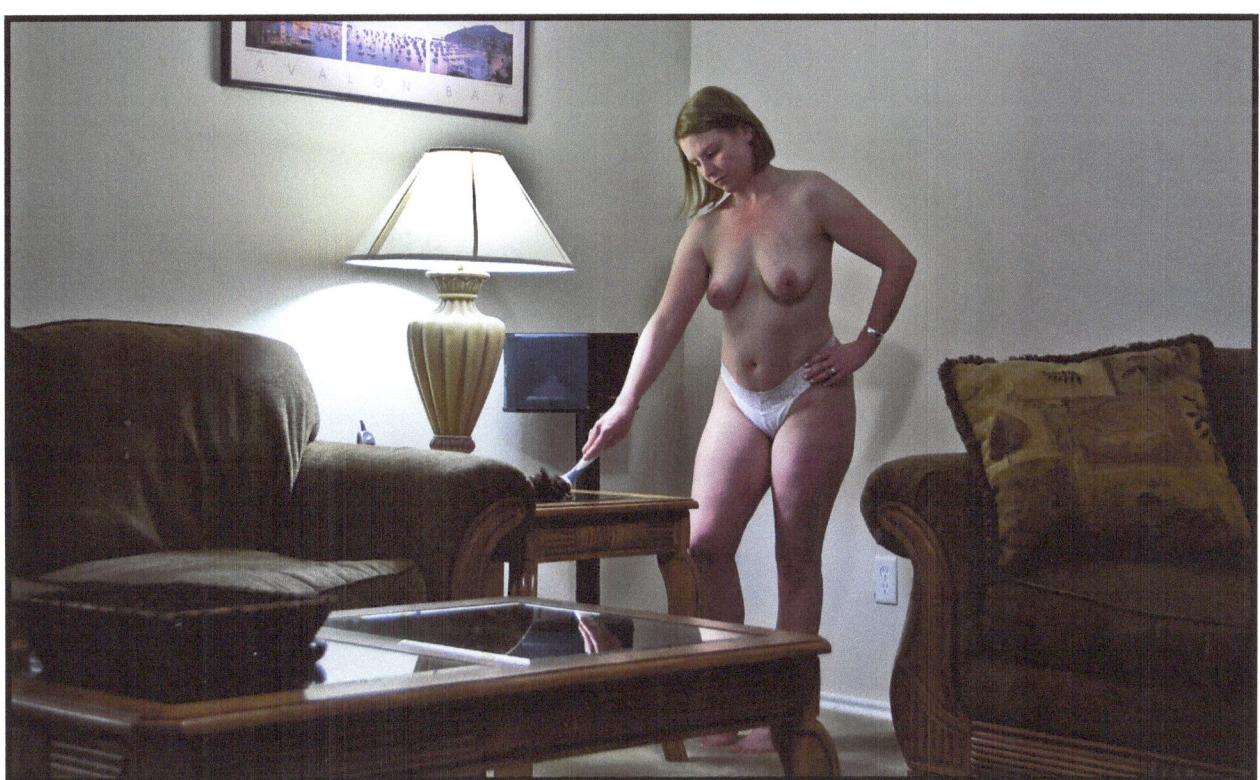

♀♀♀♀♀♀♀♀♀

I wouldn't change into a man, even if I magically could. I love being a woman!

♀♀♀♀♀♀♀♀♀

I think the best part of being a woman is the sensitivity and instincts that we have.

The worst part is the pressures we face of being women, of making memories of life as a woman...having the power, or I should say, the "powerlessness" as a woman.

♀♀♀♀♀♀♀♀♀

In most cases today, men still have a big advantage over women in the workplace - I believe many women would agree with that. And in politics - there's still the "good old boy" club. Men still have most of the power and the strength in this world.

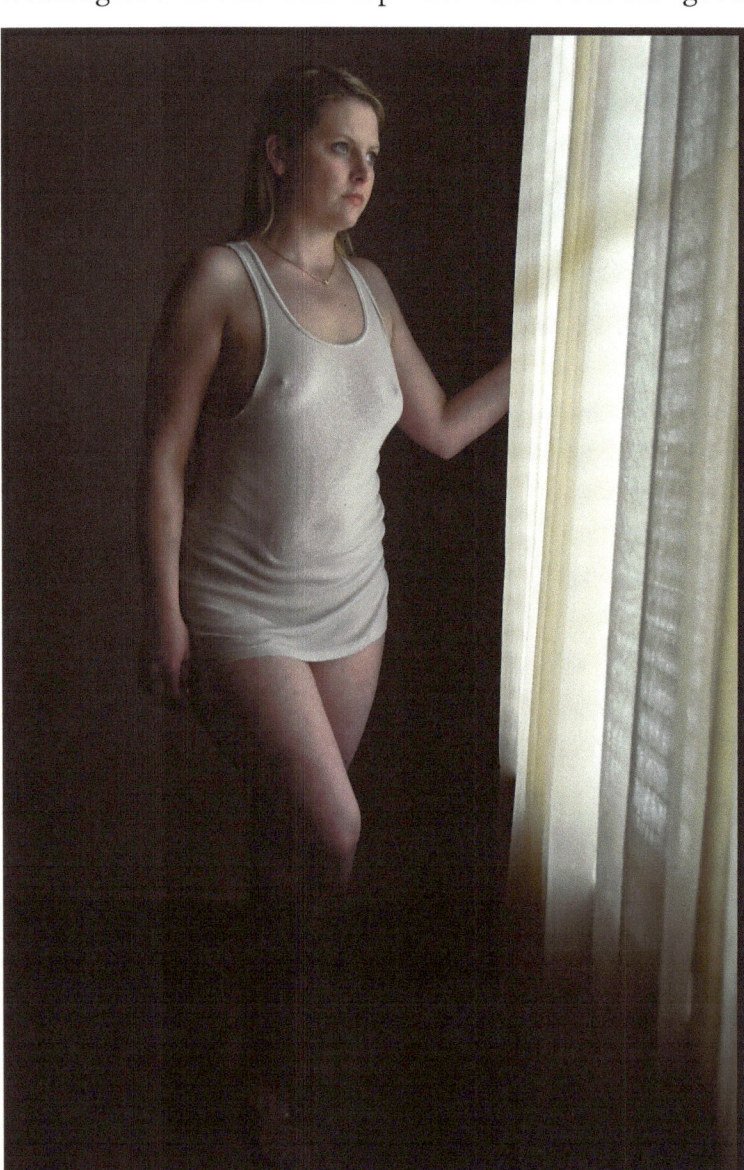

I don't think that men are as in touch with their emotions as women - even though I think men are truly, truly emotional. I think they have pressures to not express themselves emotionally, and it causes them to feel bad. Sensitivity is important for both men and women, though - men need to express their feelings, without worrying that they are weak for doing it.

♀♀♀♀♀♀♀♀♀

Star crushes? Yes - I've always had a soft spot for John Cusack. I love his movies.

♀♀♀♀♀♀♀♀♀

The biggest lessons I've learned about life so far is that it's too short - you have to live it, not just stand around on the sidelines.

♀♀♀♀♀♀♀♀♀

If I could be any animal, I'd probably want to be a hawk or an owl. It would be cool to have their keen sense of sight and be able to fly.

♀♀♀♀♀♀♀♀♀

My strengths: I love to the core, I never

give up on a friendship or relationship without trying real hard. I'm generous - I give to others, I try to help mankind and people who need help. I have an open heart.

Weaknesses: I'm not as patient as I'd like to be with my family - though I generally am with others. And I sweat the small stuff all the time - I analyze everything to death. I need to revisit all that.

♀♀♀♀♀♀♀♀♀

I always loved my mother's stories of Greek mythology. She was real creative with them.

♀♀♀♀♀♀♀♀♀

I enjoy and appreciate a gratifying sex life - I love sex. I would say that I'm a very sexual person indeed. I'd like to believe that my husband and I have the most satisfying and fulfilled sex lives possible. I've al-

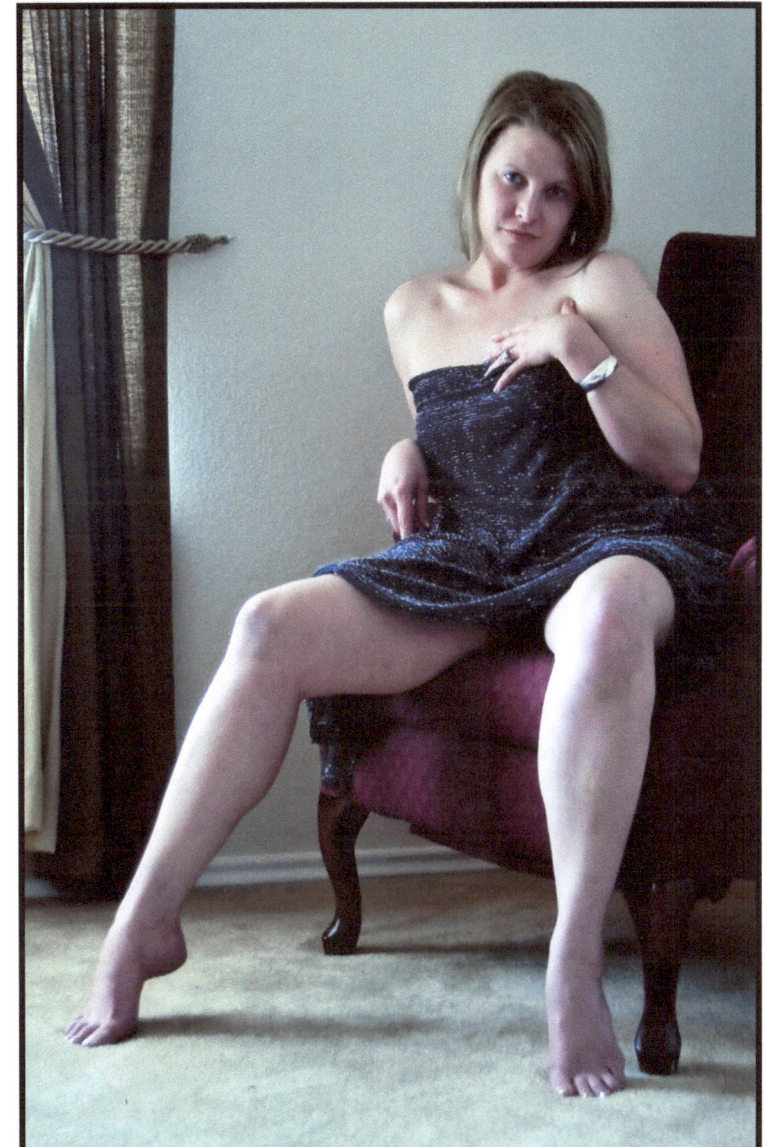

ways been sexual - even as a young child. I can remember masturbating at like age five or six. My attitudes about sex have definitely evolved as I have matured. I think it's important to maintain a proper balance about it.

My favorite sexual position is simply the standard missionary position. I like that one.

Do I have any sexual fantasies? I've actually thought about what my sexual fantasies might be quite a bit. It would probably be having sex with someone I love - my husband - while other people watched us and enjoyed themselves.

♀♀♀♀♀♀♀♀♀

My favorite sports to participate in are soccer and volleyball. My favorites to watch are football and basketball. Actually, basketball would probably be my first choice.

♀♀♀♀♀♀♀♀♀

My favorite comfort food would definitely be Shepherds Pie. It's meat, potatoes, peas, cheese - it's just this big thing that's all put together and so delicious.

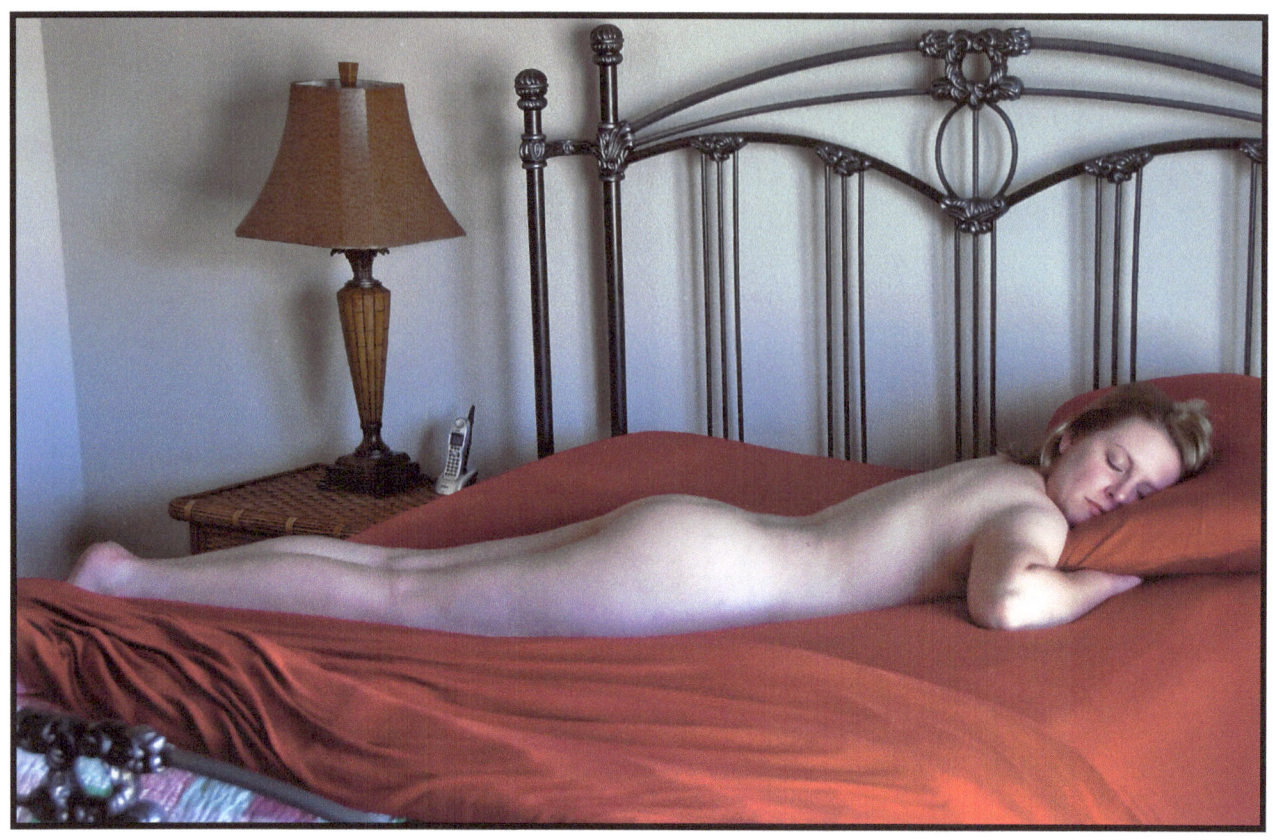

It's really comforting to eat. And I just love warm soups!

Favorite color is purple.

My favorite kind of music is rock and roll

My favorite musical group? I love Coldplay, Dave Mathews, the Beatles - I'm a music lover, I like all kinds of music - jazz, classical...just about anything.

My favorite TV show is "John Edward Cross Country" - it's fascinating, I love watching him.

My favorite movie? I have lots of favorites - "Titanic" would be one for sure.

My favorite kind of movie would be drama.

♀♀♀♀♀♀♀♀♀

To win my heart, a man just has to write something beautiful from the heart.

♀♀♀♀♀♀♀♀♀

Important qualities for a significant other to have? He has to have a good sense of humor - to be funny, to be able to make me laugh. He has to be kind, be a nice person, and someone who always puts his family first before himself.

♀♀♀♀♀♀♀♀♀

I am passionate about cooking - I love cooking.

♀♀♀♀♀♀♀♀♀

I hate it when the house is a mess - I can't stand things being out of order. It drives me crazy.

♀♀♀♀♀♀♀♀♀

My favorite season is fall.

♀♀♀♀♀♀♀♀♀

I'd like people to know that I'm not as naive as I look.

♀♀♀♀♀♀♀♀♀

My favorite subjects in school were philosophy and sociology. My least favorites were math and political science.

♀♀♀♀♀♀♀♀♀

The craziest, wildest thing I've ever done? Well, I've tried cliff diving and bungee jumping. I probably shouldn't mention this, but an ex-boyfriend and I had sex underneath the carousel at Six Flags a really long time ago. I think that was probably the craziest thing I've ever done.

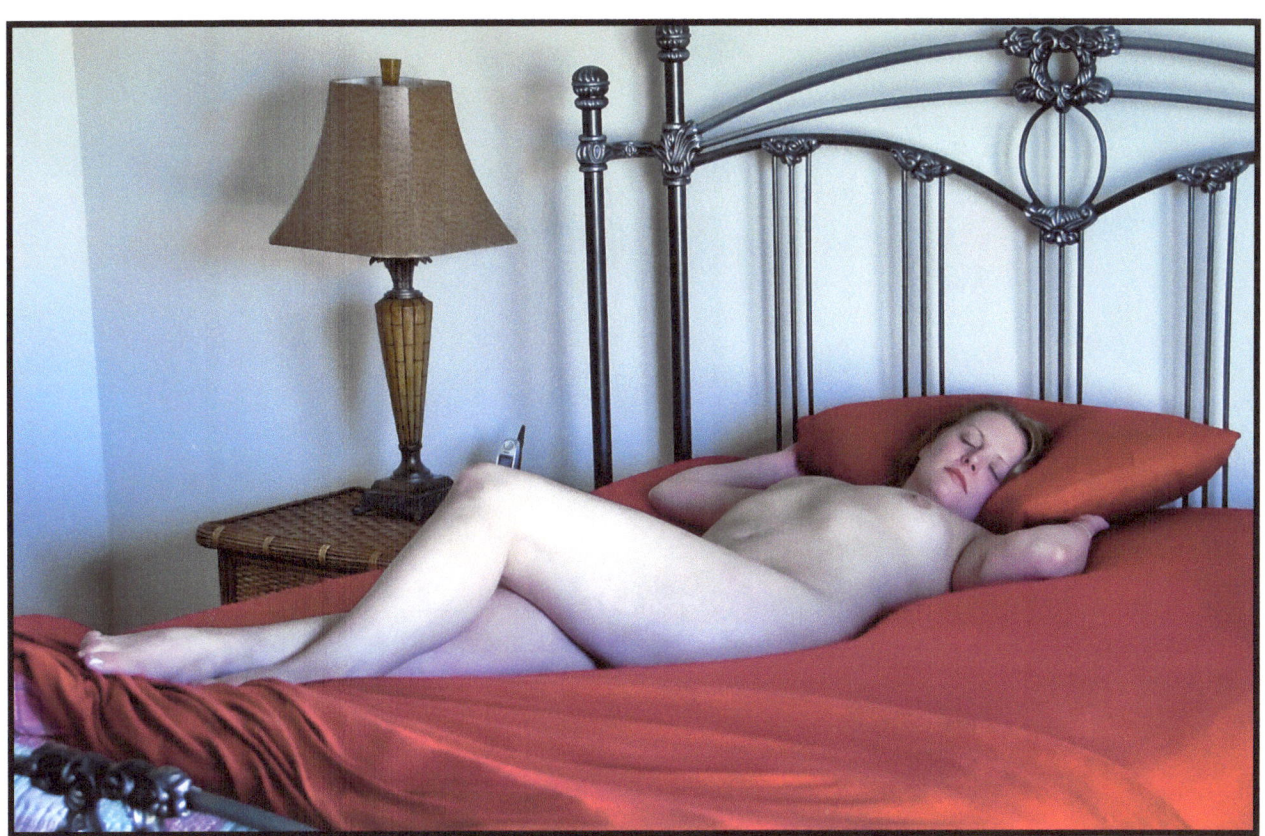

⚲⚲⚲⚲⚲⚲⚲⚲⚲

My husband is actually the person who got me into modeling. He's an aspiring photographer and loves to photograph women. He really pays attention to things like their body lines, and he has such a pas-

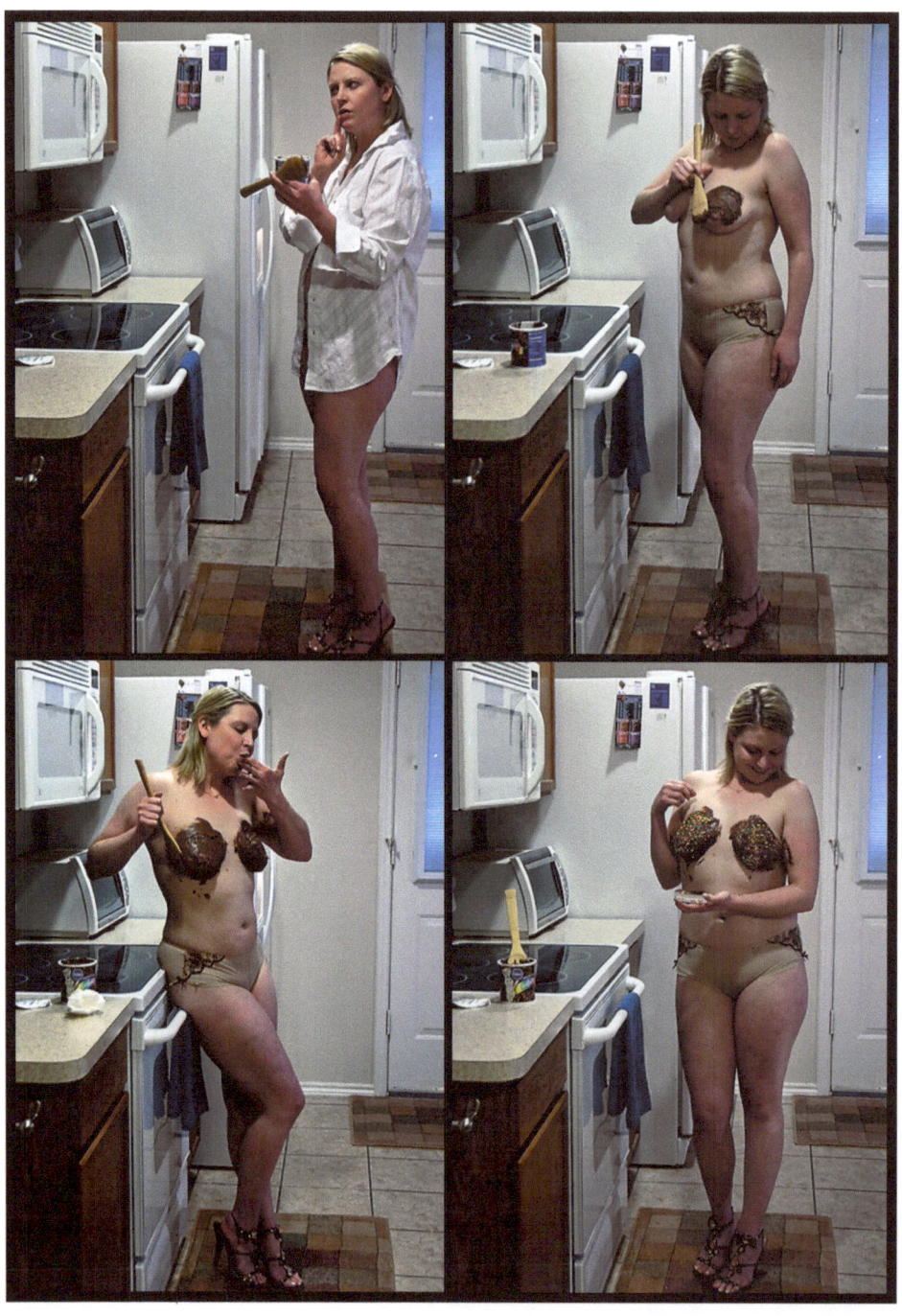

sion for it. Over time, I've developed a strong passion for both modeling and photography as well. He created an account for himself on a popular networking web site for models and photographers (the same one that Gary is active on) - then he took several pics of me and posted them online. By the time we had been doing this for about three months, he had received several comments on his photos - as well as several inquiries as to who the model was. After he told me about that, we decided to set up an account for me on that web site as well. A few months later, I started getting some offers to model.

♀♀♀♀♀♀♀♀♀

I guess the best day I've ever had was when I found out that I didn't have cancer - that was a great day!

The worst day was when my father died.

♀♀♀♀♀♀♀♀♀

The thing that scares me most is death.

♀♀♀♀♀♀♀♀♀

My favorite alcoholic drink is red wine. My favorite non-alcoholic beverage is diet coke.

♀♀♀♀♀♀♀♀♀

I try to be on time, but more often than not - I'm always late!

♀♀♀♀♀♀♀♀♀

Heroes in my life? My father was a hero of mine...and Kurt Vonnegut.

♀♀♀♀♀♀♀♀♀

Yeah, I'd have to say that I'm an exhibitionist - but the reason I model nude is simply because I believe that the human body is gorgeous! Everyone should be comfortable with their body, no matter what size they are. The human body is a work of art in itself - the greatest creation of art that exists. What could be more "human" than images of it?

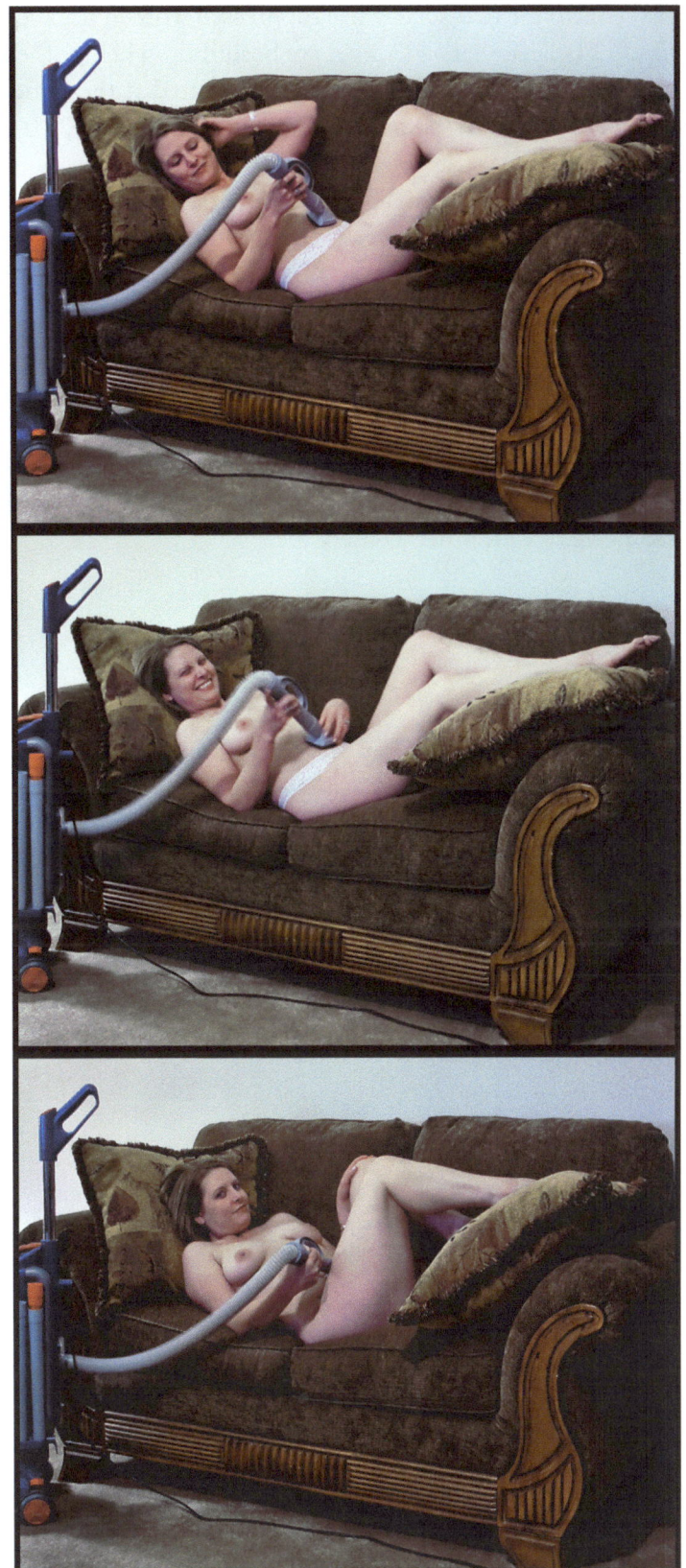

It seems to me that society has suppressed women for a long time with the attitude that "nudity is not lady like." I believe that all women are beautiful - whether they're a playboy model, a wife, a mother...19 years old...or 65. You can be classy yet uninhibited at the same time. I hate that our society generally believes that nudity (and taking photos of nudity) equals SEX. It does not!

The down side of modeling nude is worrying about my safety. It's often hard to know just who you are actually dealing with. I always check references on any new photographer before I work with them, and I try to network with other models and such. That part of it does make me pretty nervous at times, so I always try to make personal safety a very high priority when setting up photo shoots!

♀♀♀♀♀♀♀♀♀

What's it like to be a woman in today's world? I don't know - the best thing about being a woman is that we can use being a woman to get what we want in certain situations. I love being a woman - I don't complain about it. I think there's a lot of passion behind being a woman - experiences and relationships that we all share with other women.

Joelle

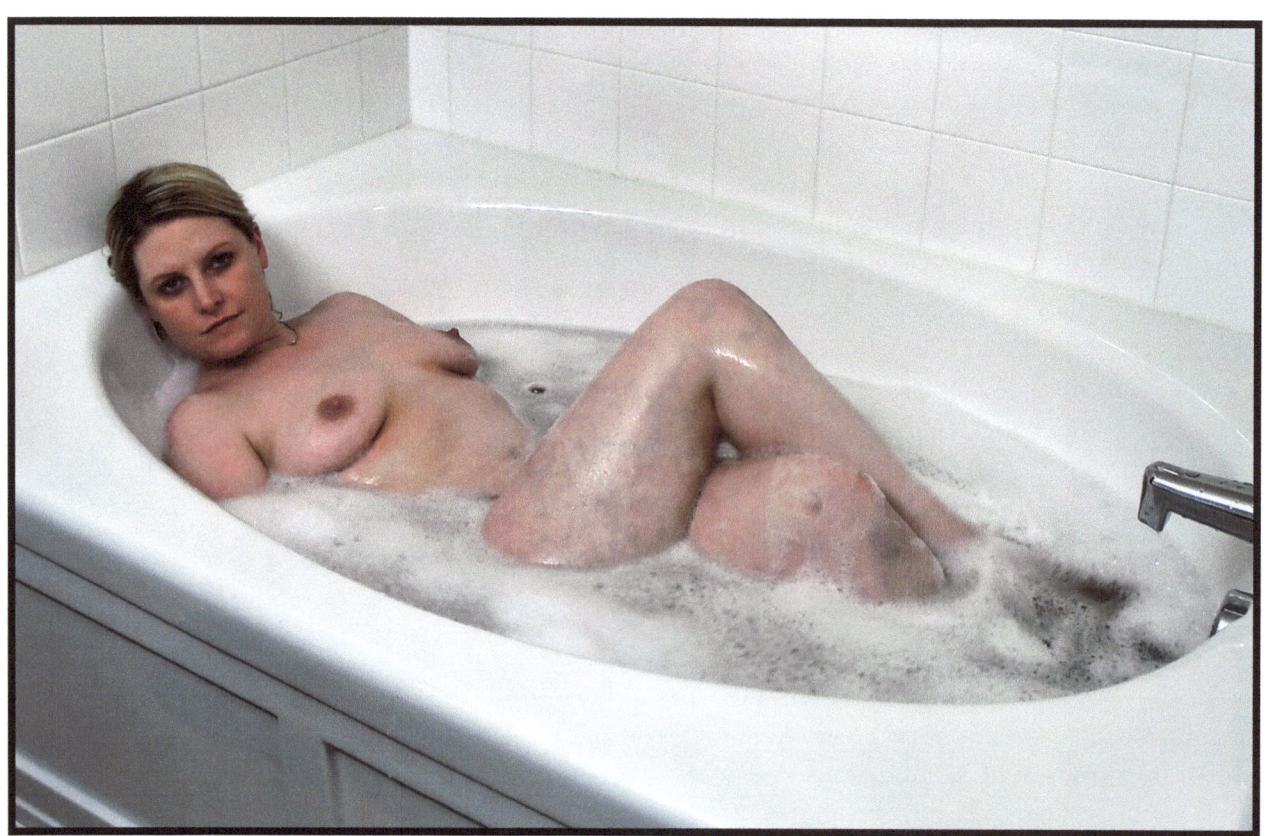

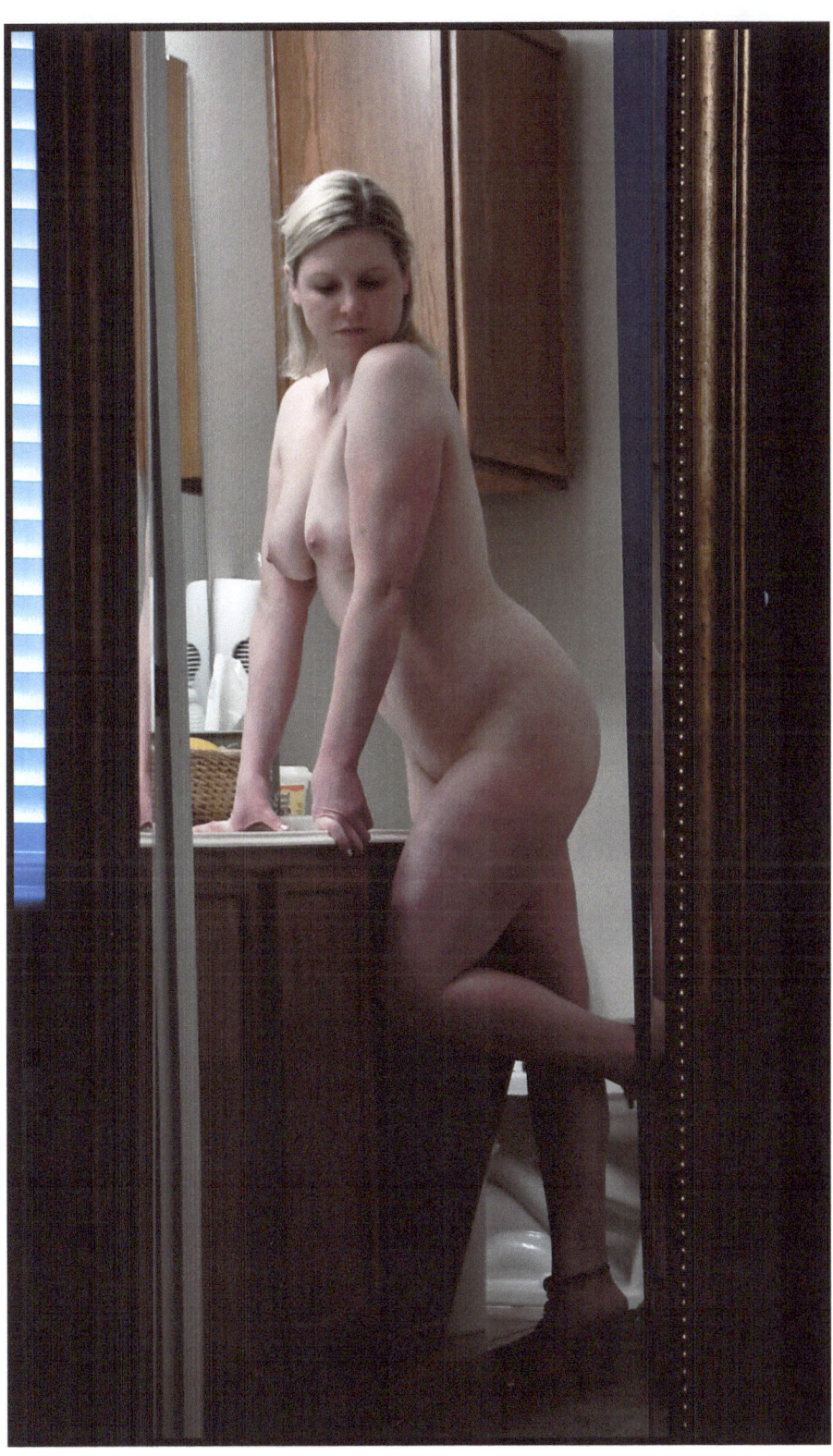

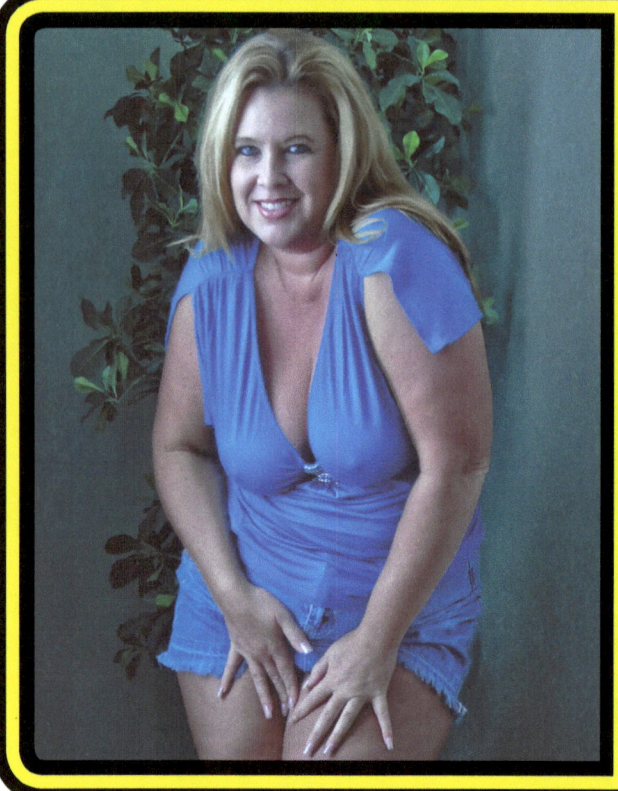

Jasmine

♀♀♀♀♀♀♀♀♀

"The best part of being a woman is the sexuality part - we've very sexual and sensual."

At 40, Jasmine is the oldest of the Nine Women - but you'd never know it to meet her. I'd seen her work for a while and always wanted to shoot with her. She didn't disappoint - she was a joy!

Growing up, I actually wanted to be an interior designer. I have a lot of craft capabilities and I thought that would be fun. The only thing that stopped me was that I didn't have the money to go to school for interior design.

♀♀♀♀♀♀♀♀♀

These days, I guess my goals are to be a good person, to expand my modeling career, and to do more jewelry design. I'd really like to become a jewelry designer at a fashion mall or something like that down the line.

♀♀♀♀♀♀♀♀♀

I was born in Texas and grew up in a small town outside of San Antonio. We were on the edge of the city, which kind of grew up around us over the years.

My childhood was great. I grew up with 2 sisters. We got to play around the yard, and do fun stuff at my grandmother's house. We did have to do our chores - I was very disciplined on making sure I got everything done that my parents asked me to do. My mother and father were hard working individuals who taught us great values. It was all pretty good - just an average growing up type of situation, average family, mom and dad both working and we had lots of summertime fun.

I'm the oldest - I have one sister who is two years younger and the another that is six years younger. I ended up being the bossy one - telling them what to do. They always said that I was too mean to them - that I was the "mean one" in the family. I really don't think that I was as cruel to them as they talk like I was.

It's kind of funny, but I don't remember any "bad news" as a child. If something bad happened in the world, I probably didn't even know it. I was very naive and led a very sheltered life.

♀♀♀♀♀♀♀♀

I've never really thought about being something truly important - like a doctor, nurse or firefighter. Actually, I'd enjoy not working at all! But if I could do anything - have any occupation - I would find it difficult to be inspired by going to work for someone else. My ultimate job would be one where I'm self-employed, doing my own thing - setting my own hours. Actually, that's kind of where I'm at right now in my life. There are days when I can be really lazy, then there are other days where I'm really strict on myself and work hard to accomplish as much as possible. Jewelry designing has become a great love of mine. I've always been creative, and now - that's my job. I put things together that I hope people will like and buy from me.

♀♀♀♀♀♀♀♀

I love to travel, and now it appears that my dream trip is about to happen. My husband and I are going to take a trip to Greece - in fact it's already booked. I've been to a lot of places in this country, but I'd really like to see Europe now. Maybe go to Paris and actually shop and buy some expensive bag or purse - something new.

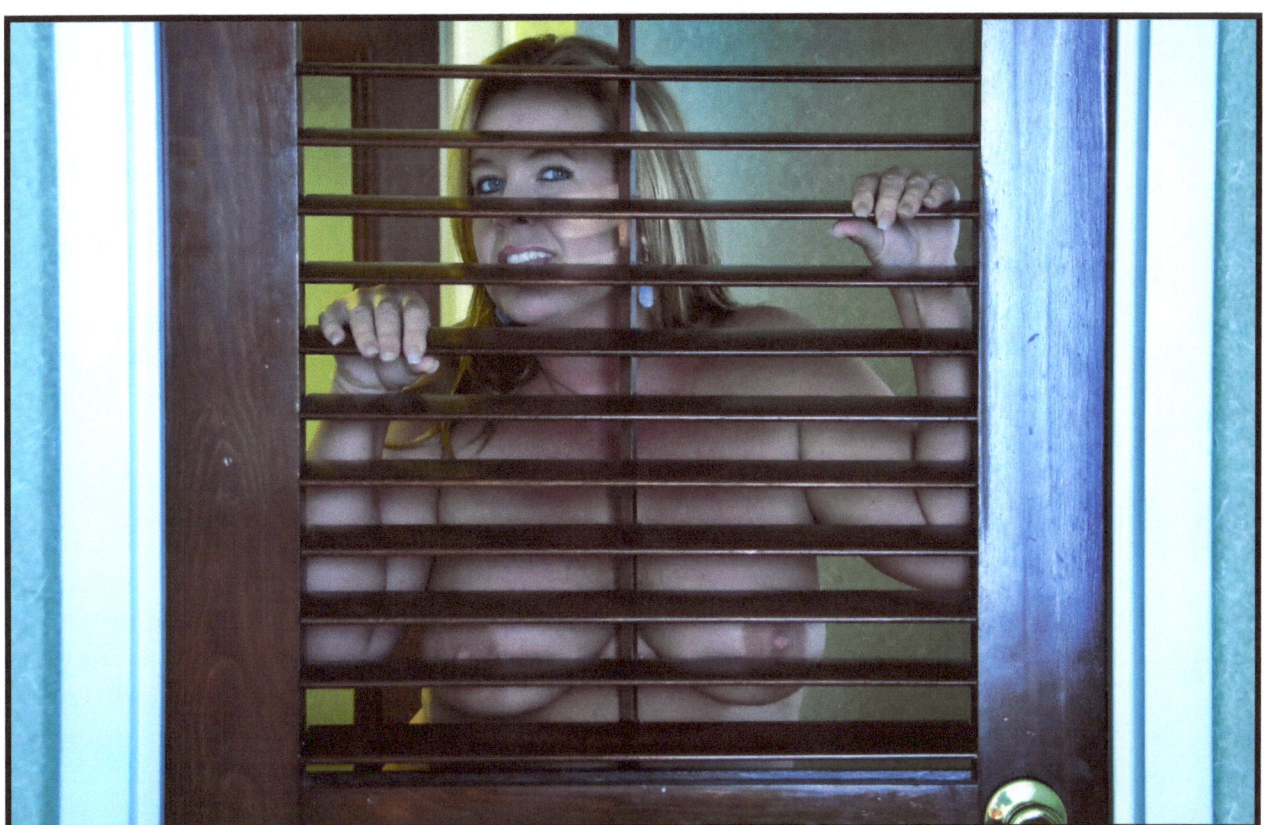

♀♀♀♀♀♀♀♀

A lot of people don't know that I pose nude. That's something secret. I've kept it that way because I worry that a lot of people won't understand - that it's strictly about art for me.

♀♀♀♀♀♀♀♀

If I could change anything about myself, I'd like to change my legs. I've always wanted to change them. People say you should be happy for what you have - after all, I have my health and I have my curves. But if only my calves were a bit smaller so I that I could wear those cute boots! Or maybe the world needs to make larger shoes!

♀♀♀♀♀♀♀♀

My proudest achievement was getting a college degree. Not everyone gets that opportunity, and I'm someone who had to accomplish that on my own. It took me a long time, including going to night school, but eventually I completed it. I'll always have that degree whether I use it or not.

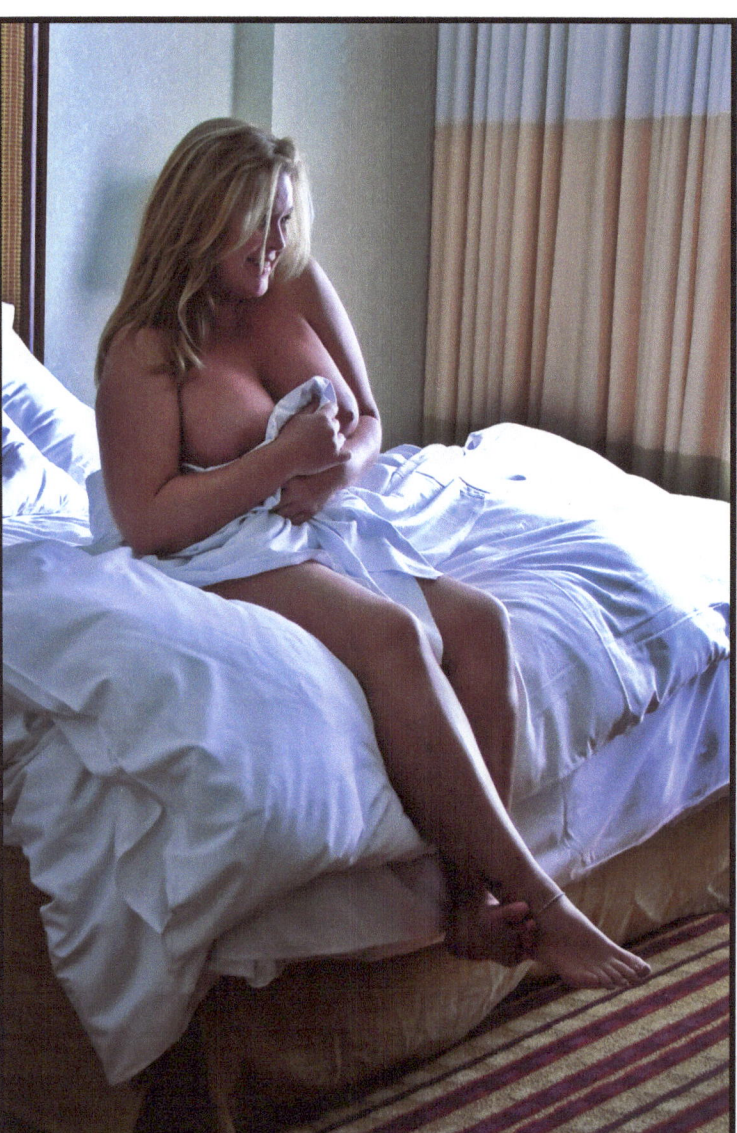

On the other hand, probably my biggest regret is that I didn't get a more interesting degree. Mine is in business management and it wasn't very exciting. If I could do it over (and if I had had the money), I would have loved to get a degree in interior design or fashion design. I feel like my creativity is a large part of me, and I would have loved to put that talent to more use. Every once in a while, I still think about how it would be nice to go back and learn something new. I'm sure I could do that still if I really put my mind to it.

♀♀♀♀♀♀♀♀

If I could magically change in to a man, would I? No way - I would never want to be a man! I am so happy to be a woman! We just have better "assets," we have more interesting clothes, we get to wear jewelry, make-up. We get to do all sorts of fun stuff!

♀♀♀♀♀♀♀♀♀

The best part of being a woman is the sexuality part - we've very sexual and sensual.

♀♀♀♀♀♀♀♀♀

The worst part is what every woman has to go through - their monthly "occurrence" and the jealousy and anger and mood changes that comes along with that. We just wish that we didn't have to deal with that crap every month.

♀♀♀♀♀♀♀♀♀

As time goes by, it seems to me that the separation between the sexes is getting less and less. I don't see that much difference in the way men and women are treated by society today. Even in the workplace - I think that women are getting equal opportunities to do what they want to do. I actually don't even think about it that much anymore. It was different back in my parents' day - when men were the ones who were

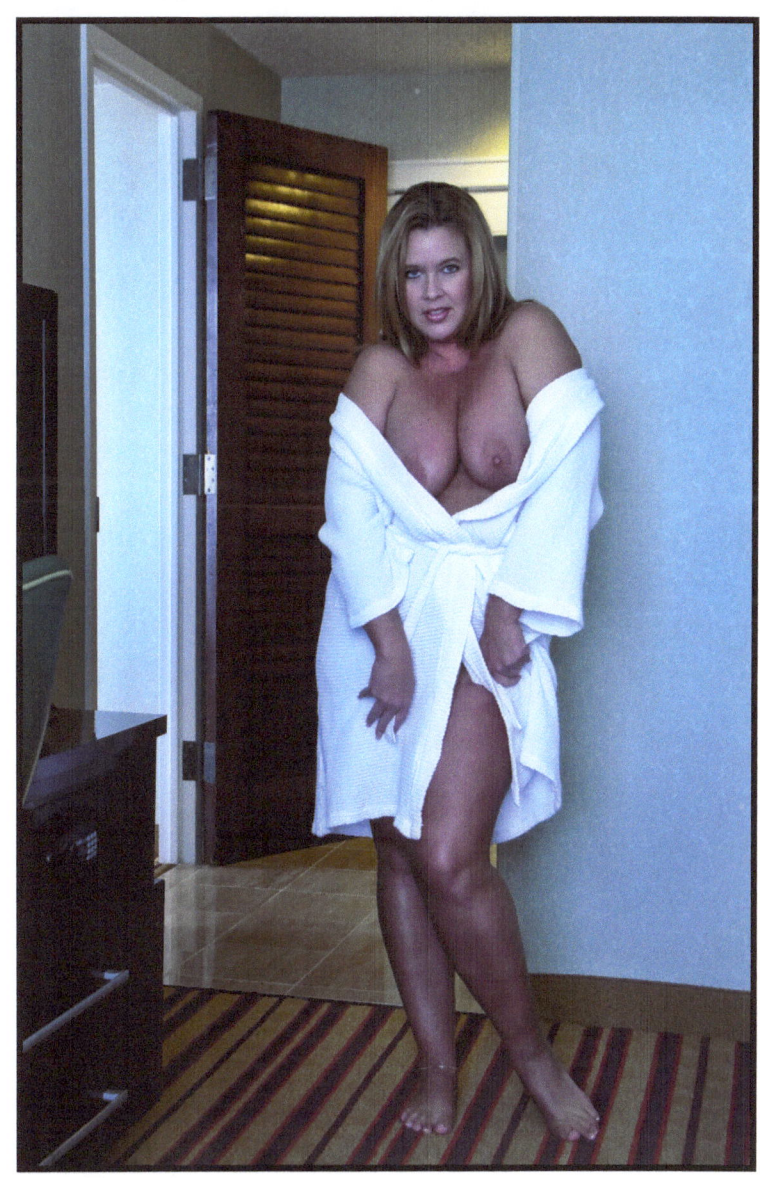

supposed to get the job and support the family, and the wife was supposed to stay at home. But now, I think we're almost equal.

♀♀♀♀♀♀♀♀♀

I used to have something of a crush on Dolph Lundgren - I think mainly for those muscles of his. But I don't really have crushes on celebrities anymore.

♀♀♀♀♀♀♀♀♀

One night I got a little too drunk, got a little too mad at my husband and wound up stepping out of a moving vehicle. It made me cool down and realize I needed to stop doing stupid things - like not drinking as much.

As I've gone through my life, I've learned to be in more control of it. I've also learned to be more confident, to be friendlier, to take pride in who I am. I think I've learned to be a better person.

♀♀♀♀♀♀♀♀♀

If I could be any animal, I'd like to be a big cat! It's funny - I was just thinking about that the other day. I love big cats - I could be lazy, just relax in the sun, and enjoy the natural life outdoors. I was

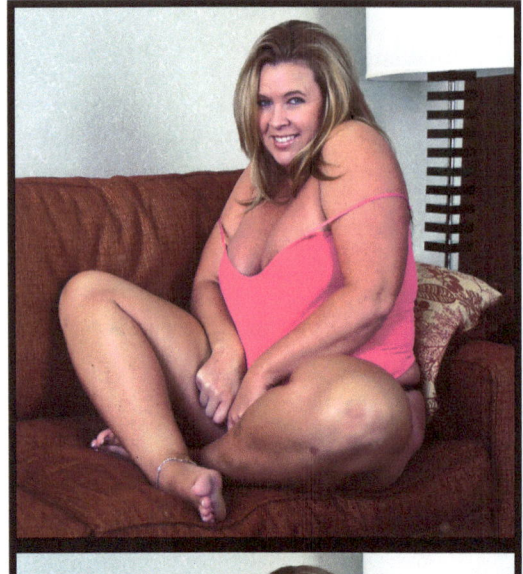

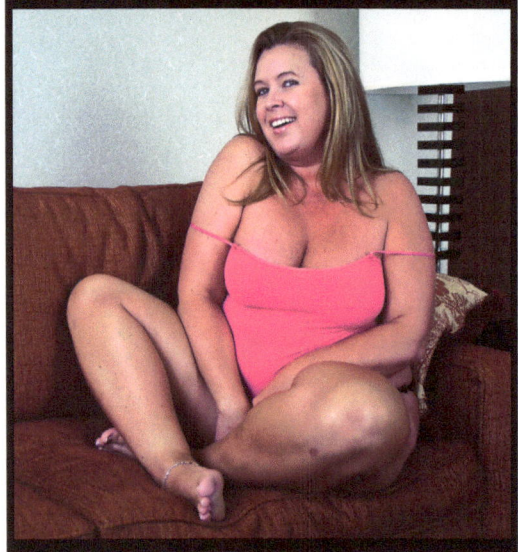

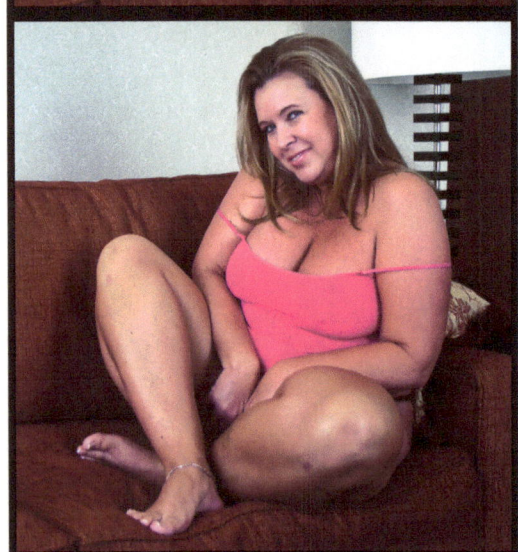

thinking that they're sexy, but I guess it could be dangerous to be one as well. I just think they're cool.

♀♀♀♀♀♀♀♀♀

My best qualities? Well, I think my best physical quality is my smile - and my eyes. Those are the two things that people are constantly complimenting me on, especially since I'm a model. My best nonphysical quality is my friendliness. I try to treat everyone the same, no matter who they are, whether I've met them before or not. I try to be equally friendly with just about everyone I meet.

My worst quality - which I think about a lot - is that I'm a very jealous person. I'd really like to improve on that. I've been working hard to be less jealous about certain things.

♀♀♀♀♀♀♀♀♀

Not much scares me. Well, I would never jump out of a plane - that would scare me! But really, I'm not easily frightened. I'm stronger willed to do things now than I ever was.

♀♀♀♀♀♀♀♀♀

I don't really have a favorite fairy tale. Reading wasn't a big part of my growing up. I don't know - maybe Cinderella? I never really sat around and thought about it that much before.

♀♀♀♀♀♀♀♀♀

I've never been all that athletic or wild about playing sports, but if I had been - volleyball would have probably been my favorite. I've spent most of my life working, so I've never had much time for sports.

And I don't really care about watching any sports, either. I'd rather do something like sit around and talk with friends instead.

♀♀♀♀♀♀♀♀♀

My favorite comfort food would be shrimp - no, chocolate - chocolate is a comfort food. Sometimes I think it's an aphrodisiac, too!

Favorite alcoholic drink is vodka - mixed with whatever. Favorite non-alcoholic beverage is iced tea.

♀♀♀♀♀♀♀♀♀

Favorite color is pink.

♀♀♀♀♀♀♀♀♀

Favorite sexual position is "cowgirl".

Do I have any sexual fantasies? Doesn't everybody? I don't sit around and worry a whole lot about having a bunch of fantasies, but I guess there are the ones that everyone wants to try: threesomes, swinger type situations, etc. Maybe just having a Dolph Lundgren type walk in and sweep me off my feet and take advantage of me. That might be fun!

♀♀♀♀♀♀♀♀♀

Favorite kind of music is dance - 'cause it's fast and fun. Dance music is something that everybody likes, you know - stuff you can "move" to. I just love to dance!

Favorite musical group, I guess, would be Bon Jovi. At least he was my favorite at one time. Oh, he still is - he sings pretty good songs!

♀♀♀♀♀♀♀♀♀

Back when I used to get occasional control of the television remote, I liked to watch "Friends". And back in the day - all the sitcoms like "Three's Company", "I Love Lucy", and the "Munsters". But these days, I'm surrounded by nothing but sci-fi. I get to watch a lot of sci-fi 'cause that's what my husband is in to.

My favorite movie? There's so many! I guess I like action movies - no, no - I get forced into watching action movies. I like drama and comedy and romance - the ones that make you feel good in the end. You know - the ones where you walk out of the theater saying "that was such a good movie!"

♀♀♀♀♀♀♀♀♀

To win my heart, a man has to be romantic and spontaneous. I think that's why I've been married so long - because I still get that today.

♀♀♀♀♀♀♀♀♀

I'm most passionate about being creative.

♀♀♀♀♀♀♀♀♀

It really irritates me when I can't get a hold of somebody on the phone - when they just don't answer.

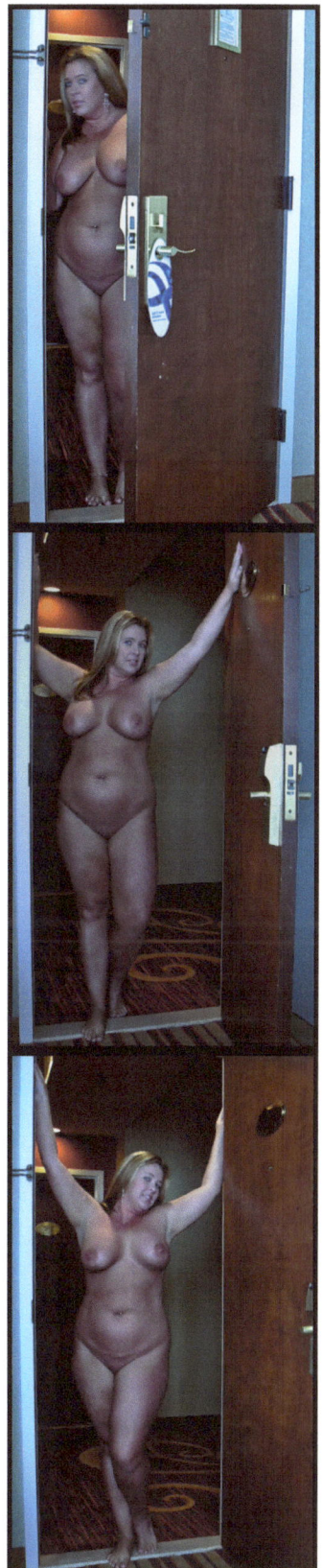

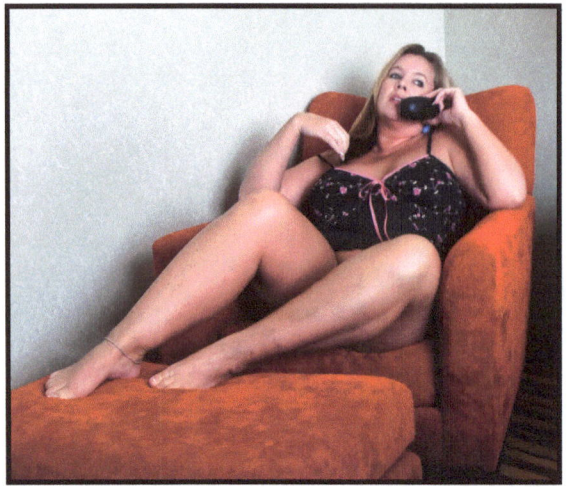

♀♀♀♀♀♀♀♀♀

My favorite season would be summer - well, make that spring and summer. I like warm weather - it's probably why I've lived in Texas forever.

♀♀♀♀♀♀♀♀♀

I wish people would judge me for what's in my heart, and not so much from my appearance. Growing up, I was always judged from my outer appearance and not my inner self. I'd like people to know that I'm a nice person - or at least I hope that I come across as one. I just want them to know that I can be their friend. I'm always going to be there for you if you need me.

♀♀♀♀♀♀♀♀♀

My favorite subject in school was art. My least favorite was English.

♀♀♀♀♀♀♀♀♀

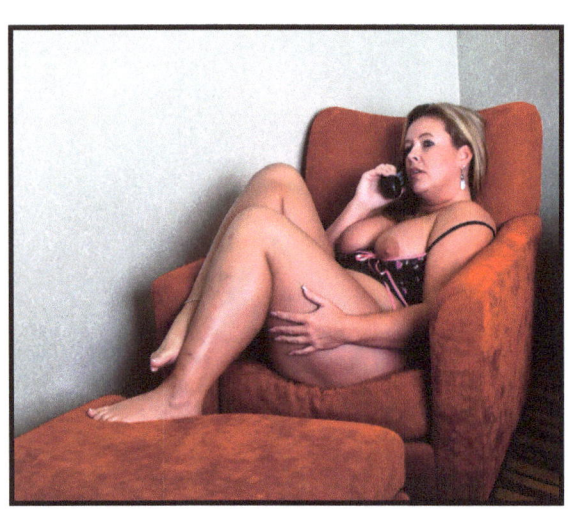

The craziest, wildest thing I've ever done was going to a nude resort. At least it seemed like a wild and crazy thing to do the first time, but then I discovered I really liked it.

♀♀♀♀♀♀♀♀♀

The best day I ever had was when I got married.

The worst day was when I discovered I'd hurt someone's feelings. There's been a few of those days - the kind where you wish you could take back what you said wrong.

♀♀♀♀♀♀♀♀♀

I'm late more often that I'm early.

♀♀♀♀♀♀♀♀♀

Oh hell yes I'm an exhibitionist! I like being the center of attention and the ham in front of the camera. I like to smile, I like to have my picture taken, I like to look at myself, I like to make sure people are looking at me. I think it runs in my family.

♀♀♀♀♀♀♀♀♀

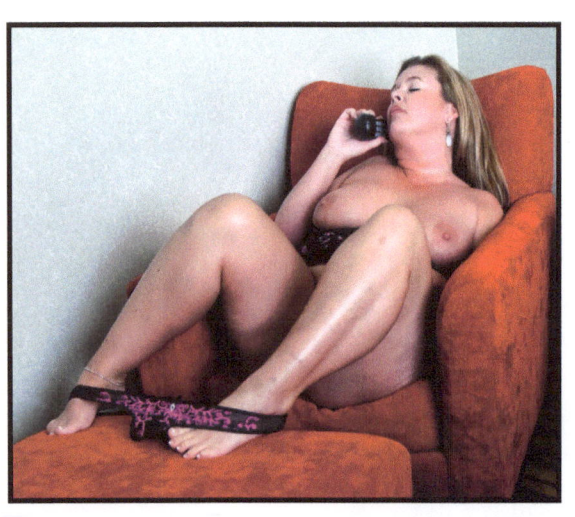

What is it like to be a woman in today's world? I think it's fairly easy actually. I've worked all my life, but I've also had the opportunity not to work. I feel like I'm a princess. I get to do whatever I want and go wherever I want. Nobody's telling me that I can't. The great thing is that I know there are several people out there who really love me for just who I am.

Jasmine

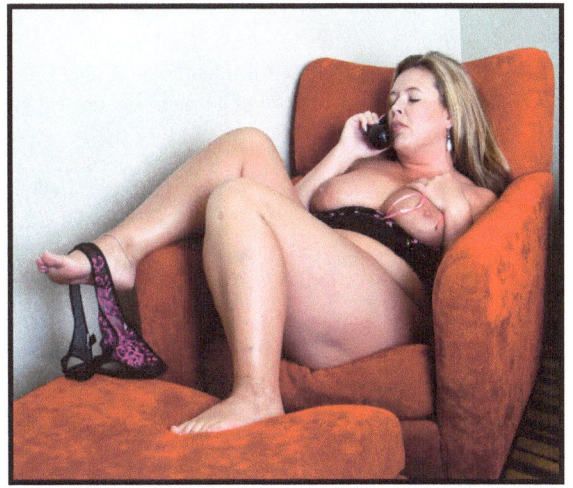

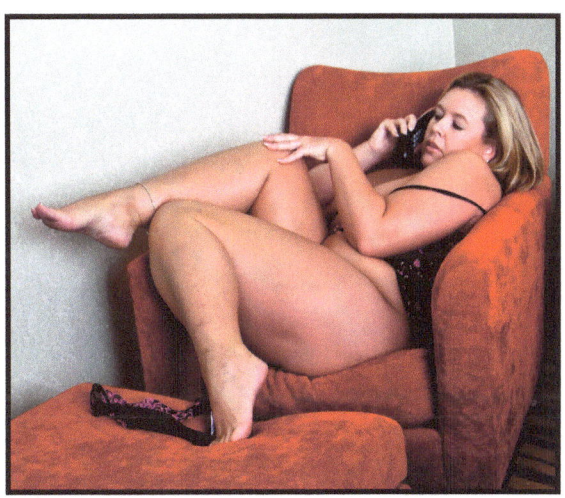

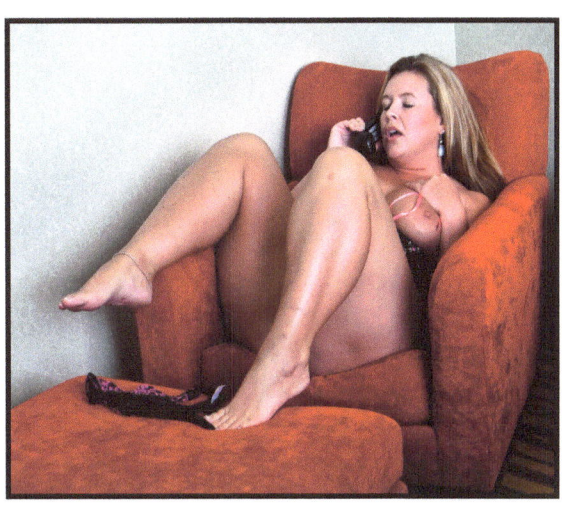

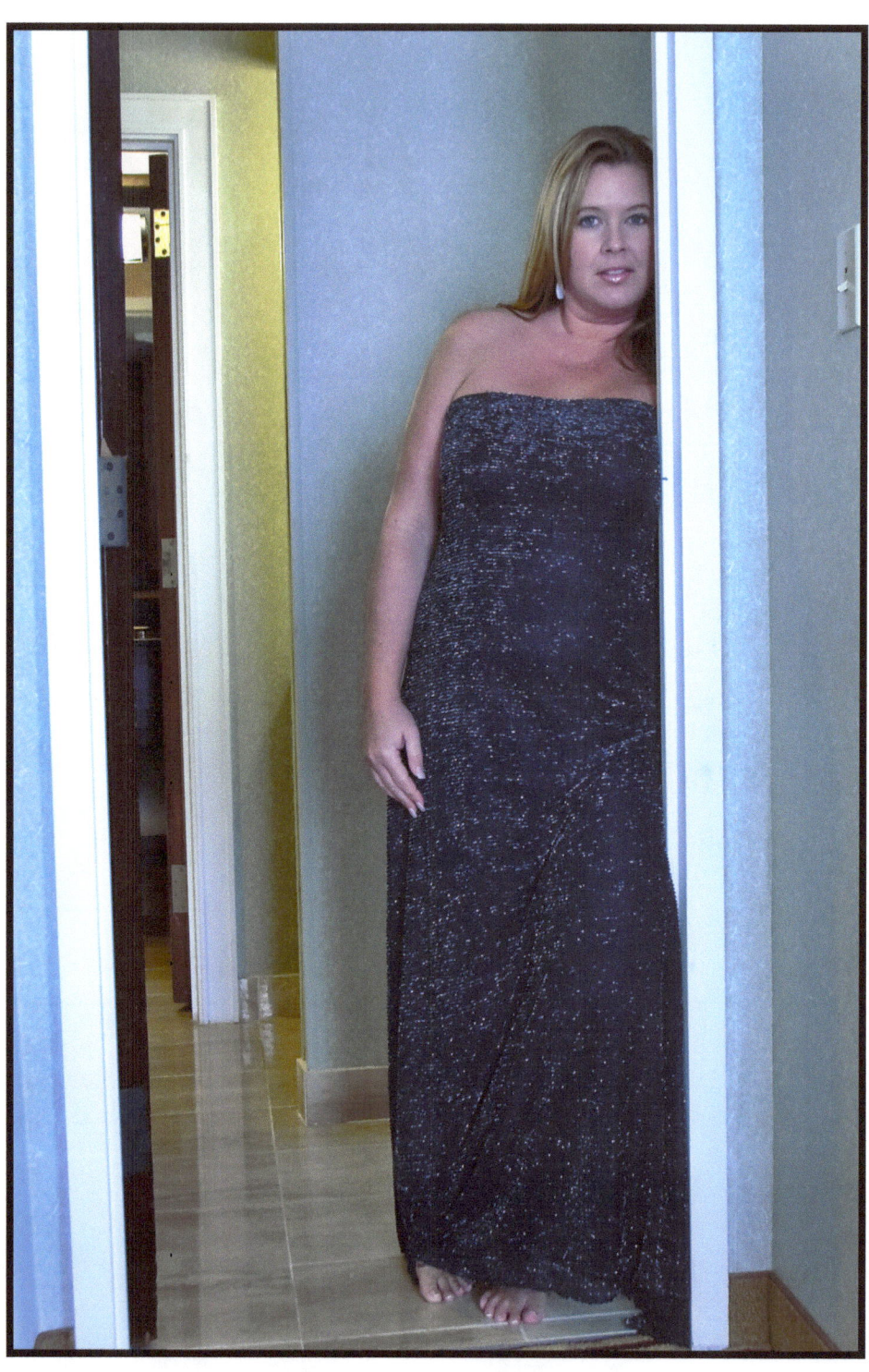

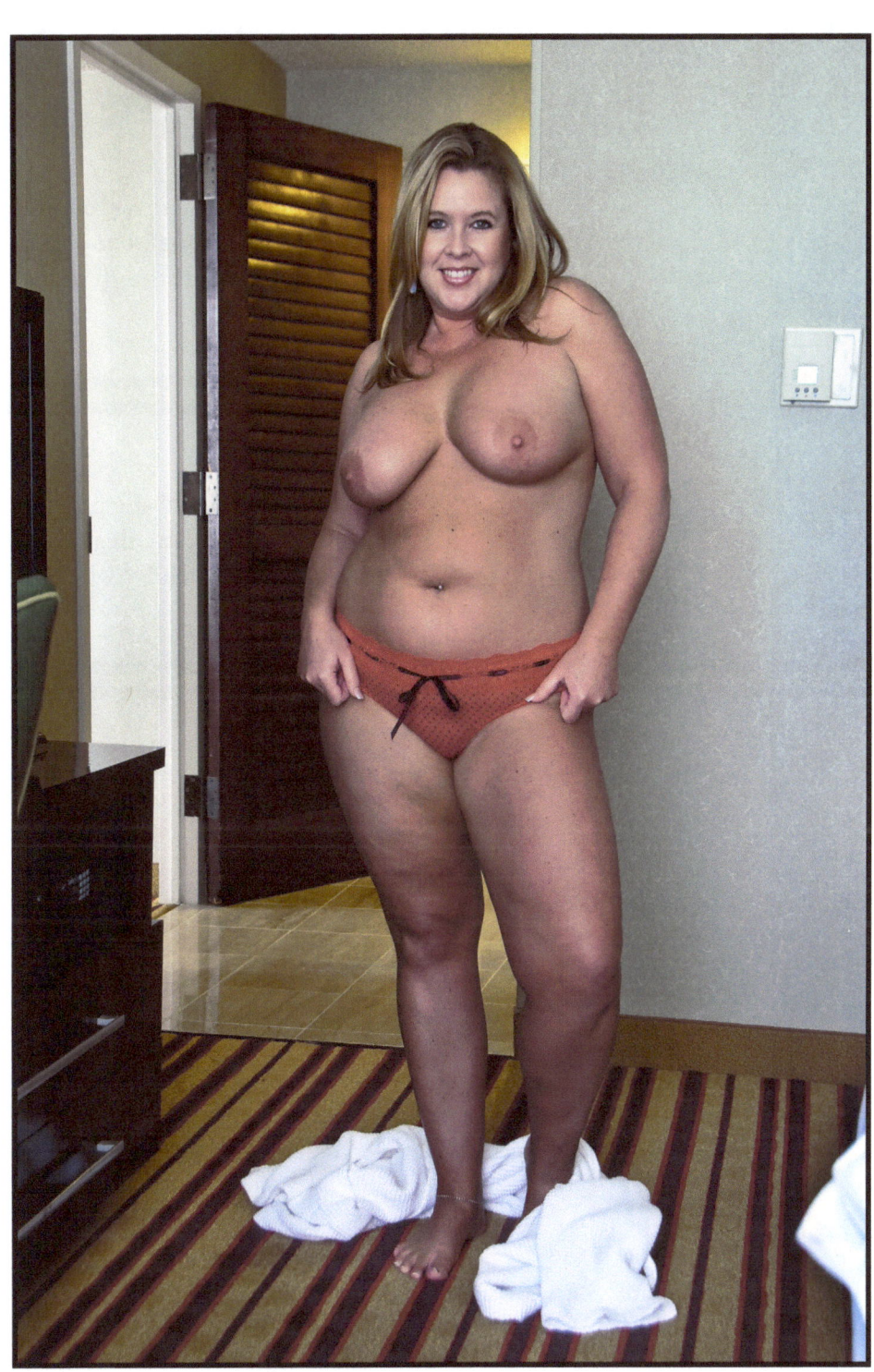

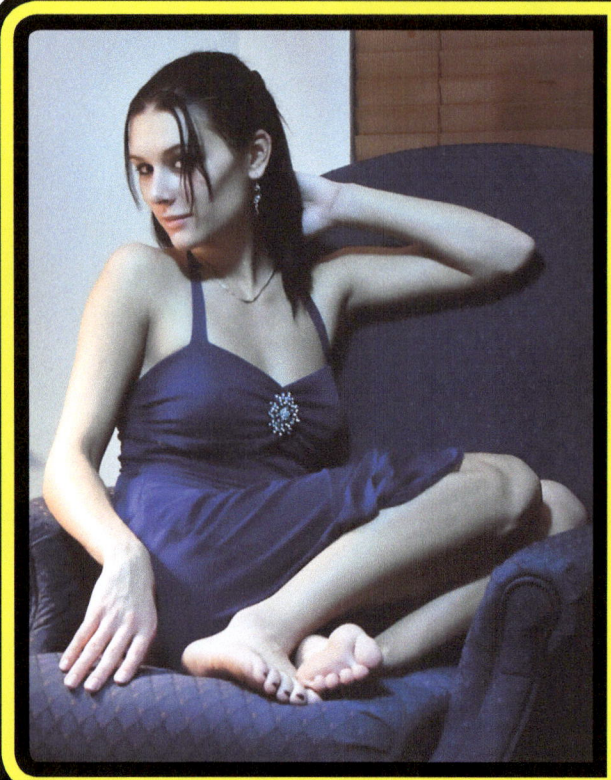

Stephanie

♀♀♀♀♀♀♀♀

"I love music - music is definitely a great thing and a big part of my life. A lot of my emotions run through music."

Stephanie, 22, joined the project late - but brought some fresh ideas to the table. She is quite the creative one.

I was born and raised in Michigan, in a little town 22 miles south of the Canadian border. I was a "yooper." People still laugh at me because my Canadian accent comes out sometimes. I lived there my entire childhood until I graduated from high school and went into the military - 17 years. We had cold, cold 15 degree below zero winters, but pretty decent and comfortable summers.

When I was a kid, I went horseback riding a lot with my sisters. I have two biological sisters, two step-sisters and one step-brother. They call us the "Brady Bunch." My step-brother is the oldest, then me, then all my sisters. It was a lot of fun up there, though I don't miss it. I love the country - I'm not a big city girl - but there's a lot more to do here in Texas than there was in that little town in Michigan where I grew up. All of my family is still up there, except for one sister and one aunt. Everybody else stayed within about a 50 mile radius of our little town - a town so small that my graduating class was only about 50 people.

My childhood was rough - I experienced a bit too much "real life" at a very young age. I learned from it though - it made me who I am today. I had to raise my sisters when we were younger, because my biological mother abused drugs and alcohol. She wasn't around much, so I really didn't have a mother figure until my father divorced her and found my adoptive mother. Then we had the complete family thing, and got into the whole step-child syndrome. It was all "he said, she said" with so many more siblings, and money was tight. But it was definitely nice having more playmates - having new bonds with new siblings. It was fun - we even lived on a horse farm for a while - that was eventful!

♀♀♀♀♀♀♀♀♀

I've always wanted to be a police officer - I guess because they were around a lot when I was a kid. My biological mother was constantly causing altercations and domestic disputes - the cops were called on a pretty regular basis. We were always going to court, fighting over this or that. I guess all that might make a lot of people go the other way, but as I got older, it made me want to uphold the law and to help people out. And of course, there's the power of having a weapon - I do like my handguns. I miss that - I spent a couple of years as a cop already.

I still want to be a police officer. I also want to be a good mom. I'm terrified of when my daughter reaches her teenage years! I wish that she could stay two forever...well, only if I can potty train her first!

♀♀♀♀♀♀♀♀♀

I guess my first real "rude awakening" as an adult was when I went through a divorce at a very young age. It was a big eye opener - I've matured very quickly since then. People tell me I act like I'm 28, when I'm barely 22. And having a kid at a such a young age quickly made me realize that once you're a parent, your life is really not about you anymore - it's definitely about that beautiful baby. I've had to sacrifice a lot of things - but I've become a better person from it all.

♀♀♀♀♀♀♀♀♀

If I could travel anywhere, I'd love to go to Scotland. I've always wanted to go some place overseas and run through hills covered with really green grass. I'd love to experience different cultures, maybe go to the Netherlands...I *am* Dutch. Maybe go to Germany, too - I've heard a lot of good things about that country. Some of my friends are stationed over there.

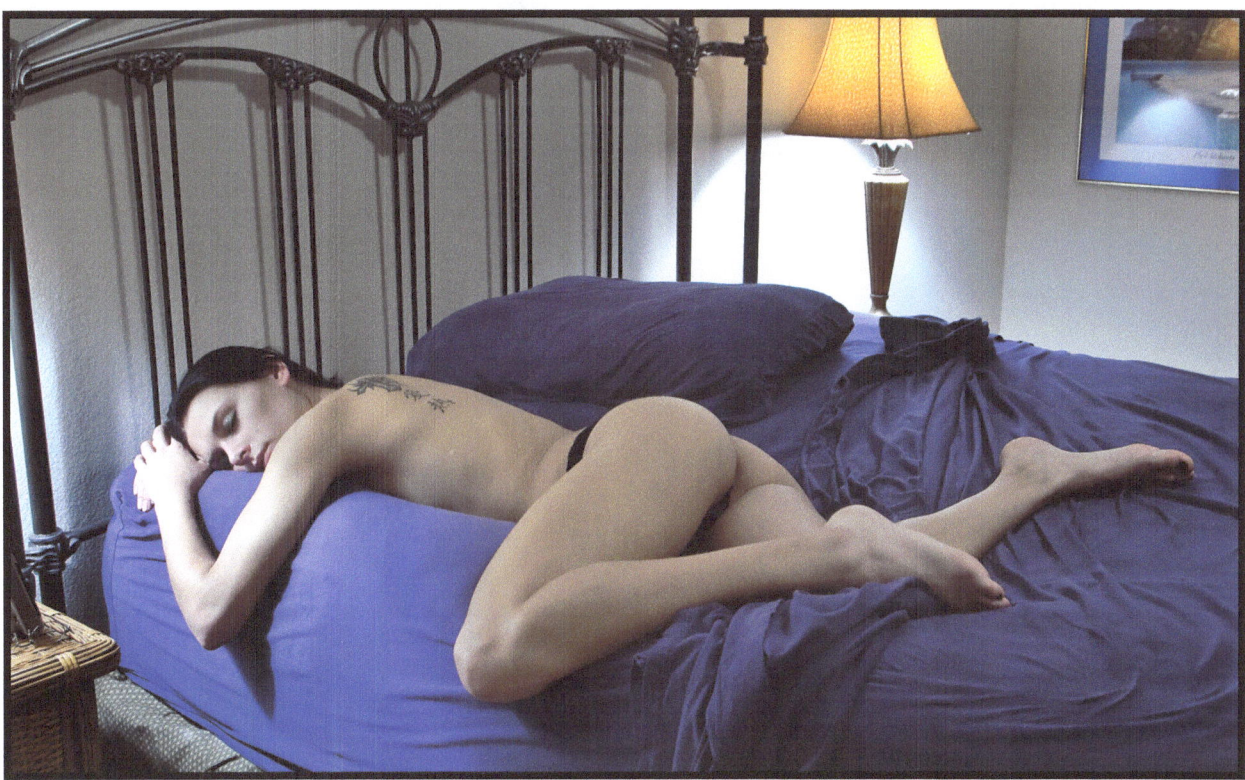

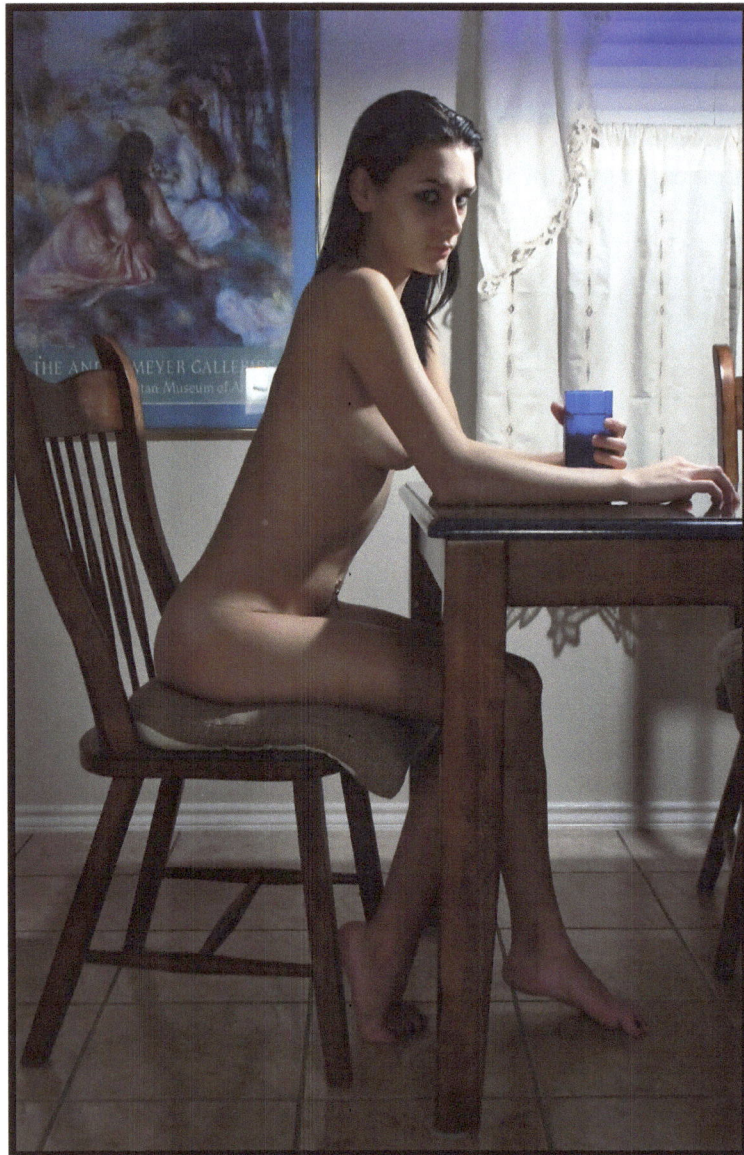

♀♀♀♀♀♀♀♀♀

Because of my usual demeanor, most people probably don't know that I'm actually very outgoing and a lot of fun to hang around with, and that I like to make people laugh. Seeing other people walking around smiling brings a smile to my face. I love happiness, I thrive off the laughter of people. You wouldn't think that I've had such a rough childhood.

♀♀♀♀♀♀♀♀♀

That I was a cop in the military totally blows people away, because I'm this slim, dainty-looking, "model type." When I tell people that I was security forces for the U.S. Air Force for two years, and that I'm air defense trained and that I can handle a gun quite well - they are pretty stunned. That I can defend myself if I need to throws them off a bit.

I joined the Air Force just two weeks after graduating high school. I wanted something with stability, and something that would help me go to college. Unfortunately, I won't get the full college tuition benefit. You have to be in for two years, and I was only in for a year and ten months. I would not have gotten any part of that benefit, but they recently passed a law that gives people with less than two years service a percentage of the benefit based on how long they were in. So, I'm going to get 80% or so, which isn't bad.

The reason I got out early was because I became pregnant with my daughter. When you're security forces in the military, you work 73 hour work weeks. My husband at the time, who was also in the Air Force security force, was working 73 hours a week, too. As you can imagine, there wasn't time to have a baby and a career. I decided to stay home so I could raise my daughter myself, rather than put her in day care at crazy hours. We got up at 3:30 A.M. because we had to be at work by 4:15 - then we worked until 6:30, 7:00, maybe 8:30 at night. No day care would take her for that long, and I didn't want to give her up for that long, either. I didn't want someone else raising her and seeing all the "milestones" of her growing up - I didn't want to miss out on all that because I was too busy working.

I was the first in my family to go into the military - that was the proudest achievement of my life. I'm sad that I wasn't able to stay in and make a career out of it. My cousin went in after I did, but I was the first.

♀♀♀♀♀♀♀♀

If I could change anything about myself, I would try to learn more from my mistakes - I've made an awful lot of them. I can't really make excuses, but being young - you just sort of do what you want, without considering everything. You don't always think things completely through, and I wish I had done that more when I was younger. I can't complain - I don't regret anything because it all made me who I am today.

♀♀♀♀♀♀♀♀

Being a woman can be so stressful - you menstruate, which makes you emotional and dramatic much of the time. I hate that emotional roller coaster. What I do love about being a woman, though, is being a nurturer and a mother. I love the fact that I'm able to experience childbirth - that was one of the most

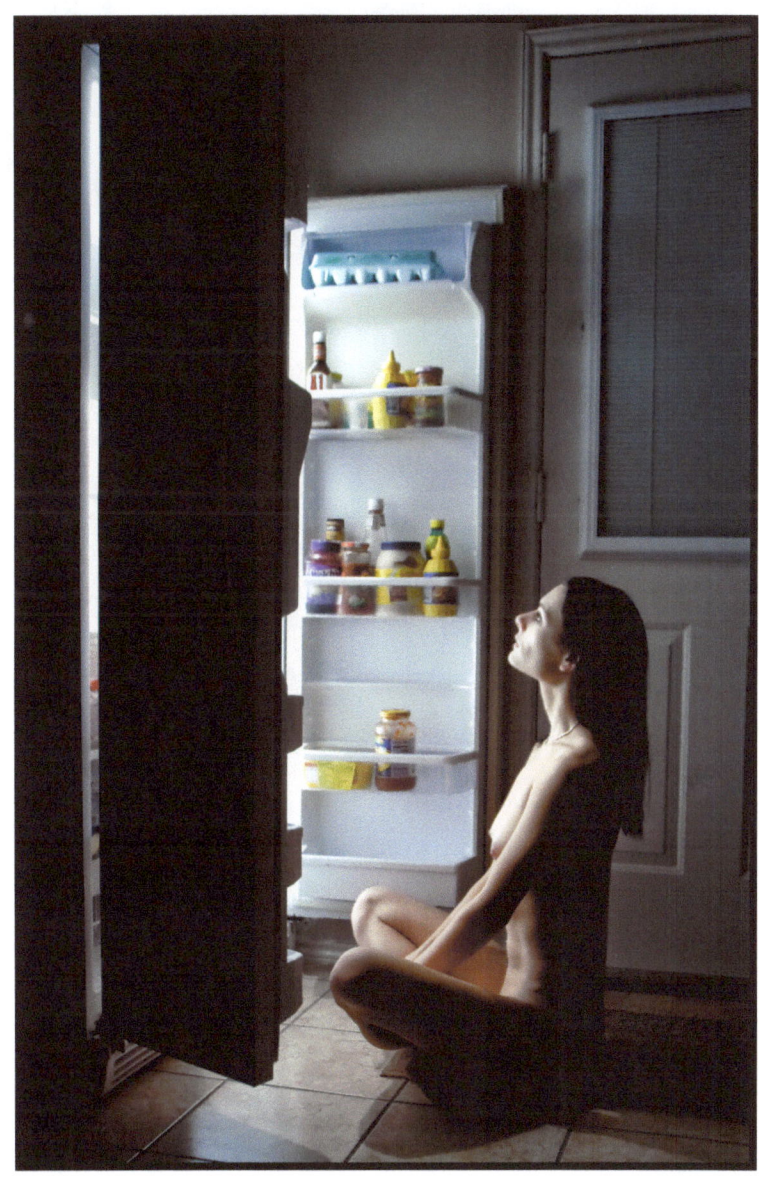

magical events ever in my life. The contractions sucked - 17 hours of labor was not fun - but it was definitely a gift. I'm glad to say I can do that. I honestly don't think men could handle it.

Everything about childbirth - being a mother, having that nesting, nurturing instinct, taking care of our children - that's the best part of being a woman. At least it is for me, and I think for a lot of other women as well. It's funny - you watch those NFL movies, where they're interviewing the MVP, and they'll talk all dramatically about how much they love football. Then the interviewer asks them who they want to say "hi" to - and it's always "I love you mom!" There's just something about being a mother and having that kind of impact on your child's life that stays with them throughout their entire life. I love that!

The worst part is the hormones - the period! If I could live without a menstrual cycle for the rest of my life - I would be very happy. Well, as long as I could still have kids if I wanted to. I hate it and I know it's happening but I can't do anything about it, except take Midol or Pamprin. Using tampons and pads is not the most fun thing in the world, either.

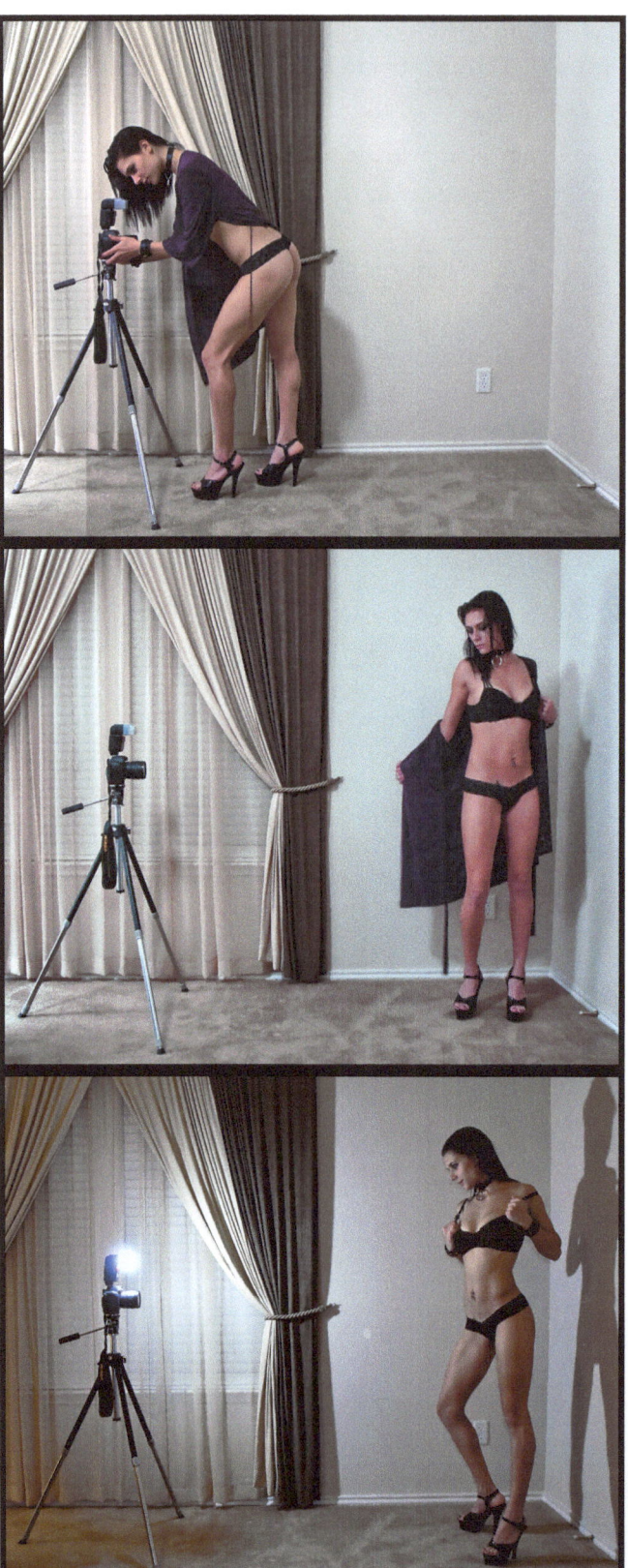

♀♀♀♀♀♀♀♀♀

Men are so lucky - they get to pee standing up! I know that's totally adolescent of me, but it's just so cool! They don't even have to use toilet paper - they can just stand up and go in the woods. We girls have to squat. We have to risk sitting on some poison ivy and getting it all over our butt. I know that must sound like a silly thing to complain about, but guys don't even have to think about stuff like that!

Some men take advantage of common stereotypes about them, like "men are lazy," or "men are sloppy." They can be all "I'm sloppy cause I'm a guy, so just get used to it" when they are perfectly capable of cleaning up after themselves.

I think a lot of men don't quite understand and grasp what women go through, and that really frustrates them. A lot of men honestly want to understand their women better, but when they can't - it's really discouraging to them.

♀♀♀♀♀♀♀♀♀

I've never been one to have star crushes. Well, unless you count Johnny Cash - I really admired him. I think what he did was amazing. His songs were all phenomenal - I'm a big, big fan. I only wish that I could have shaken his hand before he died. My senior year in high school, I dressed up as him for Halloween. You know - with the black suit and the black hat and all.

♀♀♀♀♀♀♀♀♀

Nothing much scares me - not as far as violence and all anyway. The one thing that would terrify me would be losing my daughter, like if something were to happen to her. That's pretty much it. I do have some little physical fears like needles. I have four tattoos and a couple of piercings, but if you get an IV needle around me - I get all clammy and pretty much pass out.

♀♀♀♀♀♀♀♀♀

My favorite sexual position? Oh, my! Uh - all

of them pretty much! If I had to choose one, it would probably be missionary. I know - that's so typical - but I like the closeness of being face to face and looking at each other, having that connection. It's more personal.

Do I have any sexual fantasies? Of course - who doesn't? Am I going to share them here? Well, I probably shouldn't, anyway. It might scare people. Let's just say most of them involve cuffs and collars.

♀♀♀♀♀♀♀♀♀

I don't have a favorite sport to play or watch - I've never been big on sports. I ran cross country in high school, but was more of a "fine arts" kind of girl - played the flute and piano, and sang in chorus.

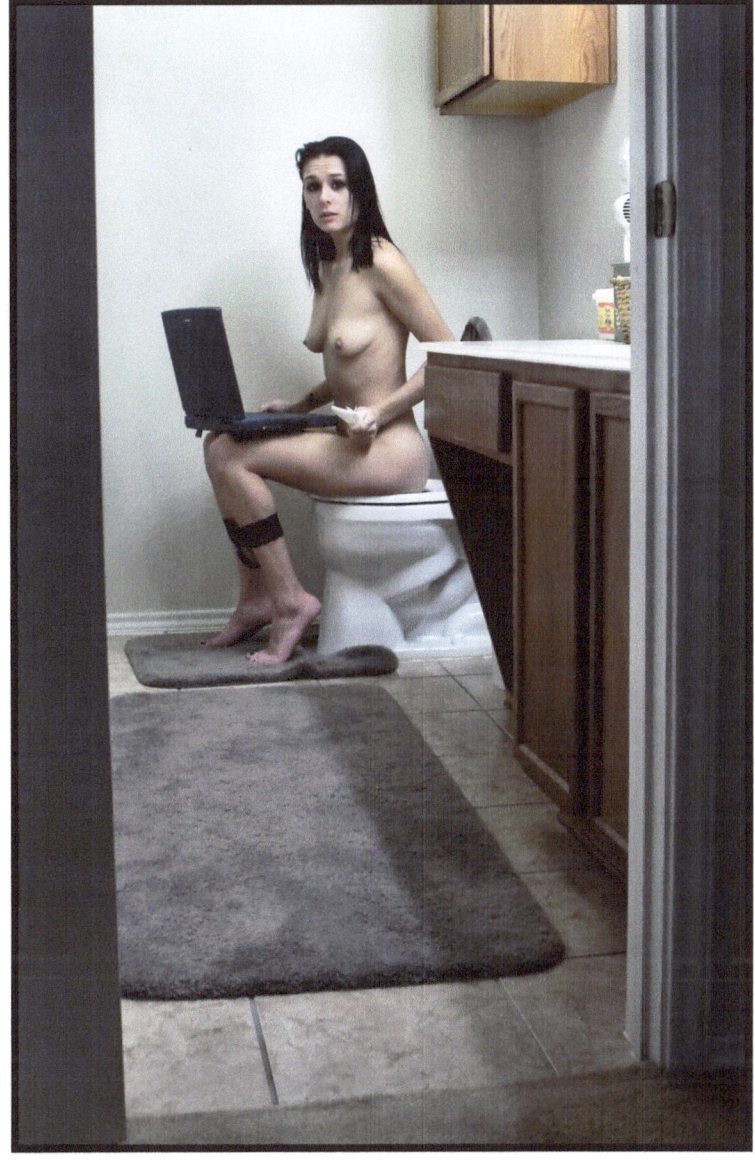

I did quite a bit of cross country running - mostly 5k runs. We used to play what we called "cross country soccer" where we'd get together and play soccer, but we'd get real rough - tackling and tripping each other and winding up in a big pile on top of the soccer ball. It was a lot of fun.

I'm definitely not someone who sits down to watch sports on TV, but I did love to watch my brother play football when I was in high school. It was always cool to be there and feel the energy of the crowd. I was in the band, so we'd play at the games, you know - march around the field in formations and stuff.

♀♀♀♀♀♀♀♀♀

Some of my favorites:

Comfort food: my own cheesecake, a family recipe. I love making it, and my daughter loves helping me.

Color: black. It was blue when I was a little girl. My hair is not naturally black like this. It's more of a dishwater blonde color actually. But I like it black like this - I think it makes my features look more exotic.

Music: "industrial." I like "stompy-stompy" kind of dance music, but I don't like any kind of "booty" music or rap or R&B - I'm just really not in to that. But I do like country, rock, metal, industrial, emo, screamo - pretty much everything but rap.

TV shows: "Dexter" and "Weeds." I was uncomfortable at first watching "Weeds" with all the marijuana talk 'cause I was a cop, but it's just so addicting! It's interesting watching them struggle - very captivating.

Movie: "Batman Forever" - the one with Jim Carrey in it. Any Jim Carrey movie is my favorite - he's an amazing actor, and he was so funny in that one.

⚲⚲⚲⚲⚲⚲⚲⚲⚲

To win my heart - it helps if the guy is an artist, especially if he can play guitar or sing. I love a musical man - someone with talent and brains. By brains, I mean someone who can hold a good conversation - someone who has a good sense of humor and understands what's going on. I don't like guys who are bland, shy and afraid. Don't get me wrong - shy people are very genuine in their own way, but I like someone who can keep up with me - someone who can challenge me as much as I challenge him.

Most important qualities for my significant other to have? First of all, he has to know what he wants from life. I don't like the young bucks who are pretty much lost and just do things on a whim. He needs to be financially stable, have a good head on his shoulders, and know what love - and a good relationship - is. Guys who are just "on the fly," and who don't know how to appreciate a woman are not for me. And I like a generally rounded person - someone who is knowledgeable about a lot of things.

⚲⚲⚲⚲⚲⚲⚲⚲⚲

My passions? I love music - music is definitely a great thing and a big part of my life. A lot of my emotions run through music. I love dancing, I love singing, I love playing the piano. I composed a few pieces of my own in high school. I taught myself how to play the piano by taking an independent study course. I've just been very musically oriented my entire life - I really love it.

⚲⚲⚲⚲⚲⚲⚲⚲⚲

My favorite season is fall - I love all the beautiful colors. To truly appreciate fall colors, though - you have to go up to Michigan. With all the leaves changing colors, and the first snow - it's just gorgeous! I used to really love it because fall was when we ran cross country. It was so quiet and peaceful running through the woods that time of year. There is just something so serene about it.

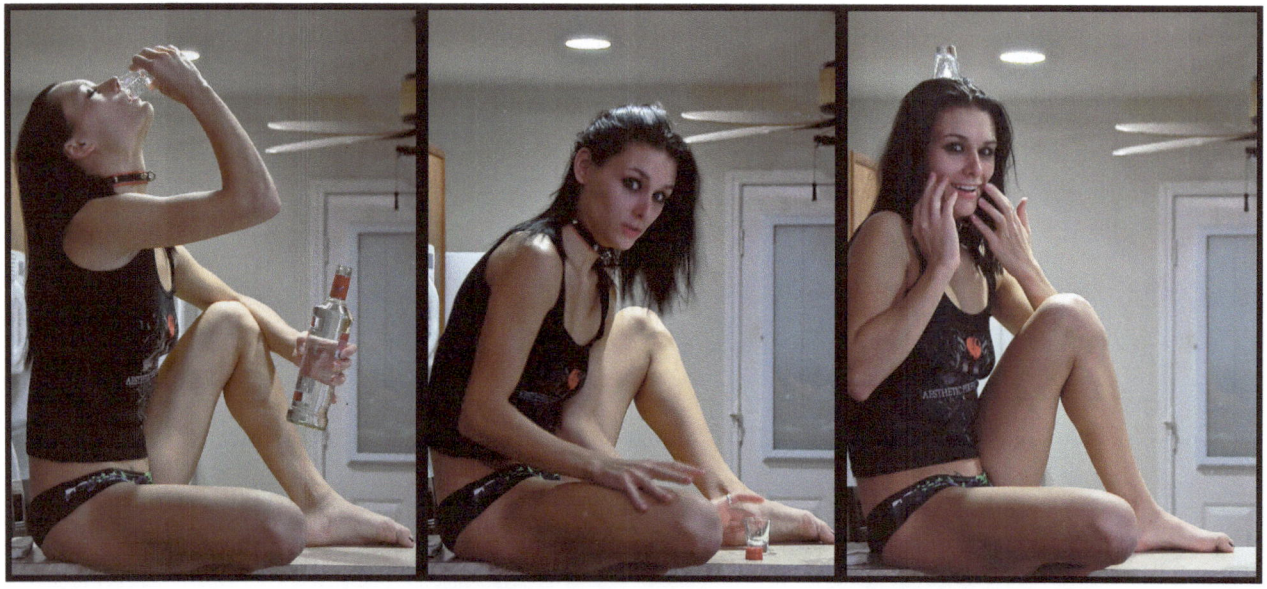

♀♀♀♀♀♀♀♀♀

My strengths and weaknesses? I care about other people a lot. I'm always worrying about them - I want to make them happy. I try to do my best - go out of my way to do the little things - to put a smile on people's faces and make them laugh. But that same strength is my weakness as well, because I totally neglect myself in some ways. I'm more selfless than I should be sometimes. I need to take a bit more "me" time.

♀♀♀♀♀♀♀♀♀

I can't stand the sound of dogs licking themselves! That noise is just so irritating. It's a lot like people chewing with their mouths open.

♀♀♀♀♀♀♀♀♀

I'd like people to know that I can be fun loving and caring, and that I can be great to hang out with; but I also want them to know that I am very passionate about getting back into law enforcement. There are two sides to me. I know when to be fun and laid back, and I know when to take things seriously.

♀♀♀♀♀♀♀♀♀

Craziest, wildest thing I've ever done? There's a lot of things. What's crazy to one person is normal to another, so I'm not sure what would be classified as crazy.

Last weekend I was involved in a fetish performance at the Dallas Fetish Ball. My boyfriend and I went on stage and did a little skit where he proposed to me and I kind of laughed at him. He took me over to the side of the stage, tied my hands up and used a bull whip on me. It was just acting - the whip mostly didn't catch me at all. Then he tied me up, used candle wax on me, flogged me, put a collar around my neck and led me off stage. It was all kind of a simulation of what happened when I laughed at him for proposing to me. I have to remember that if he does propose to me - not to say "no." It was fun. We were helping out a group of our friends - we don't normally do that all the time.

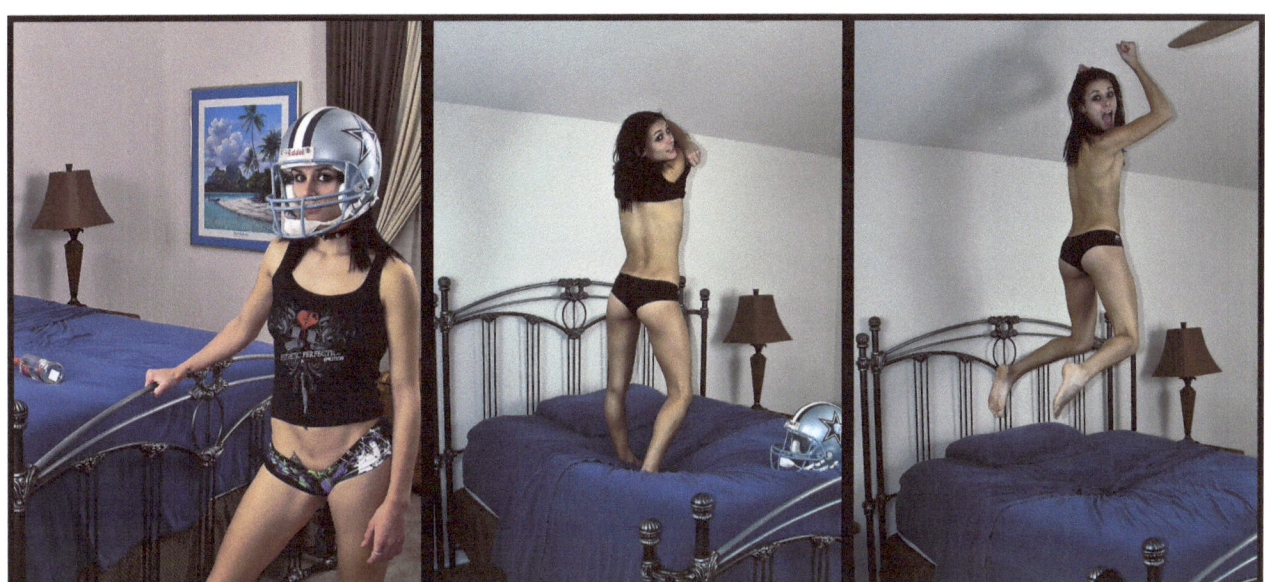

♀♀♀♀♀♀♀♀♀

The best day I ever had was the day my daughter was born. It's still like a dream. I can't believe I created something that beautiful and precious. I just feel like a big baby sitter sometimes. It's so bizarre - to have a daughter - to have created life. I loved holding her for the first time. All the pain I went through that day was totally worth it - I would do it again in a heartbeat. Only once more, though - I only want two kids.

I've had a lot of hard days, but I don't know that I've had one that really stands out as the worst. Life throws you a lot of curve balls - hard times, stressful times - times when you find yourself crying and saying "I just can't go on" - but you always do. You find that the next day is better than the last.

♀♀♀♀♀♀♀♀♀

My favorite alcoholic drink is the Pina Colada - I love fruity drinks. I don't really like hard liquor - unless I want to get drunk quick - but I'm really not into doing shots and getting drunk. I'm a social drinker. I'll have one with friends, but I've just never been into drinking a lot. I didn't even drink as a kid - I waited until my 18th birthday before I had my first one. Really - I've just never been that much into partying.

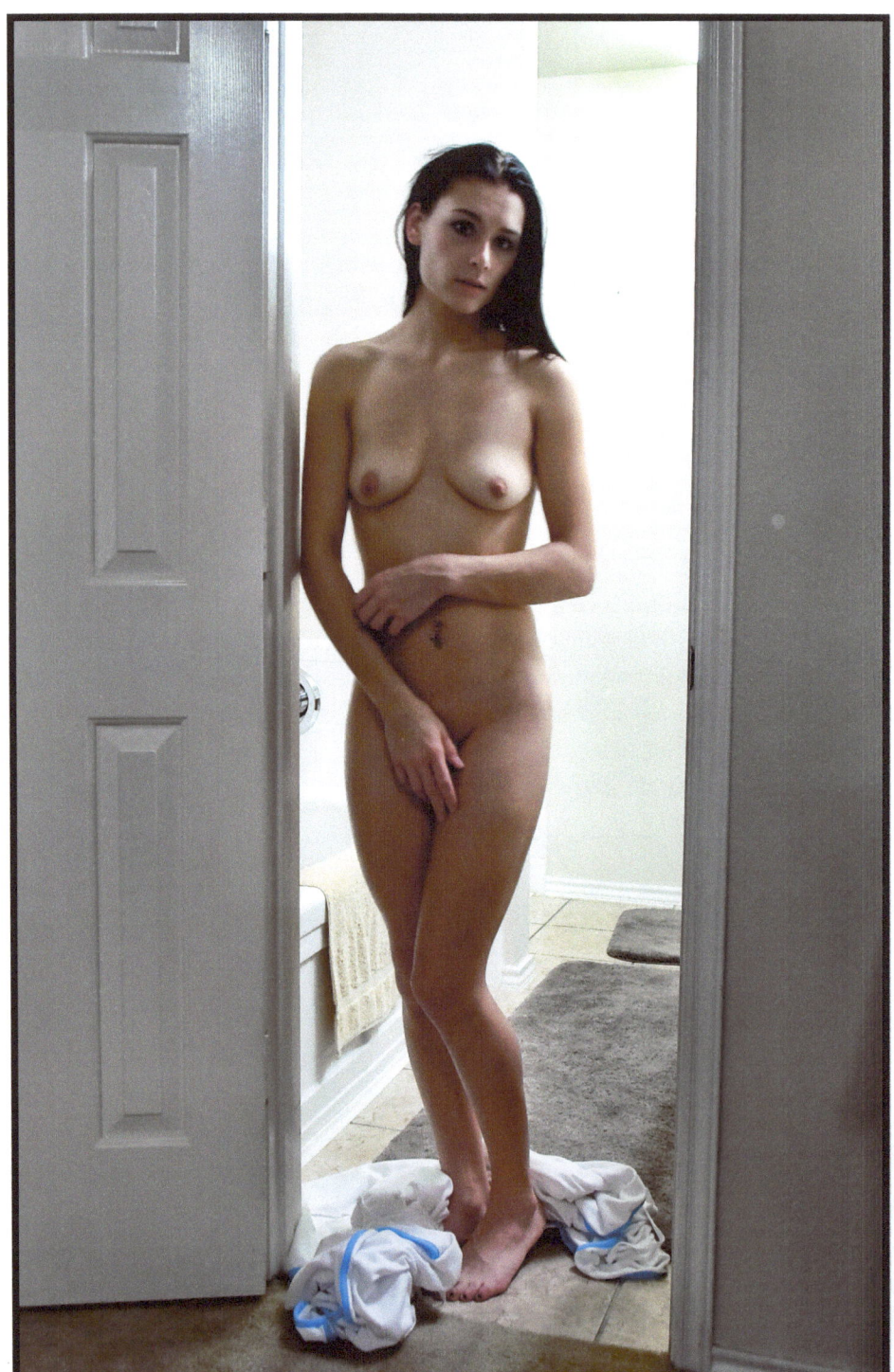

♀♀♀♀♀♀♀♀♀

I'm definitely an exhibitionist - it's a very natural thing for me. I love the attention, I love to do things to get attention from others, I love being a tease. It's just something fun to do - and I love flirting.

♀♀♀♀♀♀♀♀♀

I actually think its pretty easy being a woman in today's world. We didn't have to battle for most of the privileges we have today. I think men and women are pretty much equal now, and I like that.

There was a big controversy over Hillary Clinton running for president - some people were really upset with the idea of having a woman for president, and that upsets me a bit. It seems like a sexist way to think. Much of Christianity has preached for years that women are inferior to men. Stuff like "woman was created in the image of man, and man was created in the image of God" - some people take quotes like that out of context.

Today, I think we're pretty safe, pretty solid. Some women choose to use the rights we've gained, while others don't - and that's okay, too. But the equality is there - that's the wonderful part.

Stephanie

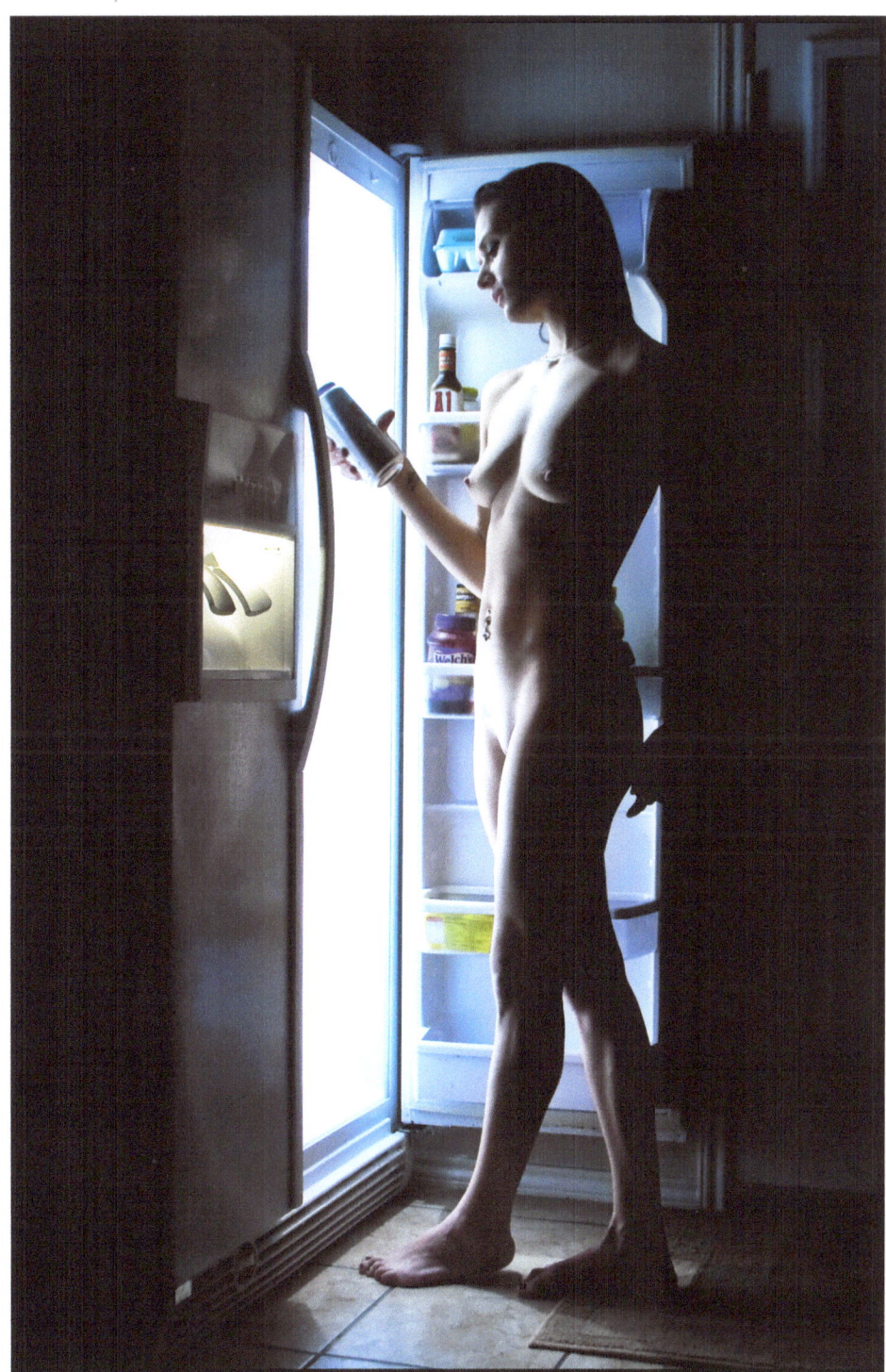

The Making of "Nine Women Revealed"

When I began working on this project, I had six major requirements for the women I would select to be in the book. I wanted women who:

1) Were average to nice looking - who looked like somebody's sister, mother, aunt, cousin or friend.

2) Had never posed nude before (other than for a significant other).

3) Were okay with me shooting them in their own homes - in their "natural environments."

4) Were comfortable with being as "natural" as possible for the shoots: no make-up (or very little), no special hair treatment - plus very little "touching-up" of their photos.

5) Were okay with being photographed while doing everyday activities, especially activities of an "intimate" nature (intimate in the sense of things that most people never see them doing - like shaving their underarms or their private area, or acting goofy in their underwear in front of a mirror, etc.).

6) Were comfortable talking about their personal lives - who were okay with revealing their "inner" as well as their "outer" selves.

As I mentioned in the "Introduction" for this book, I searched for (and found) the nine women on a popular networking web site for models and photographers that I have been a very active part of for over three years. When I ran my casting call, I had the following results in finding women that matched my six criteria:

1) Virtually every woman who replied to my casting (and I got a lot of replies) were more than "average to nice looking" - many of them were a lot more. So I had to settle for nine beautiful women.

2) I knew that only models from the web site would see my casting, but I had asked them to tell their friends and relatives if they knew any who might be interested. Not surprisingly though, I only got responses from women who had experience modeling nude. I could have tried a different source, like Craig's List, but I was worried about who might respond in a venue like that. So I had to settle for nine women who all had experience modeling nude.

3) Several women who replied to my casting were not comfortable with the photo shoot being in their homes, so I quickly eliminated this as a requirement since it was limiting my possible candidates. Still, I did wind up shooting three in their own homes, and one in a hotel suite. I shot the remaining five women in my own home.

4) It surprised me that not one woman who applied to the casting had any problems with the "no make-up, hair treatment or photo retouching" requirement - in fact, most of them really liked that part.

5) No one really had any problems with the "everyday, routine" or "intimate" activities aspect of the project. In fact, most of them had a lot of fun with that part.

6) None of the women had any problems with the part about revealing their "inner" selves". I decided to gather their "stories" by conducting an interview at the end of each shoot, and to videotape the interviews to save time (and for accuracy purposes). No one had any problems with having their interviews videotaped.

One last thing before I go into the individual experiences: I am so glad I created this book - it turned out to be an experience of a lifetime. I was so impressed with the attitudes of all the women in the book (and many others that didn't make the final cut). This project quickly developed an energy of its own that fired up the creative juices in all of us. It was an absolute joy working with all of these wonderful, amazing women! That everyone involved *really wanted to be a part of it* made the book what it is.

The Brittney Shoot

Gary's account: One of the first to respond to my casting was Brittney, the youngest at 20. I did her photo shoot at her apartment, and it was a bit of an eye opener for me. I had forgotten what life at 20 is like when you're just getting established and don't have a lot of money. The apartment was nice, but a bit small and cramped. I haven't done a lot of location shoots (other than outdoors) and quickly discovered that setting up the shots in a small unfamiliar environment was making the shoot run a lot longer than I was used to. I had planned for three hours, but it wound up taking four and a half. Luckily for me, Brittney was a total "trooper" in every way. She had no problems with the amount of time we ran over, she was open to all suggestions, and she worked hard to help me get every shot I wanted. She was just plain pleasant to work with the entire time.

One thing I have to mention about Brittney. You can see from my photos that even without hair and make-up, Brittney was still quite adorable. You should see her when she does more conventional modeling. With hair and makeup, she is a total knockout!

My favorite shot with Brittney is the one on page 13 where she appears to be shaving her private area (FYI: she wasn't really). I did not want any of the photos in the book to be too explicit, and I think the angle I shot from and her pose took care of that. But I think the last minute decision to have her put on the red stockings for the shot turned out to be very serendipitous and really made it work.

Once we finished taking the photos, she threw on some clothes and got comfy on the couch, while I pulled out my list of questions and set up my video camera. The interview went well, lasting about 45 minutes. After the interview, I packed up my gear and left.

Brittney's account: I was browsing through the casting calls, and they all seemed pretty much the same: most were for glamour style nudes - Playboy/Penthouse type of shoots - which I'll do from time to time, but that's really not my style. Not only did Gary's work jump out at me - it's so artistic, natural and unique - but the whole idea of this project was something I just fell in love with. I haven't been involved with a book or any sort of artistic project like this before, so it was exciting to find. I'm really glad that Gary selected me to work with him on it. What really interested me was how the book was to focus on the actual women in it, rather than just their figures (which is much more common). I remember that he was concerned that I was probably too attractive for the book, but from our e-mail and phone exchanges - I quickly felt that we could definitely work together, that we had similar mind sets.

Once I was selected, I was impressed and pleased with how he stayed in contact and ran all his ideas by me to make sure I was okay with them. It all got me even more excited to be really creative. The night before I meet a new photographer, I'm usually nervous about meeting them, but the night before my shoot with Gary - I was just excited about all the ideas we had discussed - nervous, but a good kind of nervous.

The photo shoot itself was awesome! Of course it helped that we were shooting at my place - but Gary had a way of always making me feel completely comfortable. Normally, it takes me awhile to warm up to working with a new photographer - but I felt at ease right away and found it easy to be myself and put my personality into the shots. I could tell he was a little nervous at first, but it started coming together very quickly. It was a really enjoyable experience for me overall.

I was a little nervous about the interview beforehand - because I didn't know exactly what all the questions would be - but I think it went pretty well. I do tend to ramble sometimes.

Oh, and when the making of this book gets made into a major motion picture - I want Evan Rachel Wood to play me in it!

The Jessica Shoot

Gary's account: Two days later, I was knocking on the door of Jessica's apartment. Her place was about the same size as Brittney's, but she appeared to be a little more into organization and order - so it wasn't quite as cramped. I told myself beforehand that I had learned lessons from Brittney's shoot that would keep us more on schedule. Oh yeah - this time, the planned three hour shoot turned into *five* hours! Jessica was every bit the trooper that Brittney had been and so was a total joy to work with as well. We had discussed quite a few ideas prior to the shoot (several that she came up with) and she was up for them all.

Like the other models, she was more attractive than I was originally looking for - but she really impressed me during the selection process with her attitude and desire to be part of the project.

My favorite shot with Jessica is the one on page 21 - I think this one shows what an incredible figure she has. I also like the one on page 27 which shows her playful side.

Jessica likes to talk - her interview lasted about an hour and a half. I have to say that I'm crazy about Jessica - she's a real "firecracker". We've worked together on a couple of things since this first shoot.

Jessica's account: I saw Gary's casting and he said he was looking for women who were not the typical beautiful model - who looked like someone's sister or cousin - and I wondered if he would think I was too attractive for what he was looking for. Not that I'm that full of myself, but I've been modeling for awhile and I've gotten a lot of compliments. On the other hand, when I'm not modeling and I'm just at the mall or something - I feel I can blend in very easily. So I thought that I might as well apply for it and see what happens. In the initial e-mail I sent him, I pointed out every little flaw that I had - trying to convince him that I was the type he was looking for. I was actually afraid that I might have come across as too "down" on myself. I was surprised when he e-mailed me back and said I was a good match for what he was look-ing for - attractive, but not too attractive.

Once he actually selected me, I was pretty excited about it. For one thing, I usually really stress about how to fix my hair or make-up, or what to bring for a shoot - but this one was about capturing me as I normally am around the house. It seemed like a very liberating thing - not to have to be overly glamorous. It was great to not have to worry about a lot of the issues I normally have to think about for a shoot.

I really enjoyed it. I liked that he let me include my cat, Roxy, in some of the shots (though there were times when Roxy included herself). I love the "cat bra" picture [page 22] - I thought it was adorable! I like the idea of the book in general, because it reminds me of the "Dove" [soap] commercials where they talk about "real beauty". I think women will be interested in this book for the way it shows less-than-perfect real women in real everyday circumstances. A lot of us get tired of seeing all the "perfect" women in magazines and books all the time. The average woman doesn't look perfect like that. I think this book could help a lot of women feel better about themselves - that they don't have to look like a "Barbie Doll" to be beautiful. I felt very comfortable with the shoot - didn't feel exploited in any way. I liked his concept of the "natural" look with very little or no re-touching, and I was actually very pleased when I saw photos from the shoot - I thought they came out very well. I really like the shots taken in the bathroom vanity area. I was worried about the harsh lighting there making me look bad, but the shots turned out great. I was somewhat concerned before the shoot, but really pleased when I saw the results.

The Jess Shoot

Gary's account: The very next day - Jess is ringing the doorbell at my house to do her shoot there. I've worked with a lot of beautiful models, but as you can see from her photos - Jess is at a level of beauty a bit above most women...or as I like to put it: "she got a winning ticket in the genetics lottery."

I was actually quite surprised when she answered my casting call. On one hand, given her experience and "position" in the modeling pecking order - I was surprised that she was interested in what I like to call "my little project." On the other hand, given my premise of having nine "average to nice looking" women in the book - my immediate thought was that there was no way I could use her. I decided to take a closer look at her portfolio and discovered that mixed in with all of the glamour shots she had - there were a lot of really nice artistic shots that I really liked (including shots with no make-up or hair treatment). Ultimately, I decided that I just couldn't pass on the chance to work with her.

So - now we're on my turf (shooting at my house), so I'm thinking we're definitely going to finish in the scheduled three hours. Nope - it took three and a half hours...but closer to being on schedule at least.

My favorite shot of Jess is the one on page 38. Like Brittney, as good as she looks in these photos without hair or make-up, you should see her all dolled up!

Jess has done several Playboy Special Editions, and in fact, is one of the Top Ten Playboy Special Edi-tion Models for 2010 (and in the running for the number one slot). The winner out of the ten will be announced in July 2010.

Jess's interview lasted about 50 minutes. As she mentioned in her interview, she has a tendency to get bored easily - and I think she was getting a little bored with our session towards the end. She was great to work with, though, and in fact I've worked with her again since our first shoot.

Jess's account: When I ran across Gary's casting for this book - it really seemed like a "breath of fresh air". I do a lot of shoots that are all about glamour and perfection - and that tends to get old, plus I find myself being very self critical about the results of some of them. I saw this project as something I could do and just be appreciated for everything that I actually am, whether I come out perfect in it or not. I responded to the casting much the same way as I normally respond to castings and was a little surprised to be getting grilled about it. Gary was telling me stuff like "Jess - maybe you're too perfect to be in this project" and "Jess - maybe you're not ordinary enough for this project"...but some women in everyday life are just like me.

The process of setting everything up with Gary went very smooth and was all very professional. It's funny - I get jobs in the "real" modeling world, and also in the "sub-culture" world of internet modeling - and the two types of jobs present different levels of responsibility for the model. In the "real" modeling world - make-up artists, hair stylists, and wardrobe stylists are all provided, so I don't have to worry about any of that. But in the "sub-culture" world of internet modeling, I'm typically responsible for my own make-up, hair and wardrobe. So this was a bit "in-between" since the support personnel weren't being provided, but at the same time, they weren't needed (given the concept of it being all "natural"). Gary and I had a minor hiccup in setting up the location for the shoot - because I have sort of a strange living arrangement, but we quickly worked it out to shoot at his house since we couldn't shoot at mine.

Gary was great to work with, but I actually found the shoot to be somewhat challenging. It's like there are two of me: "model Jess" who tries to do it all perfectly, and then there's "Jess the woman trying not to be a model". I kept finding myself trying to tweak the poses and angles as I would at a glamour shoot, which is not how "Jess the woman" would behave. There's something about having a camera in my proximity that turns me into "model Jess". I was at a friend's wedding not too long ago, and the photographer was near the bride and groom taking photos all during the ceremony. I remarked to my boyfriend that if I had been the bride, I would have had trouble staying focused on the groom. I would probably have instinctively kept turning to face the photographer - "model Jess" would have come out.

Overall though - the shoot went just fine. It was actually like going on a vacation compared to most of the modeling jobs I do. The interview with Gary went fine - it was a piece of cake. And by the way, I don't think I was as bored as Gary says I was.

And when the making of this book gets made into a major motion picture - I want to play myself in it, since I'm taking acting classes now and trying to become an actress.

The Marilyn Shoot

Gary's account: Next up was Marilyn - the last of the three that I shot in their own homes. We had to reschedule once, but still - it was just six days after my prior shoot with Jess. I had a little problem getting into Marilyn's building - she lives in one of those places where you have to call the person you're visiting so that they can let you in - and Marilyn had fallen asleep so she wasn't answering her phone. Luckily I found an open door to the building (one that was supposed to be closed and locked) and was able to get to her apartment and wake her up by knocking on her door.

Stepping into her apartment, the first thing I came upon were her FOUR cats - actually FIVE because she was cat sitting her mother's cat as well at the time. I'm a cat lover myself (I have just one), but these cats were the size of Shetland ponies (okay, maybe I'm exaggerating a little bit - but they were big)! Then, it turned out that she was out of cat food - so I waited while she went to the store to get some for them. Marilyn is a total sweetheart...but she *can* be a bit disorganized at times!

Somehow - I actually got that shoot done on schedule in three hours flat. Like all of the other women in the book, she was great to work with - had a terrific attitude, and really worked with me to get the shots.

My favorite one with her is on page 49. I don't think I have to explain why I like to say that Marilyn is the "bombshell" of the group (I think her photo is in the dictionary next to the word "voluptuous").

When it came time to do the interview, she was the only one who didn't bother to really dress for it - she just threw on a man's shirt (but didn't bother to button it, so she was mostly just nude). Her interview ran about 40 minutes - which didn't seem long enough. I did actually wind up doing an additional interview with her over the phone at a later date to fill in some blanks.

Marilyn's account: When I came across Gary's casting, I was really interested in it right away. I have a lot of photographers asking me to shoot with them, but I'm pretty picky about who I work with. I also get tired of doing the same things over and over. So I'm always looking for projects that are different and "real". I really like the way that Gary worded the casting - his passion about the project, and his views on women were apparent and I liked it. I also liked that he wanted to shoot in the model's homes - to capture them in their "own environment". When I applied to be in the project, Gary was kind of tough. He asked a lot of questions and he had a lot to say about what he was looking for, but I like that. I like that he was challenging about it. Once I was selected, I was pretty excited about it and thought a lot about it as the date for the shoot got closer. During that time, Gary asked me a lot of questions and sent me a lot of information concerning the shoot, which was good. I like to know what to expect and what will be expected of me. We talked on the phone some prior to the shoot and I thought that went very well - I could tell we were going to have some chemistry in our work together.

I really enjoyed the shoot. Even though we had discussed what was going to happen, I wasn't sure what to expect exactly. I liked how a lot of it was very spontaneous. I liked how we did a lot of different set-ups all over my apartment. And I think I did freak Gary out a little, though, when I left him at my apartment to get some cat food!

The Roxy Shoot

Gary's account: A week later, Roxy came to my house for her shoot. She was the only one of the nine that I had worked with prior to the book project (though only once, and that one time was only about a week before the first of the "Nine Women" shoots). Roxy's pretty cool - she's a housewife and has two kids, but she has an artistic side that she has to have an outlet for - which is alternately being the model and the photographer. She was someone who I really wanted in the book, in large part because she has what I call "the body of a real woman". It's not perfect - like most women, she has some flaws - but she's curvy and you can sense that she is very comfortable in it. She reminds me a bit of the actress Kate Winslet in the way she is so fearless when undressed for the camera.

The shoot with her took only three hours, though I did wind up using some of the photos from the shoot I did with her just before this project started.

My favorite shot of her is the one on page 52. I think it has a very natural feel to it - like we're watching her from a hidden location. She looks like she's just gotten out of bed and has an itch.

Her interview was about a half hour, though I interviewed her over the phone for another 20 minutes or so some days later.

Roxy's Account: Unlike the other women in this project, I didn't see and respond to Gary's casting - I had worked with him just a couple of weeks before and he approached me about being a part of it. When he explained it to me - what it was all about - I was definitely interested. I liked the concept, plus I liked that I wasn't going to have to do a whole lot to prepare for it, that I could just be myself. From working with him before, I knew that he was very detail oriented and organized - so I didn't worry about how the shoot would go or how it would turn out. I knew that he would give me all the information and instructions that I needed, and it would happen without any problems. And I was right - Gary provided me with lots of input and information about the shoot. It was very nice not to have to worry about it.

The shoot itself went very well. I enjoyed it a lot - especially the candid "unposed" aspects of it. It all felt very natural.

The Rashell Shoot

Gary's account: Rashell was next - she came to my house and we shot the day after I shot Roxy. She lives the closest to me, so it's a short trip for her. She is quite the character - very outgoing and talkative - a lot of fun to work with. She has kids and you can sense that mother "aura" about her almost instantly. I was finally getting into a rhythm with the shoots by now - this was another one that finished in three hours.

My favorite shot with her is on page 69. I think it shows her figure very well.

Her interview lasted about an hour, which kind of surprised me because she definitely likes to talk.

Rashell's account: I was immediately attracted to Gary's casting because it was different. He talked about the book being about real women, doing real things, and being themselves. No make-up, no cheesy poses - just being natural. It's not often you see a casting anything like that. So I saw it and thought "I want to be one of the 'Nine', please!" When I applied for it, I really didn't think I'd get accepted but I figured - what the heck, what's the worst he can say - "no?" When I was selected, it made me feel "special", "unique" - "selected." Between then and the shoot, Gary was really good about communicating his vision of what he wanted from the shoot and what he wanted from me. He was very open about what he was looking for and trying to accomplish. At the same time - I really appreciated how he wasn't like a tyrant about it all, but how instead he made it clear he was looking for collaborators.   He was all about "here's what I'm hoping WE can do with this" and I really liked that.

The photo shoot was so much fun - I had such a blast! I liked being allowed to do the things I would normally do myself in real life - something I don't normally get to do on shoots. I was asked to just be myself and that was cool. I liked how he was always so professional - like if he needed me to make an adjustment, he would ask me rather than barking orders. Or if he needed to adjust my hair or wardrobe, he would ask permission first - something that a lot of photographers don't do (they just adjust away). I liked how he worried about my comfort levels. That was nice.

The interview was a lot of fun. A certain amount of it was stuff I would normally talk about with a photographer during a shoot, anyway.

And I want Sandra Bullock to play my part in the movie adaptation of this book.

The Joelle Shoot

Gary's account: Joelle came to my place 2 days later for her shoot, which took three hours. Joelle was interesting. She seems kind of quiet, laid back and unassuming, but there is more to her than first meets the eye. Like the others, she had a great attitude and worked hard to help me get all the shots I needed.

My favorite shot with her is the three shot sequence on page 77. This was the seventh photo shoot, so I was beginning to run out of new ideas. She was lying on the couch and I told her to pretend she was vacuuming her belly button. I thought it came out pretty well - a combination of playfulness with a hint of sexuality.

Joelle's interview lasted about 35 minutes. Her answers were pretty short, so I had to expand our interview via e-mail some weeks later.

Joelle's account: When I saw the casting for the book project, I really thought is was a great concept that Gary came up with - seeing women as they are, no make-up, here's their life, here's what they do daily. I liked how it was about presenting women in an artistic but grounded way. I loved the idea - I thought it was some very good creativity. I don't have that much experience modeling, but I enjoy it - its a nice pastime for me, so I was very pleasantly surprised when he answered me back. I liked how he asked a lot of questions and was very organized. I was very happy that he selected me to be part of his vision. The anticipation of the upcoming shoot was exciting, especially because of the way Gary was being very encouraging, and the way he made it clear that he welcomed my creative input into it.

The shoot was definitely different. Gary was so organized and I think that helps put a lot of models at ease. I love how he had everything well laid out. I liked how he even had things timed out and he was very particular about my positioning in relation to the lighting - it was apparent that getting the lighting just right is a big passion for him. I liked how he carefully set up the shots rather than just shooting away and hoping for the best. And the interview went okay, I thought.

I want Charlize Theron to play me in the movie.

The Jasmine Shoot

Gary's account: It was almost two weeks later when I shot Jasmine in a hotel suite near downtown Dallas. Jasmine is one of only two of the women who don't live in north Texas. She comes to Dallas on a fairly regular basis, though - and this just happened to be the first time she was in Dallas since the project started. Jasmine is a model that I've been aware of for a couple of years, and she's someone who I've been wanting to shoot with for a while. She was very interested in my casting, so I was really glad we were able to work together on this. She was wonderful to work with and gave me everything I needed for the shoot. She was very generous with her time as it took four hours to complete it.

Jasmine's interview lasted 45 minutes.

My favorite shot with her is the one on page 82. She is a full-figured gal who is not ashamed of her body - I think she looks really great in this shot.

Jasmine's account: When I saw the casting, I liked the concept, so I decided to go for it - I thought "what do I have to lose?" Then being selected to be one of the nine women in the book was something I was very happy about. I think that being part of something like this - being asked to be a part of any creative work, whether it's a book or a film or playing a small part in a small play, being recognized - it's a good feeling. It made me feel like something is being recorded in my life. I'm not just another model trying to make a career - I've been chosen to do something very creative - and I'm a very creative person. So, I'm glad to be part of this. My e-mail and phone conversations with Gary totally clicked and I felt very comfortable working with him from the beginning. He gave me a very good idea of what to expect, what we were going to try to accomplish and I had confidence that it would go just as he said it would.

The photo shoot was so much fun! I had a blast, being on the "pretend" stage, just being me and being natural - and not being expected to do anything that I felt uncomfortable about. I loved the artistic side of everything that we did. A lot of it was very spontaneous, which I liked. I also liked the fact that Gary gave me the opportunity to share my creative thoughts.

The interview was interesting. I haven't done anything like that in a long time. Answering questions about your life makes you think.

The Stephanie Shoot

Gary's account: The final shoot, with Stephanie, occurred at my place about a week later. Stephanie is the other model who doesn't live in north Texas (though she did at the time of the shoot). She was actually a last minute replacement for a model that I had planned to shoot between Joelle and Jasmine (which is why there was the longish gap between those two photo shoots). I had been having a lot of trouble getting in touch with the model that was originally going to be the eighth of the nine women. When I finally did reach her just two days before our scheduled shoot - she had some new and unreasonable conditions, so I had to cancel with her. I got real lucky though, because Stephanie was a real gem. Just when I was down to the last shoot and running out of ideas, she helped me come up with a couple new concepts, plus she had a couple herself.

Most of the other shoots occurred during the daytime, but she was only available in the evenings. We shot for four and a half hours - from 7 PM until 11:30. Her interview (which was very candid) lasted about an hour. When we scheduled the shoot, I had been a little worried that she might be tired by the end of it, given that we would be shooting at the end of a long day for her - but she was great. She didn't seem tired in the least.

My favorite shot with her is on page 99 - I love how the refrigerator light falls on her figure to define her curves. As with all the other models - we got more good shots than I could fit into the book.

Stephanie's account: When I saw Gary's casting, I thought it was very creative - something I'd never seen before. So many castings are just something like "let's do a nude erotic shoot so I can post the photos on some web site" and they want you to do real suggestive poses and touch yourself - things like that. This project was the one nude shoot that was artistic and sensual instead of dirty and disgusting. It all sounded very original and like something I wanted to be a part of - something I wanted to see through to the end. I think the idea for the book is great.

I was hopeful but nervous about whether I would be selected for the final slot. Gary had told me that he was going to make a final decision between me and two other women - so when it turned out to be me that he picked, I was very happy. One of the things I really liked about Gary was how he handled the screening process. He was very clear about everything and was quick to respond to messages. Once I was selected, it was really cool how we brainstormed ideas between each other via e-mail and the phone. I really appreciated how he communicated very clearly to me what the shoot would be like. I looked at his portfolio on-line to get more ideas about what he was looking for. I really liked his work - he's a really good photographer.

The photo shoot was a blast - we kept building ideas off of each other. I loved the creativity - it was definitely a lot of fun. Like when he just glanced at the football helmet, grabbed it and handed it to me and said "here, put this on".

I enjoyed the interview and I liked the idea of having it. I think it makes the book more personal. It will make the photos more interesting, since the viewers will know more about the subjects in them.

Once the Shoots Were All Completed

I spent several weeks selecting and editing photos, and turning their interviews into their stories. As I did all that, I discovered that I needed to do an additional shoot with a couple of models, and additional interviews with a couple more. It was a lot of work - more than I had imagined it would be in the beginning. I estimate that I spent more than 500 hours altogether creating this book. Somewhat interestingly, what turned out to be the most difficult, tedious part of the whole project was transcribing the videotaped interviews onto paper. The next part - organizing and editing their answers to my questions into some kind of a cohesive and interesting story - was a lot more fun.

In the end, though, it all felt like a "labor of love". I hope you all enjoy the fruits of that labor.

♀♀♀♀♀♀♀♀♀

About the Author

Born and raised in Dallas - Gary Melton is a Texan through and through. His journey into the world of photography began at the age of 20 with the purchase of a 35mm single lens reflex camera at a U.S. Army PX in Budingen, Germany. Shortly after leaving the service, what started as a hobby and grew into a passion, became an enterprise when he started a part-time portrait, team and event photography business. The magic of picture taking lost it's charm for him, though, when it became apparent that taking photos for money was a lot more about business than it was about art, so he closed the business after a couple of years.

Flash forward a couple of decades when he decided to renew his passion, but in a different direction that he felt sure would be more interesting - female figure photography. He was right, and he was also a natural at it. It took a while to make the transition from film to pro-level digital, and it also took some time learning to find the necessary artistic connections with his models - but as I think you'll see from viewing the book in your hands, it was worth the time and effort spent.

When he decided to create a book of female figure photographs - he knew that he wanted to do it in the style that he has become most comfortable with - a style that is all about creating works that mostly resemble "artistic snapshots". He also wanted to create something that was more than just a collection of revealing images of real women - he wanted to utilize his lifetime of writing experience to capture "artistic snapshots" of the unique lives of each of his amazing subjects as revealed to him in candid interviews.

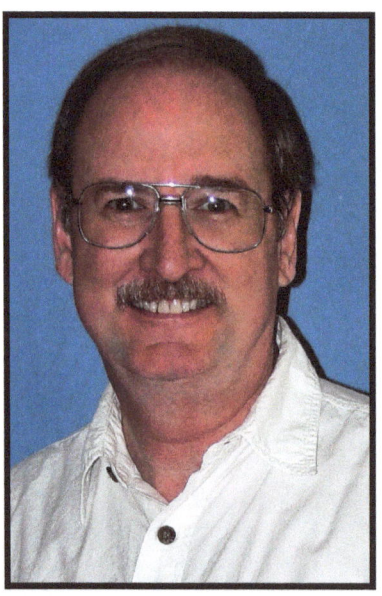

Quick Order Form

Fax Orders: 1-888-308-0462

Telephone Orders: 1-888-308-0462

Email Orders: orders@goofyrooster-publishing.com

Postal Orders: Goofy Rooster Publishing   PO Box 2904   Wylie, TX 75098-2904

Please send the following books. I understand that I may return any of them for a full refund - for any reason, no questions asked.

_____

_____

_____

Name: _____

Address: _____

City: _____ State: _____ Zip: _____

Telephone: _____

Email address: _____

Sales Tax: Please add 8.25% for products shipped to Texas addresses

Shipping/handling (US addresses only):

USPS Media Mail (2 - 8 days)   Add - $5.00

USPS Priority Mail (2 days)   Add - $8.50

[above rates subject to change as postal/shipping rates change]